HEAVY DUTY

HEAVY DUTY

DAYS AND NIGHTS IN

K.K. DOWNING

WITH MARK EGLINTON

DA CAPO PRESS

Da Capo Press
Hachette Book Group
1290 Avenue of the Americas, New York, NY 10104

www.dacapopress.com

@DaCapoPress; @DaCapoPR

Printed in the United States of America

First Edition: September 2018

Published by Da Capo Press, an imprint of Perseus Books, LLC, a subsidiary of Hachette Book Group, Inc. The Da Capo Press name and logo is a trademark of the Hachette Book Group.

The Hachette Speakers Bureau provides a wide range of authors for speaking events. To find out more, go to www.hachettespeakersbureau.com or call (866) 376-6591.

The publisher is not responsible for websites (or their content) that are not owned by the publisher.

Print book interior design by Jeff Williams.

Library of Congress Cataloging-in-Publication Data

Names: Downing, K. K., author. | Eglinton, Mark.
Title: Heavy duty: days and nights in Judas Priest / K.K. Downing with Mark Eglinton.
Description: First edition. | Boston: Da Capo Press, 2018.
Identifiers: LCCN 2018014925| ISBN 9780306903311 (hardcover) | ISBN 9780306903298
   (e-book)
Subjects: LCSH: Judas Priest (Musical group) | Rock musicians—England—Biography.
Classification: LCC ML421.J8 D68 2018 | DDC 782.42166092/2 [B]—dc23
LC record available at https://lccn.loc.gov/2018014925

ISBNs: 978-0-306-90331-1 (hardcover); 978-0-306-90329-8 (ebook)

LSC-C

10 9 8 7 6 5 4 3 2 1

CONTENTS

RENO, NEVADA. JUNE 16, 1990

Then the reality hit me.

And as it did I felt as if we'd been lulled into a false sense of security, only to be caught in a trap laid out for whichever band wasn't looking where they were going. This day felt like the culmination of a silent conspiracy that had been evolving since we'd helped ignite a whole scene in 1980—where heavy metal and the lifestyle that went with it had been viewed with suspicion, considered dangerous even—to the extent that certain activist groups were gunning for the entire culture. At that moment it occurred to me that we were just the scapegoats.

There was this uplifting outpouring of support for us for the ordeal we were about to go through. I could see the sincerity in the eyes of fans who were lining the streets outside the courthouse. They wanted us to win this case—court disposition papers claimed that two of their own, two fans of Judas Priest, had shot themselves and that our music was the cause.

Nevertheless, something still didn't sit right about the fact that the US, the country that had welcomed us with open arms back in 1977, was the same one that seemed to be trying to end our career.

As confused as I was, seeing all these pained, desperate faces as I got out of the cab at the bottom of the Reno courthouse steps, all these people yelling, "Priest! Priest! Priest!" as if the lights had just gone down at the start of one of our shows, gave me the same feeling I got every time I stepped out onstage.

It was this incredible sense of invincibility that came with being in a tight group. Whenever I felt it, I stopped being little Ken Downing from the Yew Tree Estate. No longer that shy and introverted kid with a plastic school satchel and holes in my shoes, instead I transformed into K.K.—the cocksure guitarist in the best heavy metal band there is, and my mates were there with me.

Pumped with adrenaline, as I walked up the steps and looked at Rob Halford beside me, eyes staring ahead and his thin jaw set, I thought, *We're going to be OK.*

As we got shown into the courtroom, everything changed again. The moment the big wood-paneled door closed behind us, it was as if we'd just walked into a vacuum. The feeling of loss and sadness was as palpable as the lump in my throat. I'd never experienced such a sudden change in mood. I could no longer hear the chanting voices. Their power had been removed and as a group we felt less strong.

The sound of my quickening heartbeat drowned everything out as the clerk stood up to address the court for the first time. Irrespective of how confident I felt about what we'd done and, more importantly, what we hadn't done, in an instant I felt like little Ken again, in that all too familiar position of waiting for whatever it was that was bad and heading my way.

CHAPTER ONE

WHEN THE IDEA OF WRITING AN AUTOBIOGRAPHY WAS suggested to me at various times over recent years, I think the factor that always held me back was whether I was willing to be really honest about how my incredible career played out over the forty-something years I was in Judas Priest.

From the outside, people, fans, always think, "Being in Judas Priest must have been amazing. They toured the world, playing music. There was money, there were girls—it's the perfect life."

For some of the time, it was the perfect life.

But just like anything, it doesn't go perfectly every single day of the week. If it did, it would become boring and predictable—two adjectives that I got into a band to avoid ever having to confront.

What I've come to realize in recent years is that although a person can walk away from something to present a particular impression or preserve an image and be doing that for some reasons that seemed right at the time, sometimes the need to be honest and forthright about certain happenings is much fairer not only to the fans, but also to everyone involved with the band. In so doing, it seems to me that the slate is wiped far cleaner than when things are left unsaid, incomplete and vague.

And when I left Judas Priest, things were certainly left unsaid, incomplete and vague.

So, with that being said, I changed my mind about writing about my life for reasons that I think are in everybody's best interests—and all the people who are discussed and implicated are people whose company, ability, and friendship I value a great deal and will continue to do so long after I've finished writing this book. Nothing will ever devalue my time in Judas Priest. But it is important to me that all the facts, as I see them, are laid out for the fans to laugh at, cry to, grit their teeth with frustration . . . and, of course, go out and buy more Judas Priest albums when they've finished reading.

Therefore, everything I've written in this book is either how I remember it or my opinion of events that I lived through. Obviously, I don't remember everything; a lot of these events happened a very long time ago. But as I've gone through the enjoyable process of dredging through more than five decades of memories, I've come to realize that there are aspects to my life that I'd never really thought about until now.

This delayed reaction is neither a good thing nor is it a bad thing. It's just life, and the perspective that it brings you. By and large I've enjoyed reminiscing.

When I first started thinking about writing about my life in and out of Judas Priest, as I tried to identify and prioritize all the things I wanted to say and thoughts I wanted to get across, the feeling that I just couldn't shake was the idea that a person's upbringing shapes everything that happens later.

Everything.

In my case that's especially true—to the extent that it sometimes feels like I've spent my entire life trying to escape where, and *who,*

I came from. No matter what I'm doing—and it even applied to the most exhilarating moments at the absolute height of Priest life in the late '80s—I still catch myself thinking or making subconscious decisions as if I still were little Ken from a Black Country council estate in the Midlands of England, with holes in my shoes—rather than K.K. from Judas Priest.

Sometimes that's a good thing: my upbringing taught me a lot about how not to live. But it can also be negative: on a few occasions I may have been guilty of holding myself back or unintentionally alienating people who are close to me.

If you're lucky enough to have a stable, loving family life, that's great. In theory, you're set up for life. But when you grow up in a difficult family environment, believe me it leaves indelible scars. These scars, although faded slightly, are still there—and to this day I feel them occasionally, despite the privileged and exciting life I've led. I now know that they'll never completely heal; they've had every opportunity to do so.

✦

Just being born when and where I was—in 1951, in the heart and the thick of the Black Country, in the heart of the UK as England was still dragging itself from the aftermath of World War II—meant that daily life was tough from the get-go. Everything about life in England's industrial heartland was a struggle: certain foods and amenities were still scarce, and the standard of the dwellings was basic to say the least. For most people it was all about survival.

Then there was my family. That's a story in itself.

In those days, people seemed to have kids much younger. My mum was just a seventeen-year-old girl when she had my older sister, Margaret, who is one year older than me. She was still a child, living with her parents in old terraced housing (buildings joined onto each other at both ends to form a row) in the West Bromwich area with outside toilets and no heating.

When Margaret arrived, my mother and my dad, who was six years older, went to live with his mother in a small and very old semidetached house in Hilltop, a suburb of West Bromwich where the horizon, assuming you could see it at all, was dominated by steel-rolling mills and foundries set against a dense, gray backdrop created by their filthy, gaseous by-products. As you'd imagine, Hilltop was a noisy, gritty, industrial soundtrack to accompany any life. This was the kind of place that, given time, wore anyone down.

After a year and a half or so of them living there, I arrived.

Then, just a few months later, my dad's brother, my uncle Wilfred, knocked on the door with some bad news for my mum.

"You've been here two years. Time to go to *your* mother's."

He wanted us out of that house as soon as possible. Truth be told, he was being a bit nasty about it. He and his wife had just had their first child, my cousin Christine, but they didn't have anywhere to live. In those days people were having kids left, right, and center, but there was no accommodation—that's just how it was. Something, or somebody, had to give. And it was us who did.

Not wanting to instigate a major family argument, we moved out and into my mother's mum's house for a period of time that, if my hazy memory serves me correctly, didn't seem very long. It, too, was a terraced place; and it also was pretty rough living, not least because it was here that I became aware that my mother's parents hated my dad.

They thought he was a "bad un"—Midlands slang for somebody who was (a) not to be trusted and (b) would never amount to very much. And, in retrospect, they were absolutely right about him, although I, being so young, knew very little about their reasoning.

At that time, I'm told that he spent his days driving a horse and cart. I don't know precisely what he was doing—maybe he was making deliveries of some kind. Who knows? I'll give him the benefit of the doubt on that one. Unfortunately, the concept of work ranked pretty low on the list of my dad's priorities—although he seemingly had been employed at one time.

As the story goes, my dad, who had two brothers, once worked alongside his younger sibling on one of the factory cooling towers in West Bromwich. In those days, the idea of occupational health and safety didn't exist; it was all ladders and ropes—really dangerous work in all weather and for low pay.

One day, my dad took a day off to go to the racetrack, and on that day, his younger brother had an accident and fell to his death from the tower. My dad was devastated. I think he felt some sort of survivor's guilt. But I also think he somehow felt that horse racing had saved his life. In a way I think it became a comfort blanket for him thereafter. But that skewed thinking would come at great cost to us.

Unlike many abusive parents, my dad never drank. In fact, I'm not aware of him ever having touched alcohol, or cigarettes, in his entire life. It was a good thing for us that that man didn't drink. Trust me. Living with him was bad enough as it was. But he did have two major problems that became *our* problems.

First, he had this strange mix of hypochondria and obsessive-compulsive disorder. In combination, these characteristics were very confusing for us—mainly because his paranoia wasn't always directed at himself. Instead, it was us who bore the brunt of it. The second issue was his rampant gambling habit, which I'll come back to later.

Looking back, these OCD traits of his were so unusual and, at times, absurdly contradictory. For example, when I was a child, my dad never wanted us to be around other kids. He was always terrified that we'd catch something from them.

"Leave that alone!" he'd forever be saying. "You don't know who's been touching it."

Obviously, enforcing this strange rule was always going to be a problem, particularly given that when we were toddlers and we had moved back into his parents' house again there were a hell of a lot of kids around the house.

Furthermore, I can remember many nights when I, my sister Margaret, and my cousin Christine all used to sleep together in one single bed. I can vividly recall that sensation of being lined up across the bed, which was always covered with army-style blankets with serial numbers on the top edge. It wasn't comfortable but we had no choice. Two families had to make the best of what little room there was, but my dad was always obsessed with the idea of other kids' germs being passed on to us.

From a combination of hazy memories and pieces of information I was later given, I know that—presumably to create more living space—my dad somehow converted the shed at the bottom of his mum's garden. I say it was a "shed," but I suppose it was a little bit grander than that. It was a halfway decent structure that might have once been a pigeon loft that my granddad might have made into a workshop at some point.

He'd gone to the length of putting some steps in the middle, and when you reached the top you could go left or right into separate room-like areas. In effect, he'd created another part of the house, albeit fifty feet away from the actual house, at the bottom of the garden. My hazy recollections tell me that this was where we spent the daytimes when I was very young. And then, at night, we'd all tramp up the garden into my grandmother's house where we all slept in that one bed.

Despite the fact that we slept in the same bed, as close as people could conceivably get, my dad went and built a fence around the shed in the garden to keep my cousin Christine out! He said he didn't want us to catch anything from her. None of it made any sense. But we just had to go along with it anyway.

And there was more.

Christmas, a day that most kids remember with joy, filled me with dread. I vividly remember that we never, ever got to unwrap

Christmas presents. What should be more exciting to a child than opening gifts on Christmas morning? But we never did that. Ours always arrived unwrapped and in advance, which, to me, defeated the point of it altogether. We just came downstairs on Christmas morning, it could have been any morning, and whatever presents there were for us would just be sitting there on a chair. There was no element of surprise. It all felt so empty.

And again, the reason for this was that, because of his phobias, he worried that somehow, we'd be contaminated by something that might have been on the wrapping paper! Any Christmas cards that came with tinsel on the front were immediately thrown away for the same nonsensical reason—"You never know who's touched that . . . "

I suppose he was trying to be protective, but it was so cruel to effectively do away with Christmas, not that we ever got that much of it anyway.

Whenever we left the house, things were every bit as bad. Before we'd even stepped out of the front door, he'd tie our shoelaces up in this strange, very tight knot, before proceeding to cut the loose laces off entirely "because then our laces couldn't collect people's spit off the pavement."

Anytime we were on a bus together, he'd frog-march us up the middle of the central aisle, holding us in a straitjacket-like position to stop us from touching the handles or rails. If the bus came to a sudden jolt we'd sometimes fall over because we had nothing to hold on to. Really, our dad made life complicated for us in the strangest of ways. Although I was still a kid, I'd already lived a hell of a life.

After a couple of years, because they now had two kids (and my sister Linda on the way), my parents were able to get onto the council list for a house. Once you're on such a list, it's just a matter of waiting until a property becomes available.

Eventually, when I was around five years old, we got selected for a new council house on the border between West Bromwich and Walsall on what was called the Yew Tree Estate.

This new estate, built on reclaimed farmland, was a mixture of semidetached houses and six-, eight-, and twenty-one-story blocks of flats. Even though these were all "new" houses, their build quality was very poor. They were that basic, early '50s style, with aluminum, single-glazed four-millimeter glass windows that offered very little by way of insulation. There was no heating at all except for an open fireplace, so it was freezing cold most of the time. There were no carpets or rugs on the floor, just bare lino. There was at least a toilet upstairs—something I'd never even seen before. To that point in my life, toilets had always been outside. At least I was going up in the world.

My young life revolved around Yew Tree and was largely contained within it. There was rarely any cause to leave; everything was there. As estates went, it wasn't too bad, I suppose. It was on the edge of the city, on new land—far away from the dirt, the smoke, and the grime of the more industrial areas. I remember there being a canal and an abundance of playing fields. So, it wasn't as bad as some of the older, prewar estates in the city.

In addition to a few shops and a youth club, there were two primary and two secondary schools within the estate boundaries. When I first went to the primary school—the Yew Tree School it was called—it seemed that the teachers thought that I was some kind of child genius. I was never quite sure why!

"Kenneth, come out here to the front of the class," my teacher would say while beckoning the two smartest girls in the class to do the same. "Show the class how good you are at copying this text from the Bible."

"OK, Miss."

So, we'd sit there, copying what seemed like endless pages of text from the Bible, while our classmates watched. To this day I don't know what the point of it was. I suppose it must have been some kind of aptitude test.

In the early years, I thought everything that was happening at home was normal, simply because I hadn't had anything to compare my life to. But as time passed, I became aware that my family environment was extremely unorthodox.

Looking back, I could see that my home life was missing key elements: love and positive parental input. And as much as going to school was some kind of escape from the wretched home environment, I couldn't help but bring most of my problems with me.

In retrospect, I think that I was always just holding myself together at an age when I wasn't equipped to do so. It was the little things that gradually eroded me, steadily making me feel like I was something less than those around me.

For example, as with most schools, there was a standard uniform of trousers, blazer, shirt and tie, and a satchel.

But I never quite had what I was meant to have.

Whereas other kids might have had a leather satchel, mine was never leather; it was the cheaper plastic equivalent. When kids grew out of their trousers and got bought new ones, I never did—mine were always too short and often had holes to match those in my shoes. That wears away at your soul as a youngster.

Then there was the embarrassment of free school dinners. In the classroom, you had to put your hand up if you were staying for these free school dinners. By doing so, you were effectively saying, "I'm poor."

And out of maybe forty kids, I'd always be one of only two or three who put their hands up every single time. I felt embarrassed that I needed the free meals and I had to put up with other humiliations all the way through school. I know it sounds like an Oliver Twist story but I really was an urchin, struggling to make it from day to day.

Those years between the age of five and when I went to secondary school at eleven were when the really lasting damage was done to me. At a time in my life when I most needed nurturing and support, I got bad influence, absence, and borderline abuse instead. My parents never really got along—that much was obvious. There was constant tension because there would always be some kind of battling going on, usually about money or something related to it.

Predictably, my mother left my dad several times during these years. When it happened, we'd briefly decamp to her mother's house until, as was always the case, she'd go back to him or he'd entice her back in some way.

Then, after no time at all, everything would return to how it had been and my mother would just put up and shut up while he was around. The household became delineated areas where two rival factions existed. My dad would occupy the front room; my mum, my sister, and I would mainly be in the kitchen. The boundaries were rarely crossed.

Away from the house, however, my mum seemed to take on an alternate personality. When we'd go up to West Bromwich on a Saturday, I'd stand and listen to her tell women friends she'd meet in the street about the abuse she was getting at home—"You won't *believe* what he did next . . . "

She'd be very animated as she was doing so. It was a side of her personality that I wasn't familiar with; I'd only ever seen her with her guard up. The saddest part was that, from earwigging on their conversations, it seemed like most of these women were going through something similar at home.

They'd nod knowingly when my mother described my dad's most recent antics. They'd be sympathetic and disgusted at the same time. And then they would often look at me, with my bright blue eyes and my silky blond hair, and say, "But *look* at him! Isn't he absolutely beautiful?"—while I shyly hid behind my mother. I suppose they were suggesting how lucky my mother was that such a toxic relationship had produced such a cute boy like I seemingly was.

✦

As lucky as my mother might have been to have had me and as much as she always did the very best she could for her children in difficult circumstances, she wasn't always there. I must have been around the age of seven when she developed an unusual complaint called porphyria, a kind of inherited metabolic disorder, from what I've been told.

The condition's symptoms were acute and debilitating, but unpredictably intermittent. The effects came and went, but the indirect impact on us never relented. When she was laid low, she was incapable of doing anything. She'd be bedridden for days. And instead of showing her any sympathy and pulling his weight, my dad just treated her worse because it meant, God forbid, that he'd have to do some of the things she couldn't in the house.

Margaret and I particularly were always caught in the crossfire, lurching from day to day. There was even a period of a few months when my mum was affected so badly that she had to go into hospital. I specifically remember that we were sat down and told by our dad that there was a real chance that she might never come home. As a young boy, the realities of that were hard to fathom.

During that time, my dad's worst habits seemed to be exacerbated. For a start he insisted that he and I sleep in the same bed, with him holding on to me tightly all night. To this day that still strikes me as being a very odd thing to make a kid do—although there was never a suggestion of anything untoward about what he was doing.

Nevertheless, the bed was *horrible:* greasy and dirty, with old, dusty overcoats thrown over us for warmth. I dreaded going to bed every night. To this day I don't understand his motivations. I'd like to think that maybe this was his way of showing how much he was suffering, but who knows?

Regardless, the controlling behavior continued.

During the winter months, before I went to bed, he'd make me and my sister trail round the estate with him in the evening, pushing this old pram that we had. We'd go to the various building sites, where workmen had left coke and coal they'd been using for fueling fires during the day. He'd stand there watching as we were made to load this filthy stuff into the pram and then he'd get us to push it back home for our fire. It was borderline slave labor.

Then, in the summer months, he'd put us to bed ridiculously early, at 6 p.m., while it was broad daylight. I'd just look out of my bedroom window, watching other kids play, wishing I were somewhere else. When I *was* allowed out in the sunshine, I always suffered from really bad hay fever and other allergies, particularly to the adhesive on Elastoplast, a brand of bandages also known as "sticking plasters."

Instead of being sympathetic to that, for some reason my dad would put snuff up my nose and make me lie on my back on the ground and stare at the sun! He made us terribly unhappy with all of his weird habits and phobias.

And then there was his second problem: the habitual gambling.

I can say without reservation that there was no bigger cause of constant friction between him and my mum than money. Because he didn't work as such after we moved to Yew Tree, he relied entirely on council handouts. But to bolster that small sum, as soon as he was able, he involved me in his plans.

By the time I was seven or eight, he'd drag me along with him to the dog tracks and even to racecourses around the country, where he tried to supplement, by gambling, what he was claiming from social security.

On certain days of the week, it seemed like everyone was up at the dog tracks. Dog racing back then would be the equivalent of people buying a lottery ticket now, I suppose. People just did it, hoping that somehow they'd win enough money to change their lives. They'd go to Willenhall, Perry Bar, or Wolverhampton, always in the vain hope of getting a bit of cash to help make ends meet.

As popular as this pastime was, there was no glamour whatsoever attached to midweek days at Midlands greyhound tracks. Even I could see that as an eight- or nine-year-old. Near-destitute people, most of them smoking heavily, gathered around the on-course bookmaker pitches with a look of absolute desperation in their eyes. At the weekends it was slightly better because other kids would be there, too. We wouldn't necessarily be allowed to play with them, but at least it was more colorful. For the parents, it didn't matter. They were trying to back a winner—a winner that wouldn't really change their life in any way. And, for many years, our dad was one of them.

The whole exercise was so pointless. All of the little money that ever came our way would be gambled away as quickly as we got it. He never, ever learned—even on the few occasions when he got lucky. He'd back a dog, make a few quid, and put some money in his pocket. But then he couldn't help himself; he couldn't just walk away, get on the bus with me, and go home.

Instead he'd get greedy and gamble it again and lose everything. Even then, after he'd spent our bus fare home, he'd still try to borrow a couple of quid off a stranger or ask if they'd go halves with him to bet on the last race. It was madness! Even to me, as young as I was, there was an absolute futility to that way of life and the tangible day-to-day consequences of his gambling made me really resent him.

Beyond the dog track, my dad's methods to acquire money went to extreme levels generally. I remember walking miles, literally *miles*, along the canal from our home—there and back to his parents' house with him—just so we could get the pocket money they gave us, which was just sixpence or a shilling.

However, as soon as we were out the door of their house, he'd have it off us saying that he'd give it back during the week—which he never did. But as long as he got a couple of shillings to go to the betting office on a Monday morning, that was his fix. And if he didn't have any money, it was not good.

So, it got to the point where we always wanted him to have some money, just so he wouldn't be in the house. The less he was around, the better it was for all of us.

Tuesday was the day when we got the family allowance—some shillings to help the family survive, basically. And of course, there were continual arguments and upheaval because, rather than let it be used to help the family with necessities, he wanted that money to go gambling with. Worse than that, my mother knew very well that if she didn't let him have it, he'd have withdrawal symptoms that would impact all of us.

Predictably, they fought about it every week and, inevitably, the neighbors would hear all the noise through the thin plasterboard. I remember many occasions where we had to get the police to sort it all out. It got to the point where we never had any ornaments in the house that my mother could pick up and launch at him. The house was always clinically bare; we didn't even have a clock!

And the upshot of adapting to my father's addiction was that the cupboards often were bare, too. There wasn't always food on the Downing family table. Luckily for my sister and me, we had the option of those humiliating free school dinners. Without them, I doubt we'd have survived.

The few times that my mother managed to keep her hands on the money from the family allowance, she could just about buy basic food and pay some bills, but it was never enough to buy clothes for us. Consequently, my dad would always be up there at the family allowance office, pleading poverty. He never stopped trying to scrounge. Really, the man should have been arrested for the amount of money he managed to sponge over the years.

On more than one occasion he went to the office for more money, supposedly to buy shoes for us. They'd always believe his sob story, send him the money, and then they would arrange to come around to the house to inspect the shoes and to look at the receipts.

My dad didn't really buy the shoes.

Instead he devised a plan to fake the purchase and con the allowance office. When we'd go up the town to West Bromwich High Street as we did once a week—the Golden Mile as it was called at that time on account of its row of shops—he would make us wait outside the Tru-Form shoe shop, which was just opposite the Yew Tree Estate bus stop. Then, whenever someone came out of the shoe shop and threw a receipt on the pavement, he'd get us to pick it up. Can you imagine the shame I felt? It was vile to be scratching around on the pavement, among cigarette butts and chewing gum, searching for these receipts.

And then later, when the inspectors came around, he'd get us to clean our old shoes as best as we could and would insist that they were brand new. If the inspectors asked, he'd simply flash them the receipts we picked off the pavement and say, "See, I bought these . . . "

It was pathetic, really. He was meant to love and care for us. Instead we were just pawns in his game.

Then, to make matters even worse, he'd plead poverty to our grandparents and say, "The kids have got no shoes" in the hope that they would buy us whatever they could afford, which wasn't much because they were struggling to make ends meet themselves. The man really had no shame at all. He undermined every aspect of life, particularly the parts that were meant to be innocent and good.

Although we were at school with other kids all the time, once we got home, we were never let out of the house to play with other kids on the estate—again, so that we would not come in contact with germs. We were prisoners much of the time.

It was by being with other kids at school that gradually made me realize that our family wasn't normal. And when I did realize it,

I don't think it really upset me; it was more a case of accepting that we were indeed living a life of absolute hell—and that there wasn't much I could do to change it.

And so, the habit of a lifetime began.

Whether I was born with this trait of grinning and bearing it or not, that's exactly how I'd navigate difficult situations thereafter. As hard as I tried, I was never a nasty person, or someone who relished confrontation and head games. For me the path of least resistance was the most attractive—and if that meant sabotaging or disadvantaging myself, then so be it.

CHAPTER TWO

B Y THE TIME I REACHED SECONDARY SCHOOL AGE, I THINK I was so jaded by my wretched home life that everything I did was geared toward escaping it. I had no idea what I wanted to do with my life; I just knew that there had to be something better out there than the status quo.

At Churchfield secondary school I wasn't what you'd call a bad scholar. It wasn't entirely wasted time. But I always floated in the midrange of the classes, doing the bare minimum to progress through what seemed like a factory-bound production line.

I suppose it felt like they'd already decided that I was going to live the life of a laborer. And, to hammer that point home, after two years they increased the number of metal and woodwork classes as if to acknowledge and concede to the limited opportunities of my grim, industrial surroundings.

Worse still, they increased the number of religious education classes while, to my horror, also cutting back on music and art— both of which were two of the pursuits I liked most.

If there were any careers that interested me as a youngster, I suppose the arts would have been the most obvious. When I was thirteen, I painted what I thought was a really good portrait of William the Conqueror, riding on a horse. The teacher was really impressed with it.

"Good picture, Kenneth," he said. "What else can you do?"

"I don't know. Suggest something."

Then, the art teacher asked each of us to design a safety poster for an environmental project. I did mine about littering. I drew up this colorful poster, and as a headline I wrote a message that said:

Don't Throw Litter from a Moving Car.

The funny part was that I also incorporated a cartoonish picture of someone throwing his or her mother-in-law from a moving vehicle! Other people thought it was funny, too; my poster was put forward for a competition at West Bromwich Town Hall.

Generally, though, with just a few dim highlights, I scrambled my way through school without ever latching on to subjects that interested me—although it might surprise people to learn that I did enjoy playing field hockey and chess for the school teams.

By and large I was desperate not to be there—to the extent that I often *wasn't* physically there. I regularly used to throw a change of clothes into my school bag; that would be all that was in there.

My fishing tackle was kept at my friend's house, which was miles away from mine. But instead of going to school, I used to walk to my friend's house, change my clothes, grab my fishing tackle, and go to the canal for the day to fish. Then, at three thirty, I'd drop my gear off again, walk home, get changed, and tell my mum I'd been at school. I don't think she ever knew any better.

Although I bunked off school a lot, the latter part of my time in secondary education was significant for a number of reasons. As the unpleasant situation continued at home, because I was older, I'd start spending more time at my gran's house in West Bromwich on weekends and holidays where, within reason, she let me come and go as I liked.

At first, I'd alternate weekend stays with my sister Margaret. But soon—because my dad used to pick on me if he wanted to get back at my mum about something—I was going there almost every weekend for relief.

Gran's house, on reflection, was shockingly basic. It never really occurred to me that this stark, slightly damp room with the peeling paint on the ceiling where the rain often got in was in fact my mother's bedroom, where she grew up. And furthermore, it was more or less exactly as she had left it when she left at the age of seventeen. For me it was just somewhere to sleep. Somewhere that wasn't five feet through the wall from my mother and dad's arguing and all the stupid rules that applied in that house.

Being at my gran's not only put me back in the smoke, the grit, and the grime that was synonymous with the industrial center of West Bromwich, it also represented an appealing glimpse of freedom. Looking back, it was like being fitted with a pressure-release valve. Predictably, I grabbed this newfound opportunity with both hands.

Above and beyond the relaxed atmosphere at gran's house, West Bromwich, the city, as industrial as it was, just seemed so much more exciting than the estate. These older terraced houses had so many more unusual features than the predictable, shoebox-like layout of housing estate dwellings. There was so much more aesthetic appeal in old stone houses for inquisitive teenagers: nooks to explore, discarded items to salvage.

At every opportunity, my friends and I would roam the disused cellars of nearby terraced houses, getting up to all sorts of mischief, finding what we could, until darkness or the distant call of a parent or grandparent late at night brought us home again. That's what we did, and I loved it. These weekends and holidays stand out as bright paint slashes of happiness on an otherwise dark and depressing life canvas.

As much as we were running around the city while I was at my gran's, me and a few of my mates were slowly starting to have our young heads turned toward music. My best mate, a very outgoing lad called Nick Bowbanks, was starting to get into the same music at the same time.

Nick was always a bit of a tearaway. Coming from a similarly dysfunctional family background as mine, he seemed to take out his frustrations on the world by committing random acts of petty crime—all the while with a cheeky smile. I'd inevitably get drawn in to his various schemes. For a while we were the terrible twosome. Nick and I got up to all sorts. He'd wake me up in the middle of the bloody night by banging on my window with a washing line prop, yelling, "Coming out? Coming out?"

As I fumbled around with the curtains, there he'd be with a big smile on his face as he tried to persuade me to go out with him to steal clothes off washing lines. The reasoning being that since we couldn't afford Levi's jeans of our own, why not take someone else's? The idea seemed reasonable enough, and when they were hanging up to dry they were admittedly easy targets. We never once got caught!

Nick and I did have a few minor scrapes with the law. For a while, though, we always seemed to be a step or so ahead of them. Then, after a few months, our luck ran out. We ended up in juvenile court accused of breaking into a local rugby club. Nick and I *had* been at said rugby club where there was booze and all kinds of other things attractive to teenagers. That part was true. But it was another school friend, Ian Hill, and one of his mates who were later caught there by the police.

"Which of you kicked the door in then?"

"It wasn't us, officer. It was Kenny Downing and Nicky Bowbanks."

They hung us out to dry, and I remember the sheer embarrassment of having to go along to Walsall Court with my mum, because I was still a minor, where the judge stood all four of us there like idiots, dressed us down, and then ordered us to pay a fine of five pounds each. Believe me, that was a lot of money in those days, but we were granted time to pay.

This incident didn't deter Nick, though. A year later he went to juvenile prison for something else.

◆

Whether it was connected to the rebellious company I was keeping, I found myself being drawn to, subconsciously or otherwise, bands that were either "cool" or had some kind of insubordinate quality.

So, the Beatles and Elvis Presley never interested me; those were my sister's favorites. I liked a tougher image and, as a result, when somebody came on TV—like the Rolling Stones had a couple of years earlier in 1964—it was just so exhilarating. To me, they were super cool. Their rough and tough, "ugly kids" look really appealed to me.

Hearing Barry McGuire's "Eve of Destruction" left a similar imprint on me. It was brilliant! I don't remember whether I was reading into it at the time as a protest song per se. All I knew was that *anything* that was vaguely rebellious was great—and made me think, *This is the best thing ever!*

Maybe this attraction to protest perfectly fit the narrative of my life at that time. Up until then, while I'd inscribed the names of bands I thought were cool—like The Troggs, or Them, or The Pretty Things (who were anything but pretty)—on my satchel back at school, there had never been any real substance to or thought behind my taste. I think it was the *idea* of these bands that appealed to me, much more than the music itself. But as 1966 approached, this emphasis began to change, as my hunger for music developed in line with what was happening in the area around me.

Besides the drafty youth club on the Yew Tree, which was all about listening to music, a local "circuit" of sorts was developing in conjunction with the popularity of a few different styles of music.

Everything seemed to be kicking off at once; bands were springing up from everywhere. For a young guy recently hooked on music, there was almost too much to take in. On one hand, the Motown/soul style was flying. On the other, blues and blues-rock was really taking off, too. On paper, the two just don't mix. Or so you'd think . . .

In those days, in and around the Midlands, this circuit revolved around several venues that they called "plazas" in suburban towns like Handsworth and Old Hill. These had been, I suppose, dance halls in the prewar and wartime era and, on any given weekend night, it wouldn't be at all uncommon for one of these old, rundown plazas to have a soul act and a blues band on the same night. It was always a great night out.

Nobody thought anything of the eclectic nature of these nights, least of all my mates and I. It actually played into our hormonal teenager hands. For us it was all about two things: one, the music, and two, chatting up as many girls as was possible. The girls may not have been into John Mayall's Bluesbreakers or Cream like we were but they definitely did like to dance to the soul acts. For us this was just too heady a mixture to resist: girls and great music, in one place, every weekend.

As I breathed this all in, my eyes widened. Girls, music, freedom, and approaching young adulthood titillated me all at once. For the first time I became aware of life's opportunities rather than just its limitations. I didn't have to stay at school. School offered me nothing anyway. I didn't have to live at home. Home had been a living hell by and large, so why stay there?

Although I'd yet to reach my sixteenth birthday, I knew enough to decide that I wanted out, out of *everything*—to be released into the world to fend for myself, whatever that meant. After all, no reality could have been any worse than the half-life I'd been living. I thought to myself, *It's now or never, Ken . . .*

✦

I left school in 1966 at fifteen and a few months, which was as soon as I legally could have. And because I'd taken cookery lessons with the girls for the last year and a half at school and taken to the pastries, the roux, and the béchamel surprisingly well, I walked straight into a position as a trainee chef at a local hotel called the Lyttelton Arms in Stourbridge.

This hotel was and still is next door to an archetypal country church and just down the lane from Hagley Hall, a beautiful stately home that belonged to the Lyttelton/Cobham family, dating back to the sixteenth century.

Although the surroundings were quite crusty and traditional, in 1966, the pub was a popular local hostelry and locals traveled from quite a distance to eat and drink. There was live entertainment, weddings every weekend; it was a rocking place for locals to socialize.

As you might suspect, on paper this was a dream job for most fifteen-year-olds. For me, any job would have been. With regular hours and in-house accommodation included in combination with what seemed like a clear career path, the hotel job was the first time in my life I'd felt anything resembling self-sufficiency. Hilariously, I genuinely thought I was living it up—even though the reality was that I was dropped right in the deep end and had to learn many aspects of the job as I went along.

Hotel life was nonstop hard work, and when my shift ended I usually went to my room, flopped down on the bed, switched the transistor radio on, and listened to John Peel. On reflection, I suspect I thought that what Peel was playing in those days was "weird stuff." He was a Captain Beefheart fan and a T. Rex devotee. But he'd also play all kinds of eclectic stuff; that was the appeal with John Peel. I just loved it all.

To me, Peel's radio show was like walking through a star gate. And on the other side of that portal I found Jimi Hendrix—even though I don't specifically recall Peel playing him very much. Other artists he favored led me there, though, as well as hearing Hendrix's music in the circle of friends that I had at the time. And as Hendrix's popularity soared, my admiration for Jimi ascended with it.

As dark and moody as his music could be, it was also so very colorful to me. He seemed to paint pictures and landscapes with music. With him you could listen, close your eyes, and embark on a journey. It all felt so unique, exciting, and new, and I realized that I needed all of these feelings in my life

On some level I felt that I was abandoning my mother to her horrible existence with my dad. But on another I knew that if I was ever going to make anything of myself, I had to make a clean break from the stifling world I'd grown up with on the estate.

It was hardly surprising that I'd steadily developed a deep hatred for my dad in the weeks and months before I left. In fact, I spent quite a few nights just lying in my bedroom staring at the ceiling, thinking of ways that I could kill him and get away with it. Things had become very strained, to the point that it felt like we couldn't both be in the same house. Years of abuse (and the emotional scars they left) were piling up on me, crushing my self-esteem in the process. Anger was always near the surface, especially where my dad's disregard for our well-being was concerned. But now I was a young, thrusting teenager; hormones were coursing through my body.

The culmination of it all was a moment that I suspect happens in every young man's life—that one when you wake up one day and decide that you may just be a physical match for your father. You look in the bedroom mirror, shirtless, the embryonic traces of chest hair sprouting, and you think, *I reckon I could probably have him . . .*

One day when things really kicked off about something, I almost acted on the in-the-mirror rehearsal. As my mum cowered in the kitchen after another argument, I squared off with him in the front room. I was hardly muscular but I was a tall enough lad. As the tension between us crackled, I was close enough to smell his breath and sense something that resembled fear for the first time. It was a defining moment for us both: for the first time I was genuinely ready to lay into him.

Of course, now I realize how unnatural an idea it is to want to hurt a parent. But equally, a parent like my dad must also understand (but often doesn't) how his behavior affects a parent/child relationship. Any degree of trust, respect, and love is reduced to nothing, leaving, in effect, two unrelated, emotionless alpha males to contest territory and loved ones.

Even as a teenager, I acknowledged that while this was a very sad situation, it was nevertheless a predictable result of how he'd treated me. The sad thing is I don't know if my dad ever understood anything of how I felt. At that time, all I could do was put a marker down that clearly said, "I won't be tolerating your shit any longer."

Once I was gone and working in the hotel, I never went back home for an entire year. I think I wrote my mum one letter. For once I was more focused on *my* life—and in it, music was becoming more and more important.

CHAPTER THREE

B Y THE LATTER PART OF 1966 AND INTO 1967, AS MUCH AS I was a huge fan of Hendrix's, his music was still very much an acquired taste; only a select few were into it—which for a youngster is always a good reason to get into an artist. In a way it felt as if the timing of it all had been crafted just to suit me. And then I read in the *Melody Maker* that he was due to play a show nearby, at the Coventry Theatre.

The first time we played Coventry Theatre with Judas Priest many years later, with me standing stage right, I couldn't help but think about when I'd first seen Jimi Hendrix play there in 1967 on a November night that nobody who was there will ever forget.

Back then everything was different.

I took a night off from the hotel, jumped on the train with a couple of my mates without paying. And when we got off at Coventry, we looked around to figure out a way of evading the ticket collector who was blocking our exit.

"There," I gestured, pointing toward what looked like a route out.

I thought that if we ran up this really big, steep embankment as far as we could go, eventually we'd probably be able to get out of the station without paying or getting caught.

My assessment was correct. And that's what we did, reaching the street in ten minutes with the lights of the station far below us.

The whole outing was an experience, seeing Hendrix, Pink Floyd, the Move, and three or four other bands. As I recall, there were half a dozen bands on the bill for a ticket price of just seven and six pence. Not that I paid. When we arrived at the theatre, one of us just snuck in and opened the exit door—that's how we used to do it!

The feeling I got when the gig began was like what I would imagine taking acid would feel like. Compartments of my mind that I never knew existed opened up at once; they were bathed in the most vivid, fluid colors

As Jimi took the stage, my heart raced.

He opened with "Foxy Lady" with his back to the audience and wearing purple trousers with pink swirls like flames below the knees, facing the cabinets with just a Super Trouper spotlight on him. Then, building the tension, he instigated that familiar, resounding note, turned around, and went straight into it.

It was unreal—my mind exploded like fireworks.

Holy shit! I thought.

The whole night was insane because the audience literally went mad. There was just this huge surge of unfettered awe and excitement all around me when he combined these crazy shapes he threw with his body with what were undeniably otherworldly sounds. Normal individuals like me came out for the night and were just compelled to lose their minds. People stormed the stage and I was one of them. They were jumping from balconies, landing on people below. Faced with such aural excitement, it seemed the entirely natural thing to do. Everything about Hendrix was such a turn-on. And the effect of such sonic arousal stayed with me forever thereafter.

Two weeks later I saw Hendrix again at Bristol Colston Hall. That night showed me another side of the Hendrix effect, how he instinctively knew how to turn it on or off at will, as if he controlled the collective emotions of his audience.

I took mental note.

Instead of starting the set with "Foxy Lady," for which people always just went absolutely fucking crazy, I remember being so dismayed that he opened not with one of his own numbers but with "Sgt. Pepper's Lonely Hearts Club Band." The reaction was totally different. It just wasn't right and the audience knew it. Looking back, maybe it was his way of curtailing things for the sake of health and safety, but to me it was an anticlimax.

✦

Part of the Hendrix effect involved me summoning up the cash and the courage to buy my first acoustic guitar. Ever since that first time I realized that something about the sound of John Mayall's Bluesbreakers appealed to me, I suspected the acquisition of a guitar was always going to happen. All I needed was the collision of a light-the-blue-touch-paper moment like seeing Hendrix to be combined with there being some money in my pocket.

Working long and relatively well-paid hotel shifts made sure these two events occurred before too long. And so, one day, while I was staring into a music shop window, that week's wages burning a hole in my pocket, I just thought, *I'm doing it.*

I bought an inexpensive, no-name acoustic without really knowing what I was buying. All I knew was that it had six strings, made noise, and could be carried around in the plastic case that came with it. Even then, I liked the idea that I could be seen *carrying* an instrument. On reflection, this guitar wasn't very good, and, at this point in 1968, neither was I. So, this guitar and I made a pretty good pair.

At first, I wasn't taking what I was doing too seriously. I did, I suppose, what most novices do and strummed away with absolutely no aim or direction, trying to figure out what a chord was and occasionally playing on one string in the hope of finding something that might approximate a solo type of sound.

Alas, unlike electric guitars, which, with a little more expenditure but no more expertise or dexterity can be plugged in, turned up to ten, and create the illusion of sounding quite good, an acoustic in the hands of a novice is actually a discouraging way to launch a rock star career. The neck is wide and the action is high, making it difficult for young hands to apply the required pressure to form chords. Nylon strings are hard to manipulate. Regardless, out of sheer determination and will to improve, I persevered in those days and nights at the hotel.

On occasional weekend trips back to see my gran in West Bromwich, I began to notice that a couple of my friends who also had acquired guitars seemed to be up for a bit of competition over who could play what chord, or who could play bar chords at all, all of which was very difficult to execute on the guitars that we had at the time.

This friendly competition was important on two levels. One, I was very competitive, so I naturally wanted to be better than my mates. Two, by virtue of the fact that three or four of us were trying to achieve the same thing, the law of averages meant that we were unwittingly creating a pool of expertise, if you could call it that, from which we could all extract some or other scrap of something to add to our repertoire.

Gradually, as the summer of 1968 approached, I started seeing the fresh shoots of what approximated improvement.

And then, as if he knew what I was doing, Jimi summoned.

One weekend, while I was at my gran's house, my friend, Nick—who by that point had also been hired as a waiter at the Lyttelton Arms—broke some significant news while flicking through a well-thumbed copy of that week's *Melody Maker*.

"Ken . . . Jimi's playing Woburn Abbey on July 6," he said. "We're going."

"We've got to be there," I said.

I knew that the prospect of seeing Hendrix again was too good to refuse, particularly given the modest progress I'd made on the guitar since the Coventry Theatre gig. Somehow it felt as if I *needed* to see more, to feel the rush again, to continue my progress.

In the back of my mind was what my boss at the hotel might be thinking. It wasn't that I was slacking on my assigned tasks—if anything I was cementing my position there with my hard work and ability to take on new responsibilities. To reward that, the hotel boss even felt the need to invest in my future by sending me on day release to nearby Halesowen College of Food and Domestic Science to get some degrees that would, in theory, further my culinary career, regardless of where I was working.

However, at this point, as much as I liked the job and appreciated that someone had identified my potential, I can't deny that, for the first time, I felt an intangible force tugging me somewhere else. This destination, even though I was just a novice seventeen-year-old kid with extremely limited guitar chops, was a career in making music.

By July of 1968, I had accrued a week or ten days of holiday, so I went to my boss and told him I wanted to use it to see Hendrix at the Woburn Music Festival, as Nick and I had planned.

That was it, really—Nick and I just went.

While we were at Woburn, Nick, who had quite the eclectic taste in music, said, "Captain Beefheart is playing at a festival in Belgium next week. Let's go."

"Belgium? We've got hardly any money! How the hell are we going to do that?"

"We'll hitchhike—and then I've got enough money to get us on a ferry."

"OK, count me in."

As soon as I said that, I felt two things at once.

One was, here I was, throwing caution to the wind, walking onto a ferry to Europe with no money and no ticket for the festival at the other end—basically with just the clothes I had on my back.

It felt euphoric.

The other was this sense that by doing it, nothing would ever be the same again. The latter would later prove to be especially prophetic, but because this idea seemed to be the culmination of every rebellious thought or feeling I'd had in seventeen years of being alive, there was just no way I was not seizing it—regardless of the potential consequences.

And with that, a mini-odyssey began, characterized by a nomadic sense that time, worry, and rules just did not exist. It was as if, by stepping onto that cross-channel ferry at Dover, I had also stepped outside of my former self.

In continental Europe, Nick and I lived off the land. Not one sit-down meal was consumed as we traveled around, eating whatever bread and cheese we could lay our hands on, thumbing lifts as we went, covering miles and miles at a time, with just a two-man tent that we'd acquired for shelter.

As a result, the festival in Belgium—where Beefheart was just one of a couple of dozen artists who played that weekend—became a mere sideshow. As enjoyable as it was, it was the freedom and the possibilities that were exciting us far more.

But it was cold. Damn, it was cold—particularly in Austria, our next port of call. At one point I seem to recall, as we were trudging through the Austrian countryside one evening, this rural church loomed up in our midst.

Even at that age, I was a realist, and an ardent nonbeliever. The religious affiliation of this building therefore paled into insignificance in relation to the opportunity it now provided for shelter. Freezing cold, with nowhere to pitch a tent in sight, we walked in through the unlocked front door.

"I've got an idea," I said as my eyes were drawn to the six-foot-wide sections of rug that ran the length of the central aisle, all the way up to the altar.

"Grab an end, mate." I beckoned to Nick as I peeled one end of one section off the cold, stone church floor.

Nick grabbed the other end and we lifted the rug section and dragged it into an anteroom probably used as a cloakroom or for after-service receptions.

"Now let's get another . . . "

Nick and I dragged another section back into the room, positioned them side by side and then rolled ourselves loosely up in each.

That church wasn't the most comfortable night I'd ever spent, but it did the job. The next morning, we folded the rugs up, tied them with string we found, and carried them with us.

Somehow, we managed to hitchhike into Germany, and on the first night there in Cologne we pitched our two-man tent in a public park, rolled ourselves up in carpet, and went to sleep. We had the routine perfected.

In the middle of the night I remember being woken up by lights and an almighty noise outside the tent. Suddenly, the zip of the tent goes up and fucking machine guns and torches get poked in. I kid you not!

"Don't shoot! Don't shoot! We're just kids!"

Suddenly it occurred to me that maybe this was the police, and that somehow they'd found out about us stealing the rugs from the church in Belgium and had only just now caught up with us.

"We'll give it back, we promise!"

The German policemen looked bemused, not least because of the two dirty, hippy-looking guys captured in the glow of their torch beams, wrapped in maroon carpet. They looked at each other, said something in German, and then laughed.

Still unsure, we didn't laugh.

But when they switched off the torches, called off the machine guns, and zipped up the tent, we looked at each other, burst out laughing, and said, "Fuck! What was all that about?"

As we wended our way back to England over the following few days, time ceased to mean anything. Any thoughts of the hotel or work had evaporated in Europe as quickly as the wanderlust grabbed ahold of us. The act of living and traveling with no purpose was all so easy in those days.

Somehow, along the way we'd made contact with a ginger-headed friend of ours called David Foster, or "Floss" for short, and we'd arranged to meet him somewhere on the South Coast after we disembarked the ferry at Dover.

As it turned out, our paths converged at Babbacombe, rather a picturesque seaside town not far from Torquay and identifiable by tall, steep cliffs that towered above the beach below. Like a scene from a movie, the three of us met at the top of these cliffs whereupon Nick had a brilliant idea.

"Why don't we throw our stuff off the cliffs so we don't have to carry it down?"

"Seems like a good idea to me . . . "

On paper, it wasn't a bad idea. Logic suggested that rucksacks would somehow find their way down, with the help of gravity, to the beach a hundred feet or so below.

One by one we threw our gear over. And one by one we watched as our respective belongings bounced down satisfyingly for a while, before losing momentum and being snagged on a bush or such, like at different points on the descent.

"Now what?" I said.

"We'll all walk down, and then we can climb up and get the stuff down," Nick said.

"I see what you're saying. But I don't like the sound of it."

At the beach, it was decided that Floss and I would go up after the gear. It was a hell of a climb but we did OK. But inevitably, when you're climbing up rocks, you're soon faced with overhanging parts that, while getting you higher, also stop you getting back down.

Realizing we were climbing toward probable disaster, I thought, *We're idiots.*

We got pretty close to the stuff but by that time we had started to panic a bit. It was hot, we were committed with no way down, seagulls were shitting all over us . . .

So, we sent out the alarm call to Nick, who was safely down on the beach, watching potential disaster unfold above.

"Get help!" we shouted.

Nick took off to the village for help.

As I hung there by my fingertips and toenails, I thought, *Cool! At least this'll be a helicopter rescue . . .*

I only realized that I was wrong when I heard this great big thud, followed by these great big ropes just missing my head and landing by me—followed in turn by these chubby firemen scooting down them toward us.

As we got hauled up, as we breached the brow of the cliff it became apparent that the whole village was on the other end of the rope!

"Hi, everybody!" I remember saying, embarrassed and slightly disappointed that it hadn't been a helicopter rescue.

They took us all to the police station, asked us a bunch of questions, and sent coppers to our respective homes (in my case a home that I hadn't set foot in for more than a year). But we didn't know any of this at the time.

"Good afternoon, Mrs. Downing. Were you aware that your son has just been rescued off cliffs in Babbacombe?"

"No . . ."

"Did you even *know* he was in Babbacombe?"

"No . . ."

"Well . . ."

After a couple of hours in the police station, they put us in a car and dropped us off at the roundabout at the top of the town and told us to go home—an instruction we blatantly ignored. Instead, we hitchhiked to Weston-super-Mare for no good reason that I can remember. And then from there we hitchhiked up the A1 to Durham to visit Nick's grandparents, where we managed to sleep in a bed for the first time in God knows how long, possibly two or three weeks. The next day Nick and I had a big falling out about something and made our separate ways back to the Midlands.

This trip of a lifetime had ended on a slightly sour note . . .

When I arrived in the vicinity of the hotel, as I walked along the lane, I could vaguely see something red outside the back door. I remember thinking, *What the hell is all that?*

As I got closer, it became apparent that what I had seen was my earthly belongings, which had been gathered up and dumped outside in red polythyene bags.

I'd lost my job.

As disappointing as this was, I could hardly blame my boss for sacking me. I was meant to have been away for ten days, but those ten days had turned into a month. He had no idea where I was, so he had no choice but to find somebody else, regardless of how good an employee I had been.

With no other options available, I just got on the bus and made my humble way back to my parents' house on the Yew Tree Estate. Given the circumstances under which I'd left, I was a little unsure as to what the lay of the land might be when I got there.

As it turned out, I had every reason to be apprehensive.

CHAPTER FOUR

W HEN I WALKED THROUGH THE FRONT DOOR OF MY parents' house, the first thing my mother said after hello was, "Here's your baby brother . . . "

Because I'd been away for so long, with just that one, token letter of contact, I had no idea that my younger brother, Adrian, was even in the pipeline, much less living and breathing.

I didn't know what to say.

Life had moved on in my absence, just like I, too, had undergone changes of my own since I'd left. Yet, here, being handed to me was my own flesh and blood, just weeks old. Within a few minutes of being in that house, things felt different. Yet at the same time, everything felt exactly the same.

I felt like I'd outgrown the wet-behind-the-ears fifteen-year-old lad I was when I left. After all, as well as having navigated some of those tricky years that any young man goes through on the way to adulthood without the benefit of parental support, I'd also held down a job, passed college courses, and traveled under mostly my own steam. To that end, I was essentially a different person.

However, one look at the familiar expression—a mixture of fear and disgust—that crossed my mother's face when my dad barked an instruction from the nearby front room told me that nothing much had changed for her.

Regardless, if I was to survive however long it was I stayed at home, I knew that my newfound maturity and work ethic were both going to be important factors. I just thought, *If I'm never in the house, I'll never have to deal with my dad.*

◆

The important thing that distinguished my second stint at home was that this time, at the age of almost eighteen, I had the freedom to come and go as I wished. When I had work to go to, I got up early in the morning and left the house before anyone else was up.

In the evening, I'd come home, get changed, sit in my room playing on the guitar before going out with my mates until late—late enough that, by the time I returned, everyone was asleep. Thankfully, I rarely saw my dad.

Around this time, late 1968 or early '69, I recall walking around the estate in the evening whenever I felt like it, to and from the youth club, sensing that little groups were forming around me, all of them into music of some kind, many of them carrying vinyl albums under their arms and a good proportion of them wearing trench coats.

While the hippy scene was generally in its last throes, the Yew Tree Estate seemed to be maintaining some of the movement's last holdouts. I absorbed myself in this scene while at the same time looking for a job that could pay my rent and, ideally, further my music career.

After reading a newspaper advertisement, I decided I'd apply for a position—in the first instance at a gentlemen's outfitter called

Harry Fenton's in Walsall. What I didn't realize at that time was that a bloke going by the name of Rob Halford worked there, but the day I walked in to ask for a job, it happened to be his day off. I didn't see him, but it was a close call.

"We've got no jobs here just now, but we're looking for someone in the Bullring," they told me—referring to the well-known shopping center in Birmingham city center.

I was hired straightaway as a shop assistant in the Bullring branch, tasked to measure people up and sell clothes. I enjoyed the work; I don't really know why. But the best thing about it was that Birmingham city center was a great place to spend a dinner hour, so I'd always be in the music stores, looking at guitars and searching through vinyl records, before going back to the shop and getting the measuring tape out all over again.

On reflection, it was a great job, but I left six months later to become an electrician's mate on a hospital development in Sutton Coldfield, where they were building a new wing. I couldn't ignore the fact that the money was very much better: I jumped up from six pounds a week to eleven or twelve.

Although I had no experience suitable for this job, I learned fast and did well. While all the lads used to go and play football on the dinner hour, it was here that the foundation of what I later did with a guitar came to be.

I broke things down to the absolute fundamentals. It seemed absolutely necessary to do so.

With just a picture I'd torn out of a magazine for guidance, I spent every lunch break analyzing the fret board, identifying and memorizing all the individual notes. Because it's not exciting, this is a discipline that very few people undertake when learning to play the guitar. It's much simpler than people think, and it's absolutely vital, in my opinion, to making progress. It certainly was for me.

I soon found that, while there are six strings on a guitar, if you joined all six up, in theory, as one string, the notes all made sense.

Alphabetically, it just goes A through G and then back to A again—with sharps and flats in between. I have no idea why I had the forethought to put in such diligent groundwork at the time. I just thought it might be beneficial to know where all the A notes are, where all the B notes are, and so on.

I suppose that I looked upon it in the same way as I did on my cooking in that if I had any aspirations to become a really good cook, I'd have to spend the time learning to make a very good, basic roux. There was just no way around it. Then, thereafter, all I figured I'd have to do is add more skills to augment these basics. The principle seemed exactly the same to me and all I was thinking in terms of these notes was, *Well, it's going to be beneficial to know where all the A's and the B's are, so I might as well learn now.*

And that's how I proceeded for those few months on the contracting job. I can't overstate how important this period of my life was. Every dinner hour I'd study the paper fret-board. Then, that evening, I'd go home and attempt to replicate what I was learning on the neck of my makeshift guitar. It was laborious but steadily I improved—until the job came to an end.

Before it did, because all the other lads went to play football at dinner break and were always late coming back, the boss said one day, "If you're late back again, I'll sack every one of you."

Nevertheless, they were late and, true to his word, he sacked every one of them on the spot. That left just me and an Indian lad—who used to go home for his lunch instead of playing football—to finish the contract.

✦

Meanwhile, Hendrix was calling again . . .

He was due to play two sold-out shows at the Albert Hall in early 1969 and I found some way of being at both of them.

On the first night I recall sneaking in with my mate Nick to watch the sound check and nobody even bothered us. Very specific details stayed with me about those events; I was never more impressionable than when in the company of Jimi.

The road crew had this big box full of Vox wah-pedals and Fuzz Faces because that's all Hendrix played through at the time: a wah pedal and a Fuzz Face. I stood there staring, hairs on the back of my neck on end, as he, Jimi Hendrix, right in front of me, went through this box meticulously, trying all the pedals until he found one that he liked. He'd play a few licks, stop, change the pedal, and rip into something else, never altering his expression.

I was transfixed.

"Can you believe we're here?" I whispered to Nick.

I was close enough that I genuinely could smell him. And he smelled how I had always imagined he would: cigarettes, a little unwashed, but somehow acceptably offset by patchouli oil. As he stood there, I could almost reach out and touch his unbuttoned paisley-patterned shirt from where we were watching. But I didn't dare do it for fear of our intoxicating moment being ended by a security guy or roadie.

Later, a little while before the show and still on a high from the sound check, I remember being round the back waiting, hoping to get an autograph. After twenty minutes, Hendrix pulled up in a car. He had a guitar case with him. And in that case was the white Gibson SG with the three pickups; it had just come out. I had only ever read about it. It was a very expensive guitar; he'd apparently just gotten hold of it and quite rightly he had it with him, carrying it to the gig. He signed a poster for me with, simply, "Jimi."

Incidentally, years later, I did exactly the same thing when we played the Albert Hall for Roger Daltrey's Teenage Cancer Trust Tommy Vance Tribute in 2006. I pulled up in a car, with a guitar, because I'd been practicing in the hotel. Subconsciously or not, I was copying Jimi. There were a few fans waiting for us, just like there had been for Jimi in 1969. It felt so right for me to be humbly following in his footsteps, occupying the same space.

More significantly, seeing Hendrix in a few different situations over a couple of years made me realize, again, that he could turn it on or turn it off whenever he felt like it. And all of this accelerated the idea that maybe—just maybe—little old me could do the same thing someday.

Of course, the conditioned part of me thought, *Dream on, Ken.*

But another, bigger part of me thought, *Come on, mate, let's have a go anyway.*

At that point, me actually becoming a rock musician seemed as far-fetched as winning the lottery nowadays. Nevertheless, I just kept on practicing.

And I got better.

✦

Not many people know that I auditioned to be in the Al Atkins–fronted version of Judas Priest. The year after we left Churchfield Secondary School, Nick and I took a night off work to gate crash the school's end-of-year dance where, unbelievably, the bones of a band that would become Judas Priest were providing the entertainment. At that time, they were called the Jug Blues Band.

As good as they were, they weren't exactly the right band for a supposedly upbeat, feel-good school dance. They were an out-and-out blues band at the time, and I think they were playing only covers. Even then, their vibe was undeniably serious—and you couldn't help but notice that their singer, Al Atkins, was a pretty dark character among a bunch of guys who did, I admit, look really good.

The bass player was this guy called Bruno Stapenhill: really big guy—great bass player—and I seem to recall that he'd broken his foot and sat there playing on this imitation tree or log. The story went that he'd done it playing darts! Seemingly it was he who would later come up with the band name Judas Priest, having heard it in the Bob Dylan song "The Ballad of Frankie Lee And Judas Priest."

In addition to Stapenhill, a lad called Jim Perry was on drums, with a pretty good-looking double bass drum kit, and the guitar player at the time was his brother John Perry. Although they didn't, as I recall, play any original material, I still couldn't help acknowledging that everything that the band had going on at that time was extremely cool.

Sometime later, their guitar player, John Perry, died tragically at the age of eighteen. People said that he intentionally drove a van into a telephone kiosk on Hampstead Hill. I heard that it might have been because of a relationship with a girl. As the story goes, apparently the police found a book on his person with telephone numbers in it, and so they were led to the various homes of Al Atkins and the other guys. It hit them all very hard.

I didn't know the guy, but it was a real tragedy. I later got to know the girl in question a little: she was understandably very reluctant to discuss what had happened.

The upshot of it all was that they didn't want to carry on as the Jug Blues Band, but instead were auditioning guys for a band they wanted to call Judas Priest. I responded to the advertisement—totally prematurely, in retrospect. And when I turned up and auditioned at Al Atkins's house, the glaring difference in vision and ideology was clearly confirmed.

Basically, they wanted someone to come into the band to play conventional twelve-bar blues changes. That wasn't my thing at all at that time; my foundation was anything but twelve-bar. Instead, mine was a mixture of long improvisation, or a progressive style, simply because that's what was happening at that time. I had neither the ability nor the range of effects required to emulate a Hendrix type of sound, but that was nevertheless the direction I wanted to go.

Unsurprisingly, sitting in Al Atkins's front room, we soon reached an impasse. I just wasn't right for his band. We both knew it. In the end, he and I shook hands, wished each other the best, and went our separate ways. Rejection, as hard as it was to take, was definitely for the best. They hired a guy called Ernie Chataway instead.

✦

There was a moment related to that failed audition that has stood out in my mind since the second it happened. One night, as I was walking through the estate on my way back from seeing some mates, I heard a vehicle approaching along the street. As it got closer, I could just about make out the shape as being that of a Ford Thames 400E van. Then, as it drew up alongside me, I could see two things a bit more clearly. The first observation was that the words "Judas Priest" were crudely sprayed in green aerosol across the side of the van. That alone was cool enough. If it had been done in any way professionally, it wouldn't have looked nearly as good.

Judas Priest . . . Fuck! What a name that is . . .

Then, when I caught a glimpse inside the vehicle, I could see that the van was full of the coolest looking hairy guys!

I could see enough through the front window to know that the driver was John Ward, an extremely long-haired and well-known member of the local music scene at the time. John was from West Bromwich and he lived behind the town hall.

As far as I know, he was never actually in Judas Priest so I have no clue why he would have been driving that night. But he'd later go on to become a roadie for Deep Purple and Led Zeppelin prior to managing Whitesnake for a time. In the other front seat was the band's de facto leader, Al Atkins.

As the van rolled down the road into the distance, I thought, *I'd love to be in that van!*

Just witnessing this van scene and getting a brief insight into the imagined lifestyle that went with it was so incredibly motivating.

So, having seen this forerunner version of Judas Priest play live, auditioned for them, and then seen that van later, as much as I might have felt that I'd love to be a part of it, the inescapable reality was that the music I was attempting to play at the time was worlds away from what they were doing.

◆

Looking back, I was at a more profound crossroads at that time anyway. Until my second cousin Brian Badhams tossed a coin in his bedroom and said, "Heads, you play guitar. Tails, you take up the bass"—to decide which of us would continue with the guitar and which would switch over to bass—it wasn't even certain that I'd continue be a guitarist at all.

Although he was the same age as me, Brian had always been a companion in a healthily competitive sense when I was growing up. When I was a youngster, he and I used to go fishing together whenever I could escape the house on my bike or was staying at my gran's.

Brian was also an able musician, although he wasn't overly keen on the piano lessons his parents made him take when he was a teenager. I remember many occasions where I'd be waiting for him on my bike outside his house, listening to him playing piano scales over and over again. Frustrated, I used to think, *Will he ever finish!?*

As time passed, Brian started accumulating a few old acoustic guitars, spurred on by his and my shared love of Hendrix. Then, later still, Brian joined a band called White Rabbit with a well-known and well-liked Brummie player called John Thomas.

John (who passed away relatively recently) was one of those players with intangible abilities that I used to really admire as I was finding my way. He possessed what I like to call "ingredients," and he knew what to do with them. He could put a series of notes together in a way that I, at that time, was just not able to. I was jealous of how John could improvise, and Brian's and my musical directions diverged as White Rabbit became more popular in the local area.

However, now that Brian's coin had landed my way, I decided that if I was indeed going to continue playing guitar, as fate or luck had dictated, I'd really need to join a band of some kind (a) to get some live experience and (b) to earn a bit of money so that I could continue to pay my mother some rent.

The pop band that I ended getting together with was called Stagecoach. I would be one of two guitarists in the band. On the very first day I joined, they gave me sheet music for various shit songs by Engelbert Humperdinck, and other pop songs like "Tie a Yellow Ribbon," and said: "Here. Learn these."

We played workingman's clubs around the West Bromwich and Walsall areas, and, as exciting as it was to be playing live at all, I have no hesitation in admitting that the standard of my guitar playing was really quite crap at the time. Regardless, people came to see us, I honed what few live chops I had, and I got paid for doing so.

Soon, driven by this unquenchable need to at least have the tools of the rock guitar trade, sometime in late 1969, I walked into Ringway Music on Moor Street in Birmingham with just one thing on my mind: a proper electric guitar

Even though I was flat broke, I was determined to get my hands on an electric guitar of some kind. I was on a mission and, one way or another, I was going back home with something to replace the DIY assembly of random, unrelated guitar parts thing I had: the Stratocaster replica with unrelated pickups, no scratchboard and all the wiring visible.

In truth, anything would have represented an upgrade at that point. But the red Gibson SG Junior with a single-coil P-90 pickup that stood in the window was the equivalent to swapping a Morris Minor for a Rolls-Royce. Even though I really had my heart set on a Flying V, this wasn't a bad alternative. I had to have it. There were no two ways about it.

After I picked it up and put it down probably a dozen times, the salesman, clearly sensing my desperation, ushered me away from the sales floor and back into the smoky office where he positioned himself behind the desk, eyeing me up and down throughout, with a book of paper invoices on the desk in front of him. He laid out his cards.

"You can take it, but I'll need a small deposit," he said. "And then you'll need to come back in every month with a payment."

As he spoke, I saw him scribble the words "Ken Downing" on one of the invoices. I thought, *That's a good sign!*

"I'll take it," I told him. "Is a pound enough to get me started?"

"Sign your name here . . . "

Unbelievably, a pound was enough.

I had persuaded him, via a combination of youthful enthusiasm and unadulterated poverty, into allowing me to enter into some kind of crude credit agreement. To this day I have no idea how I did it.

Not only that, I also persuaded the guy to let me have quite a big, fifty-watt Marshall amplifier with a cabinet on the never-never!

Then I thought, *Now, what about effects?*

I couldn't do it.

I just didn't have the heart to ask the guy for anything else. There wasn't much in the way of pedals and effects around in 1969 anyway. As fate would have it, I wouldn't have to wait long until I got my hands on something far better than I could have bought.

Noel Redding's solo band, Fat Mattress, were due to play Mothers club in Erdington not long before Jimi passed away a few months later. Located above a furniture shop on Erdington High Street, Mothers wasn't a big club by any means; it probably accommodated a couple of hundred people at a stretch. It was one of those venues where the band either played on the floor itself, basically as an extension of the audience, or, if they were really pushing the boat out with production, they might have arranged for a platform to raise them eighteen inches or so above the floor itself.

This night at Mothers was one such occasion and Brian Badhams and I made sure we were as close to the "stage" as anyone possibly could be—even though Fat Mattress were, in my eyes, a bit lightweight. The Hendrix association was still enough to entice me in.

As the gig went on, I felt my eye being drawn to a Fuzz Face pedal sitting near the front of the stage. Feeling opportunity tug at me, I thought, *I bet Jimi's played through that at some point.*

I was convinced that this was, without doubt, one of the pedals I'd seen Jimi's roadie tip into the box when I snuck into that Albert Hall sound check a couple of months prior.

"You can't just take it, Ken . . . "

"I have to. It's a chance in a lifetime."

After the gig, as people were leaving, I crept onto the platform, grabbed the Fuzz Face, and slipped it inside my jacket. Then, rather than take it home, for some reason I decided to hide it inside an old upright piano in another room in the club. I came back for it a couple of weeks later. That's the kind of thing that thieves do: if you nick something, leave it in the establishment and then come back for it. Sometimes it's not worth the risk at the time for someone to see you nick it and pounce on you. And technically it's not nicked until someone sees you leaving the establishment with it anyway—"It hadn't left the building, your honor . . . " Leave it a couple of weeks and it's a slam dunk!

I'm not proud of nicking that pedal, but it wasn't just a simple case of theft either. I've always thought of it as fandom gone absolutely mad. I played through that pedal a few times, then it got lost. I never did find out if Jimi actually used it. I like to think that he did.

✦

My days in Stagecoach were some of my last at home on the Yew Tree. I continued to play the workingmen's club circuit for money while using any spare time I had at home to develop my technique.

Reading sheet music is not an easy way to go as a guitar player. It's very hard and laborious going, principally because, in these

days, although you'd have people like John Williams doing inter-
pretations on guitar, sheet music in the '60s in general wasn't really
created for guitars, but more for pianos and violins, etc. Not to say
it wasn't doable; it was just very hard work. (Years later, the introduction of guitar tabs would be a game changer.)

Nevertheless, I can remember sitting there in my bedroom with
the sheet music for an entire Leonard Cohen album, telling myself
that I couldn't leave until I'd perfected the entire record. Although
I was far from a sight reader, after what seemed like an eternity, I
got through the album. I look back on those days as paying my dues.

While my standard of guitar playing was improving, the atmosphere at home was not. Nothing whatsoever had changed in the
relationship between my mum and dad. He was as bad as he ever
was. I just hadn't witnessed much of what had been going on because I really only slept there.

One day, that all changed.

I was in my room one evening when I heard this huge commo-
tion downstairs. By the time I got down there, it transpired that
my mother had somehow fallen down the stairs while carrying my
brother Adrian, who was still basically a baby. Although I didn't actually see the blow land, it was also pretty clear that my dad had
punched my mother full in the face.

I flew at him.

This time I really was ready to punch this man, but then, out of
nowhere, my mother flew at me!

"Leave it alone, Ken," she screamed at me. "Go back to your
room."

"Why? He *punched* you?"

"Go back to your room, Ken."

I stood there thinking, *What are you doing, woman?*

On one hand, my mother's reaction made absolutely zero sense.
I was trying to protect her, yet she was flying off the handle at me!
However, when I thought about it later, I realized why she'd reacted

in the way she had. She knew that once I'd left the house for good, she'd still have to live with the wretched man. That was the bottom line.

So, as much as I'm sure she wanted to side with me against him, to do so wasn't in her best interests going forward. At the time I didn't see that standpoint at all, of course. I was just furious and left.

Because I'd had jobs in the past, when I went into the local council benefit office I was informed that I'd racked up enough working credits to be eligible to sign on the dole for welfare benefits.

"I'll actually get money?" I asked.

"Yes. Five pounds fifty a week," the cashier said.

This news was a relief, not least because, having stormed out of the Yew Tree, I now had to look for somewhere permanent to live—and that would require more money than I was earning playing the occasional gig with Stagecoach. So, I went on the dole, and that was enough to pay rent and kind of live off.

The place I rented was a bedsit on Lodge Road, which runs all the way right behind West Bromwich Town Hall. It was part of an old Victorian house that had been divided, so the room itself was very, very tiny: a bed, a table, and a one-ring cooker. That was it. The rent was two pounds sixty per week. I remember that number vividly because I kept having to find it from somewhere, every Thursday.

The building was rough, too; it was cold and there were mice everywhere. The only carpet was the piece I stole from the church in Austria and had kept ever since. I thought it was luxury. Also, the owners—an elderly couple—lived on the floor below me with their Down's syndrome daughter who must have been in her thirties. My abiding recollection is that all night, every night, the daughter made all kinds of strange noises. As sympathetic as I was, it was terrible to listen to all night!

Yet, I was happy on Lodge Road. As small and noisy as it was, it was at least mine. Furthermore, anything was always going to be an improvement on living at home.

With little money to spare, buying my first second-hand television set for two pounds felt particularly satisfying. The problem was, I soon found out that the vertical hold had packed in, so the screen was permanently rolling! Sometimes it would stop for long enough to let me watch something, but pretty soon it would start rolling again. I used to throw my shoes at it.

When I got tired of that I'd just get my transistor radio out and listen to Kid Jensen on Radio Caroline. At that time, he was playing bands like Budgie every single night without fail, as well as Deep Purple and the early stuff by Skid Row with Gary Moore playing guitar. He was just seventeen at the time.

I just absorbed it all while sitting there, night after night, plonking away on the guitar. For the first time in my life I felt liberated in the sense that I no longer had a boss overseeing what I was doing. Furthermore, as I signed on to the dole as an eighteen-year-old in 1969, I couldn't have possibly known that I would never have a traditional, nine-to-five job thereafter.

Along with this newfound sense of independence, my Lodge Road days signaled the beginning of a lifelong romantic odyssey. While I had had experiences with girls in those crazy plaza-music-nights days with my mates—a drunken canoodle here, a one-night stand there perhaps—there was part of me that always felt that maybe there had to be something more substantial and worthwhile to be discovered within a relationship with the opposite sex.

Whether having to observe my parents' awful relationship throughout my childhood had made me a bit gun-shy, I don't really know. But when I met a local girl that I really liked, Carol her name was, I remember thinking, *Maybe you're the one-girlfriend-for-life type after all, Ken.*

As if it was the most natural thing in the world, Carol and I immediately started living what I remember to be a very quaint little devoted life together. As young and inexperienced as we were, we both seemed to know exactly how to do it. I spent most of my days in the bedsitter, playing on guitar. Then, if I wasn't playing a gig at night, I'd meet her out of work, go over to her house in Bloxwich where she lived with her dad, maybe get fed a bit of dinner, and then I'd walk back home up Lodge Road. There wasn't much of me at the time. It didn't take a lot to feed me.

Although neither of us had anything in the way of money, there seemed to be enough value attached to our budding relationship to keep us both blissfully happy, day in, day out.

Better still, Carol liked music.

Although she didn't have the broad range of taste that I had, she knew what she liked. Beyond that, she was always willing to learn as I continued to be guided by whatever was on the radio. In fact, as I remember, it was her encouragement that got me to absolutely perfect—to the extent that it was note perfect—the Leonard Cohen album, after she'd asked me if I could play the song "Suzanne" for her. She was always a very encouraging influence on me.

✦

As well as these rather unfulfilling but paying pop gigs that I was committed to with Stagecoach, around this same time I was also trying to play music with a good buddy of mine, John Ellis, in a band that, when I saw a photo of us all at the time, looked like a bunch of hairy dudes!

John lived near me, had long blond hair like I did; we became very good friends and started knocking around together all the time.

Regardless of our looks, this band John and I joined was at least playing some form of rock, which was much more in line with what I was interested in at the time. They had a guitar player, a bass player, and a singer, so, in addition to John and me, we became a five-piece with two guitar players. We messed around a bit, but we never played any gigs.

The hairy-dude band just fizzled out.

Shortly afterward, via John, a quietly determined lad called Ian Hill came onto the scene.

I'd known Ian slightly for many years; he'd shopped me into the police a couple of years earlier. We'd actually been at school together since we were very young and hung out in broadly the same circles for many years. In the latter years I often skipped school to go to Ian's to listen to vinyl albums because some of my other friends were in his immediate circle. But we'd never really been close friends—simply because nothing had ever brought us together.

Now, however, a love of music was throwing me, John Ellis, and Ian Hill together as an aspiring three-piece, with Ian taking to the bass on the back of a love for Jack Bruce and the fact that his father had been a bass player.

The three of us started jamming together quite regularly, scratching together a few cheap little amplifiers to play at a local school hall up the road from where John lived. Not long afterward, having decided to call ourselves Freight for some reason, we started to feel the need to broaden our net in terms of finding a regular and suitable place to rehearse the music we were playing. Following suit with what I'd seen, we also sprayed the word "Freight" in aerosol on the side of our van we used to get around!

"There's this place in Wednesbury I heard someone talking about," Ian said one day.

"OK, let's find out what's going on there," John and I said.

At that time, an old Victorian school hall attached to a church in the nearby town of Wednesbury, between West Bromwich and Dudley, was the rehearsal place of choice for all manner of local bands. At certain times of night there'd be numerous aspiring acts jockeying around there; Slade would often pull up outside with their gear in a semitrailer. It was a real hive of activity, night after night.

This unorthodox venue was known as Holy Joe's, after the vicar of the church who lived in part of the building. He was an odd, older chap who reputedly liked a bit of the sherry, and he oversaw the rehearsal space on a first-come, first-served basis. As a steady stream of bands showed up each evening, he'd go around collecting cold cash—which probably only amounted to four shillings per session.

Really there was only one viable rehearsal space at Holy Joe's—one of the smaller classrooms that had a wooden floor and wood paneling all around. Obviously, this was where everyone wanted to rehearse, and if that room wasn't available, Joe would even let some bands rehearse in his own front room for a bit of extra money.

For several weeks, maybe even months, Freight occupied Holy Joe's for as many nights as we could get in there. We'd go in, set up, and then I'd go off on these long, improvised guitar solos armed with a new-to-me Gibson SG Standard for which I'd traded in the SG junior, plus some of the money I'd made playing Stagecoach gigs to sweeten the deal. With what I'd call a serious guitar to play with, I threw myself deeper and deeper into the world of progressive playing that was anything but blues. We'd just go in there, set up, and I'd wail away.

As if I needed any more encouragement and motivation, I saw Jimi Hendrix for the final time at the Isle of Wight Festival in the late summer of 1970.

Although he had toned his performances down considerably since those halcyon Coventry Theatre days three years earlier, seeing and hearing Hendrix was just so inspiring.

Meeting the man in person properly was even more incredible.

"Ken, I think that's Jimi's caravan," Nick Bowbanks said, pointing toward a white trailer set apart from some others.

"You reckon?" I replied. "Should we go and find out?"

"You're dead right we should, mate. We might never get such a chance."

Nick and I walked up to the end of the caravan, where there was a vertically opening window. It was ajar, and through it we could hear quiet voices talking and laughing. One of them was instantly recognizable as that of Jimi Hendrix.

Nick and I looked at each other. We both nodded simultaneously. We had acquired a lot of shared intuition of the years. Like a pair of idiots, we opened the window and stuck our two heads in. I've no idea what the people inside must have thought.

"Hi!" we said, suddenly feeling that we were invading their personal space

"Hey, guys," some American hippy-looking girl replied. "What can we do for you two?"

"I don't really know," I said. "We just wanted to see if Jimi was here."

And there he was, sitting on a bench at a square table, drinking from a Coca-Cola bottle. A brief, awkward chat followed. I have no recollection of what was said; it was a blur of fandom gone mad— the culmination of years of adoration.

As we left, he went back to the table.

"Here," he said, handing me the empty bottle he'd been drinking from and the metal cap.

"Thanks very much!" I said, shaking his hand.

Three weeks later he was gone.

By November of that year, the version of Judas Priest that I'd auditioned for a year or so earlier wasn't happening in the way Al Atkins had hoped. At that point I'm sure he was looking to do something else. Whether they were actively looking for new people or whether they'd disbanded, I don't really know.

Regardless, on one of these many nights we rehearsed at Holy Joe's, Al appeared outside our rehearsal room, where he stood and apparently listened intently to what we were doing. Then he knocked on the door and came in while we just continued with whatever number we were playing.

Pretty much straightaway Al said, "Are you lads looking for a singer?"

"Err, what?" I said, more out of surprise than anything else.

After all, it really hadn't been that long since my rather embarrassing audition. I was delighted! Even though Al was a bit older than the rest of us, I considered him to be one of the most respected singers in the area.

Where other singers might have been a bit more colorful, Al Atkins was a much darker and introspective guy than anyone I'd come across before and that, to me, was a good thing. *This dark, moody side could be a really good addition, you know . . .*

"Shall we go up the pub to discuss things?" we suggested.

"All right," Al replied.

So, Ian, John Ellis, Al Atkins, and I walked up the street to the old pub on the corner. It's now an Indian restaurant. Pretty soon, the subject of a band name was raised.

I must say that I always considered Freight to be a distinctly shitty band name. I always felt that it had very bluesy connotations—and I didn't like that at all given the direction I wanted to go in.

But Judas Priest conjured up entirely different images in my head. You can imagine what I was thinking now that Al Atkins, singer in a band called Judas Priest, was making himself available to play with us.

But I didn't say anything.

I let the conversation go on and on until I couldn't hold on any longer.

"Oh yeah, what's happening with the name Judas Priest?" I said. "Why can't *we* just be Judas Priest?"

Looking back, I bided my time for so long because I just didn't want rejection. Ever since I'd seen the van on the estate with the crude spray-painted logo, I *knew* what a great name it was. To me, those two words weren't just a name. They were a huge statement.

"Yeah, why not?" Al said. "We can just call ourselves Judas Priest."

Fucking hell, I thought, *now we've got a real chance to do something.*

When I think about it now, I'm not certain that the others had the same understanding of its value. I think they might have felt that they'd plagiarized it because of its origin, who knows?

✦

Almost straightaway, Al Atkins and I settled into being a tight and productive songwriting team. We'd convene for our sessions in the living room of his mother's house, where he lived with his mother, wife, and young daughter. From the start it became apparent that Al was quite the prolific writer. Not just that, he also played guitar, so he and I immediately could communicate in that language.

Even though I was the one who had a more fixed idea of the direction I wanted the music to go in, it was convenient that Al, too, wanted to shift away from the blues, perhaps having been influenced by the music he heard us rehearsing. For me it wasn't all about the blues at all, despite the fact that there were still, in 1970, a lot of bands focusing on that style. As much as I appreciated blues bands like Taste, Free, Chicken Shack, and Savoy Brown, I really felt that bands should be moving on from that—simply because Hendrix had done so a few years prior. Unfortunately, a lot of bands didn't know how to move on.

In contrast, I was all about moody, dark and heavy riffs along the lines of that great band Quatermass, whose self-titled debut album had been released that same year. Al was completely on board with that. It felt like we were both buying into the future.

When Al first played it to me, I thought, *This is great . . .*

Hearing them changed everything. Whatever you called Quatermass, you couldn't class them as blues. In fact, tracks like "Post War, Saturday Echo," and "Black Sheep of the Family" were anything but blues. Their vibe was darker and altogether more exciting.

My immediate aim therefore was to steer our four-piece band away from any blues influences, toward a style more akin to what Quatermass (and very few others at that time) were doing.

That didn't prove difficult to achieve.

Consequently, early Judas Priest live sets around 1970/1971 consisted of a few Quatermass covers and a selection of original numbers. We may have played Hendrix's "Spanish Castle Magic" once; I can't recall that we played any other covers. And that was it, really.

From the start, my thinking was very much: Don't cover other people's songs. Do your own stuff, and then hone your skills on original material.

By and large, I've felt that way ever since 1970.

Of the early original material conceived by Al and me, what became the song "Victim of Changes" was one of the first. We formulated it together and then we played it live, as "Whiskey Woman."

Thereafter, Al and I wrote the early versions of songs like "Winter," "Dreamer Deceiver," "Never Satisfied," and "Caviar and Meths"—all of which would resurface later, cocredited to him.

With a growing list of songs to showcase, these live shows with Al Atkins came thick and fast once we were confident enough in our showmanship. We became a fixture on what became known as "The Midlands circuit." We also went farther afield, to Scotland once, as I recall.

The first official gig we played as the Al Atkins–fronted version of Judas Priest was at St. John's Hall in Essington, a workingmen's club between Wolverhampton and Walsall. The date was March 16, 1971. As first gigs go, it was as inauspicious as it gets.

Workingmen's clubs in that area were known to put on small gigs, once or twice a month, specifically as "entertainment" for the workingmen's children. Whether we were exactly what they had in mind at the time, who knows. Regardless, we played this little gig—me, Al, John Ellis, and Ian—to a room packed with young kids who just danced the night away in spite of the fact we were playing

Quatermass covers and a few originals. It felt very strange—and we got paid six pounds for the privilege.

As good as it all was, gigging as a four-piece was extremely hard work. Sometimes these places would be empty, and when people did show up, they often clearly didn't quite get what we were trying to do, particularly with this evolving, original material of ours.

Nevertheless, we persevered. I was just happy that I was able to do what I wanted to do. Although I wasn't making much money, that was still far preferable to working in a shitty, dead-end job, answerable to a boss. The primary reason that I joined a band in the first place was to gain a sense of freedom and—as we gigged with that Al Atkins–fronted four-piece for the first three years of the '70s—I finally felt, *You've made it, Ken. Keep going . . .*

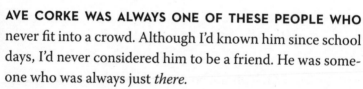

CHAPTER FIVE

DAVE CORKE WAS ALWAYS ONE OF THESE PEOPLE WHO never fit into a crowd. Although I'd known him since school days, I'd never considered him to be a friend. He was some- one who was always just *there*.

"Corky," as he was known, was a strange-looking lad: wore bi- focals, didn't have looks or muscles, and had no apparent talent for anything.

But he'd soon find his niche.

Corky was always mad into his music. He never actually played anything but he was always one of those guys who perennially seemed to be at gigs and hanging out with bands in general. When- ever anybody was playing in the local area, you could guarantee that Corky would be there.

As time passed, it became apparent that he saw himself as something more than a hanger-on in Judas Priest's world. We wel- comed him and soon he was traveling around with us to gigs while deftly shoehorning himself into the position of being our de facto manager/booker.

We did nothing to stop him. He was a laugh a minute. Better still, he had a gift for gab in a big way.

"Hello, this is DCA in Birmingham calling," we'd hear him saying on the phone. "Might you be interested in booking my transatlantic recording artist, Judas Priest?"

Transatlantic recording artist?! Who's he kidding?

He even told that to the people at the Cavern in Liverpool and they believed him. We played there twice in the space of a couple of weeks in October of 1972 and I'll never forget when I saw the advert in the *Liverpool Echo*:

> ### Tonight! Judas Priest, Transatlantic Recording Artist playing live at The Cavern!

It sounded great, but it was all bullshit.

As if that wasn't funny enough, the best part of it all was that Corky was conducting these professional-sounding business interactions from a telephone box outside his flat!

He didn't even have an office at the time. If anyone asked (in those days you could tell when someone was calling from a phone booth), he just told whoever it was that his offices were being renovated at that particular time. We could only admire the man's ingenuity. It was all mad stuff with Corky.

Unbelievably, bookers (a) never knew and (b) booked us anyway. He had clearly kidded them. Corky got us a hell of a lot of gigs in those days—with Budgie and also, because of his various London connections, with a band called the Heavy Metal Kids. What a band name that was!

We also appeared third on a bill that included Thin Lizzy and Strife, a three-piece band from Liverpool that was doing quite well at the time. To my great dismay, John Ellis quit after that gig, having decided that a career in music just wasn't for him.

In truth I was absolutely gutted when John left. I liked him, rated him highly as a drummer, and thought he looked really good. John was briefly replaced by another local drummer friend called Alan Moore.

Then, when Alan departed, Chris "Congo" Campbell came along.

I have no idea how we found him, this big, muscular, mixed-race lad with a huge Afro. All I know is that the house he lived in with his gran looked directly into the back wall of the main stand at Villa Park football ground. I remember stepping inside and feeling like I'd just walked into my gran's house in West Bromwich.

But he was perfect. He looked good, was a powerful drummer; it was great. Again, in this updated lineup with Congo, we thought we had something viable and unique.

Around the same time, we were getting gigs from IMA, an agency co-owned by Black Sabbath's lead guitarist, Tony Iommi, which was run by Norman Hood, a well-known Midlands promoter and booker who lived in Litchfield and who would later become a cartoon artist of some repute.

Although I'm told that he showed up once at a gig where we supported Budgie at Birmingham Town Hall, I don't recall ever meeting Tony Iommi at that time. What I do recall is being near their offices on Hurst Street in Birmingham and seeing Tony's Lamborghini parked outside on a couple of occasions. That sight, of course, appealed to the young petrolhead in me no end. *Somebody's obviously doing all right!*

Anyway, in early 1973, we were at least fortunate enough to be affiliated with a reputable agency that was finding us regular but small gigs to supplement Corky's freelance efforts. We'd go wherever anybody would have us.

One night, as we arrived in Inverness in the freezing February cold, I noticed that the parking lay-by outside the venue was coned off in what looked like a very official capacity. As we pulled closer in the van, this guy appeared in the middle of the road as if he was landing an aircraft. He appeared as if he was a traffic warden.

"Judas Priest, I assume?" the guy said as Ian rolled down the window to ask where we should unload.

"Who are you, mate?" Ian asked.

"Oh, I'm also the bass player in the support band—we just wanted to make sure you could park! Just pull in here," he told us, pointing us in the direction of the reserved space. "I coned this off specially for you lot," he added.

Even then, at the other end of the country, people were getting to know about us. It amused us no end. We had thought we were in trouble as he waved at us but he was a big fan.

But everything was about to fall apart again.

After a gig in Birmingham where we supported the Leicester-based progressive rock band Family, Al Atkins and Chris Campbell walked into the IMA office the next morning and basically said, "If you don't give us some money, we're quitting the band."

Money was obviously very tight and unpredictable—as it still was for all of us. Gigs weren't getting any bigger and there was no record deal in sight. They were only expressing what all of us probably felt at the time.

"Sorry, we don't have any money to give you."

We got no money; everyone was despondent. True to their word, Al and Chris drifted off to do their own thing. I should stress that they weren't forced to quit. They chose to do it. That left Ian and me, who, as much as we needed money, were both young and commitment-free enough to not walk away, too.

Instead, I focused on finding a new singer.

Fortunately, because of my girlfriend Carol's friendship with Rob Halford's sister Sue, a go-go dancer at the Dirty Duck in Walsall, I had already been giving thought to the idea of approaching Rob to see if he'd join.

From what I'd been told, Rob's band, Hiroshima, may have been playing the kind of progressive stuff that was becoming pretty popular around the Midlands at the time. That was a good start. I suppose in the back of my mind was the thought that, one day, Judas Priest was going to need a vocalist who had more range than Al Atkins had.

The way I saw it, having great musicians could only take a band so far. But if you then added a great voice, there was no limit to how successful you could become. Both Ian Gillan (Deep Purple) and Robert Plant (Led Zeppelin) had successfully proved that theory in their bands.

I couldn't swear to it, but I don't think I'd ever seen Rob's band Hiroshima play before I met him. But my girlfriend Carol had.

"You should hear this guy," she said. "He's like Robert Plant and Ian Gillan rolled into one."

"Really?" I said.

"Yeah, and he's available . . . "

At that time Rob lived with his parents and his brother Nigel in a council house on the Beechdale Estate between Bloxwich and Walsall. It was a very modest existence, the kind that we were all entirely used to.

I'll just go and knock on his door.

When Ian and I knocked on the door the following Sunday afternoon, Rob's mother answered.

"Yes?"

"I've come to see Robert. Is he at home?"

Just as I said that, behind her a figure appeared dressed in jeans and a denim shirt. With a head of very short hair.

That's not good.

He was holding a harmonica.

That is good! Could come in handy.

Then, and Rob has denied this, but my recollection is that after I'd been invited into the front room of the house, he went upstairs for something. And while he did so he was singing harmonies to whatever happened to be on the radio at that time. It was a female artist along the lines of Doris Day.

OK . . . this guy has potential.

Thereafter, I seem to remember that we went straight into rehearsals and took it from there.

◆

In the middle of all this band upheaval, sometime in late 1973, I moved out of the bedsit on Lodge Road after a phone call from Corky.

"I've got this one-bedroom flat in Handsworth Wood," he told us. "You lot can move in if you want."

I have no idea how Corky had managed to get his hands on this property, but it seemed like a good idea. In retrospect, I think he was probably looking for Ian and me to help him out with the rent but I'm pretty certain that that never happened.

The front door would hardly open because of the bills piled up behind it and I seem to remember seeing debt collectors up ladders, trying to look inside!

Nevertheless, that flat became rock 'n' roll central. Five of us were living there at one point, even though there was only one bedroom: me, Ian, Carol, Ian's girlfriend, and Corky.

There was a garage underneath where we stored our gear. Whenever we had a gig, we'd rent a van, pay a roadie, come back in the early hours, unload it, and go to bed.

All kinds of friends and women would call in at all times of day and night. One night, while I was lying in bed, I heard a knock on the door.

"Ken, Ian, let us in, won't you? We're on our way back to Wales from Newcastle."

Budgie had arrived.

We cleared some space on the floor of the sitting room and they all dossed down to sleep. Whenever we were in Cardiff with nowhere to stay, those guys would return the favor.

Rob would often come over to visit Ian and me at Corky's flat, and seeing all the comings and goings, he must have realized that we were a bit further up the ladder in terms of gigging experience than Hiroshima had been. Even then, Judas Priest was a bit of a name in the area—at least for a local band. After a week or two of rehearsals, it was apparent to everyone that the partnership was going to work.

"I'll join," Rob said. "But can I bring my drummer with me?"

Not having a drummer at that time, Ian and I nodded, said yes, and from that day onward Rob Halford and John Hinch were in Judas Priest.

Corky seemed even more enthused by the new line-up than we were. He was always doing things that he thought would advance us in some way—and that extended to giving us stage names of his choosing just a few days after Rob officially came on board.

One day he knocked on the door at Rob's house, where we were working on some song ideas, with a poster in his hand.

"What do you think of this?"

He showed us this promotional poster he'd mocked up, with pictures of all of us. Ian's might have said something like Ian "Skull" Hill. (Ian's head had always looked like a skull, ever since secondary school.) Then there was Rob "the Queen" Halford. It's easy to figure out where he conjured that one up from!

And finally, there was Ken "K.K." Downing.

Seeing it in bold on the poster, I thought, *Oooh. I like that . . .*

I remember being particularly attracted by the idea that I could be called two names. It seemed like quite a rock 'n' roll thing to do. Little did I know that the nickname would stay with me from then on.

So, just when we needed a creative mind in our camp, Corky was a nonstop font of ideas. We were all very grateful for what he did for us. Rob liked him a lot, too.

On a personal level, I took an instant like to Rob Halford. He was clearly a gay man—which didn't even register with us as an issue—and he didn't quite look like a rock star. Whether he even wanted to be one, who knows?

In those early days I don't recall ever having a discussion about what his ambitions were. Truthfully, when he got together with us, I think that Rob had probably only recently discovered that he had a voice at all by being in Hiroshima. Being a singer was obviously still very new to him.

Having said all that, after just a few weeks with Rob in the band, I had no doubt whatsoever in my mind that he was the best singer I'd ever heard.

Better still, he was still young, very inexperienced, and his voice was still maturing—as it tends to do with singers. I remember saying to Ian one night after rehearsal, "There's no limit to how far this guy could take us."

I remember thinking that Rob would probably need to be twenty-four or twenty-five for his voice and physical stature to be fully mature. And when I listen to those very early recordings now, I can hear that he didn't quite have the volume or the strength that he would acquire later.

The problem, of course, with having a singer as good as young Rob Halford in your band is that there are always other bands out there ready and willing to take a great singer away. I remember quite clearly saying to Ian and John, "Listen, it's on us to keep up with him. If we don't, we'll lose him."

I'd seen it happen with other bands. Just weeks prior to Rob joining I was at Birmingham Town Hall the night the Deep Purple guys came and saw Glenn Hughes performing with Trapeze. They were playing there as a three-piece, nice big venue, this, that, and the other. But Deep Purple showed up, saw him, and then he was gone.

I knew these things could happen.

So, for us it was a matter of getting good, and then making damn sure that we stayed good. And we did. Things went very well for us as a four-piece. Before there was even a hint of a recording contract, we were fortunate enough to tour the UK extensively, up and down the country in a Ford Transit van, often supporting Budgie.

Not only that, doing thirty-odd shows with bands like Budgie undoubtedly helped us improve as a band—to the extent that, on the back of Corky's enthusiastic urgings, David Howells, the boss of a small independent record label in London called Gull, started showing an interest in signing us to a record deal. I recall that he came to see us at a gig at London's Marquee Club and said words to the effect of, "I don't mind how they look. But I love the way they sound."

Not long afterwards sometime in mid-1974, Priest had a record deal. Not a great one, but a deal nonetheless. I was over the moon!

✦

"Would you consider a saxophone player?"

"Nope."

"Keyboard player?"

"No chance!"

"What then?"

"I don't know, really. But I'm not having any of that shit in the band."

That's pretty much how the conversation played out.

It's safe to say that David Howells at Gull had a few bizarre pre-conceived ideas about (a) the band continuing as a four-piece at all and (b) which particular musical ingredient could be added to enhance our sound for our label debut.

They suggested everything, and I must confess that I did feel the need to try and appease the record company at that time—if only because I thought that doing so might result in them offering a bit more in the way of financial backing.

As it turned out, Corky's suggestion that we consider hiring Glenn Tipton as a second guitar player was something of a masterstroke. I'd never really explored the idea of harmonies, and the problem I possibly had was that harmonies tend to make music sound sweeter given that most players go for the major scale triads. At the time, I wasn't looking for sweet. I wanted dark.

"We'll think about it," I said.

Although I didn't know him well at all, I was aware of Glenn's band, The Flying Hat Band, since like most Midlands band at the time, they had crashed on our floor in Corky's apartment, having knocked on the door one night with a bunch of girls in tow. I think Corky was maybe getting Glenn's band a few gigs around that time, too, hence the connection.

Anyway, as little as I knew him as a person, I knew enough about Glenn to recognize that he was a good, tight player with a nice sound. At that time, he was probably more bluesy than we were looking for but, as it happened, his band soon dissolved, he became available, and Corky intervened and said, "Do you want me to ask Glenn if he wants to come down and audition for you?"

We said, "Yeah, why not?"

Even then, I felt that we had created a bit of a name for ourselves. We were gigging, developing a bit of a following; I felt like we'd be an attractive option for any local musician at that time. Furthermore, the more I considered it, the more I thought, *I quite like the idea of two guitar players, you know.*

Let's be honest, the timing could not have been better. It was a fantastic opportunity for Glenn, too, to happen upon not only an established band but also one that had just signed a record deal.

Even from those earliest first awkward interactions, I never found Glenn to be particularly easy to get along with. Even as a youngster, I was very much a heart-on-the-sleeve type of person. If I felt a certain way or was thinking something—positive or negative—I'm pretty sure that my face would always give it away. Looking back now, I see that my upbringing and family life could have pushed my personality in one or two directions. I could have easily been guarded, bitter, and angry, I suppose. But instead, while I was always strong-willed and stubborn, I generally went about it with a smile on my face.

Furthermore, unlike most of the male relationships I'd had where there was an element of jocular horseplay, that kind of interaction was never on offer with Glenn. Very early on I was fully aware of the limited conditions under which he operated: if you were going to relate to him, you would do so entirely on his terms. These early observations have been confirmed by time and experience.

Despite not clicking straightaway as kindred souls, I could not for a second deny that Glenn was a very able guitar player whose abilities would massively complement not only my own playing but also give some welcome versatility to the overall sound of the band.

Up until then, the problem I had with playing solos was that the rhythm had to temporarily drop out while I played them. However, soon after Glenn started rehearsing with us, I remember really seeing the benefits of having two guitars playing a tight heavy riff in stereo, almost as you would do on an album where you'd put one guitar on the left and one on the right. Suddenly I realized that by approaching it this way, we could really fill out space. Any solos could just go on top.

With Glenn on board before we went into the studio to record an album, which essentially was already written, everything started to feel really solid. Whenever I was practicing a solo, even if it was just on an acoustic guitar with no amplifier, Glenn would be there beside me, chugging away on the rhythm. His presence felt powerful and reassuring. And the same applied when Glenn played his solos. We were gelling as a guitar duo and we focused on staying away from major scale triads in favor of sevenths or minor thirds. This period was the start of everything for Priest.

Funnily enough, up until the very last session, everything about our debut album, *Rocka Rolla*, sounded great—which was a miracle given that it had all been a tough process, recording in a proper studio for the first time. Not only that, because neither the technology nor money was available, there was so much pressure to not make a mistake, to not screw up.

For a guitar player, the stresses of the studio can turn what seems like the simplest riff into the most complicated thing in the world. The more times you try, the more times you get it wrong; you can just start overanalyzing and then you seize up completely. On many occasions, I had a total brain-fart while trying to nail something very straightforward, to the point that I've had to step away and come back later. These moments happen to all musicians.

I remember that we had to go in and play songs like "Run of the Mill" live on the studio floor, and get it bang-on in one take. There was so much nervous energy in the air that, subconsciously, maybe we lost something of our performance. Even the solos had to be played live on the floor—that was especially tough given that my solos were almost all improvised. The last thing you'd want after the take would be for the producer to say, "Actually, I'm not happy with that solo. Could you play it again?"

One, you might not remember what you played, and then two, the rest of the guys would get pissed off having to keep going back. But regardless of all of these challenges, we thought we performed well on those tracks under a great deal of pressure.

Then the real problems started.

Every band will tell you that albums almost always end up going right down to the wire. Studio time runs out because another band is booked in behind you—and then money starts to run out along with everyone's patience. Then everything spirals out of control.

A lot of bands end up having to work through the night like madmen, or even through two nights. In our case, all of the above happened, and then, during the last, manic thirty-six-hour session, our producer Rodger Bain fell asleep on the couch while we worked. He was comatose. Didn't hear a thing. I don't blame Rodger at all (bless him, he has passed on). We were all completely wiped out.

Anyway, we did the last mixes as best we could and I'm pretty sure that it all sounded fine. Just as we finished, Rodger decided to stir from his slumber, opened one eye and said, "Oh, OK, right . . . so you're done then?"

It must have been five or six in the morning.

"Yeah," we said. "You missed it all."

Ordinarily, finished records would go to a professional cutting (or "mastering," to use the posh version) engineer. But instead—and we didn't know any better—Rodger, having just woken up, went upstairs to cut the record, right there and then. Studio time had run out on Rodger; he was doing the very best that he could.

Bleary-eyed, we looked at each other and said: "He's going to cut it here and now?"

On reflection, there's no doubt that Gull had done right by us by getting Rodger and his engineer, Vic Smith, on board to work with us. Rodger had done an excellent job with the first three Black Sabbath albums and the first couple of Budgie records—most of them on shoestring budgets. All of them had been received well and to that end his production skills weren't in question.

For the record, I *loved* the first Black Sabbath album when it came out. I loved the songs and I loved the dark imagery that they were projecting. The only gripe I had was that there didn't seem to be much in the way of musical color in there. And by that, I mean the kind of color that Hendrix always had loads of. Maybe that was nothing to do with Rodger Bain, of course. His production skills stood up to scrutiny.

But what the precise extent of Rodger Bain's experience in a cutting room was or wasn't, I have no idea. The two, while interlinked, are totally different disciplines. But both have to be spot-on.

Were they with *Rocka Rolla*?

Well, all I know is that when we got one copy of the finished album between us to take home, when we put it on the record player we all said in unison, "What happened? It doesn't sound as we expected it to."

Last time we had checked, "Winter", "Run of the Mill," and "Never Satisfied" were and are great tracks but somehow, in between when we recorded the music and it got cut into plastic grooves, something disappeared.

The thing that grated most was that the sound on the record bore no resemblance to what we thought we'd done in the studio. Granted, some of the tracks on the album had been reworked slightly so that they could be presented in a way that was intended to give Glenn a gentle introduction to the band—one where he'd feel welcome and part of something that he'd been drafted into at the eleventh hour. But that did not explain the sound of the record we were holding in our hands.

Rocka Rolla, instead of being this great statement of intent, sadly had no balls at all. It just wasn't punchy or energetic in any way. And with that we were learning a tough music industry lesson: you can make a good record sound awful if it's not mastered properly. The reverse is also true, albeit to a lesser extent.

So here we were, with barely a pot to piss in, some of us working part-time jobs, with this record that we didn't particularly like the sound of. Not only did it not resemble us in the studio, it didn't in any way capture anything about what we did live either. And we thought we were a pretty good live band by then.

On reflection, *Rocka Rolla* was fairly typical of first albums in that you're willing to prostitute yourself because you've done an album, put in huge amounts of effort, and there then comes a point where you just want the thing out and in the shops. If people wanted to start putting their oar in along the way for one reason or another, you just go along with it for the sake of just getting the thing on sale.

And that's what I think happened.

I always used to think to myself, *Did Gull ask the production team and Rodger Bain to lay off the heavy metal for the sake of commercial appeal?*

Commerciality was always, understandably, at the forefront of Gull's mind from the start. It was a way for them to hedge their bets a little. I know for a fact that they saw something of a sales opportunity with the album cover.

The artist John Pasche won awards for that cover and I honestly never really liked it. I think they thought it had a commercial edge to it because of the play on words with Coca-Cola. In the end, the cover added nothing to the commercial appeal of the record, simply because, at the heart of it, *Rocka Rolla* wasn't the best-sounding album in the form in which it was released.

Regardless, we went out on the road anyway and gave it a bloody good go as we always did, starting the UK leg of the tour in September 1974 at the less than salubrious surroundings of Huddersfield's Jubilee Centre prior to going through Holland and parts of Scandinavia in early '75.

As I recall, we set off from Newcastle on a ferry to Stavanger—us, two mates along for the ride to help as makeshift road crew, one of them Nick Bowbanks, and the new-to-us Mercedes van that also served as home to all of our gear. Luxury it was not!

All I remember about departing Newcastle is that instead of us driving the van on, the ferry operators told us to all get out while they lifted the thing up on a crane, swung it round, and deposited it on the ferry deck. I'd never seen anything like that!

The Scandinavian leg was an experience: small clubs, good beer, food you've never seen in your life. I remember few things specifically about Norway, but I do recall that it was freezing cold all of the time.

As we traveled across the country, getting increasingly cold and miserable, we began to take certain, shall we say, "shortcuts" to avoid being outside. One such shortcut woke me up from my familiar back-seat state of unconsciousness.

One afternoon, as I hovered in that half-awake and half asleep state that you get in when your head keeps lolling sideways and banging off the window winder, I became aware of a smell wafting from the row of seats at the front of the van.

What is that?

Now, it should be said that unpleasant smells aren't uncommon in vans containing seven grown men, but this was something else.

What became apparent was that a member of our group who shall remain nameless was contorting himself within the limited confines of his seat into a position whereby he could drop a seemingly long-overdue shit neatly into an A5-sized brown envelope! How he achieved such accuracy, I'll never know. But he did—and all I remember is seeing the envelope being whanged out the window into the snow!

We were quickly learning about life on the road

On the back of the good reviews we were getting for our live performances and TV appearances (including showcasing "Dreamer Deceiver" and "Rocka Rolla" on *The Old Grey Whistle Test*), Corky got a call from the Reading Festival organizers, sometime in 1975.

"We'd like the band for Reading this summer," they said.

We were over the moon. Reading was a big deal; I think we were to play the first night, with UFO and Hawkwind as headliners. All I remember about it is that I spent quite a while hanging out with

UFO guitarist Michael Schenker and that we were pretty happy with our performance. Appearing before one of the biggest festival crowds ever did us no harm at all.

There was a downside, however.

After the show, John Hinch quit the band. I don't personally remember the precise circumstances surrounding John's departure. All I know is that he'd been a bit pissed off for a while after our sound system packed up two nights in a row at Scarborough.

Then I think he and Glenn had an argument about an aspect of John's playing. Whether he quit or was told to go, I don't remember. All I knew was that with the studio beckoning again, and fast, we needed a new drummer.

"Let's get Alan Moore back," I suggested. "He was fine, and he's local."

And everyone agreed.

CHAPTER SIX

THE BUSINESS ARRANGEMENT FOR OUR SECOND ALBUM, *Sad Wings of Destiny*, was identical to that of *Rocka Rolla*: two grand up front—take it or leave it.

Faced with no alternative, we took it.

What *was* different was that we knew considerably more about the recording discipline than we did a year earlier. Furthermore, with Glenn having been in the band for almost a year and having played with us live, we were more settled not only as a lineup but also as a songwriting team.

Some of the songs that hadn't made it onto *Rocka Rolla* became the bedrock of *Sad Wings of Destiny*. "Victim of Changes" was case in point—it became not only the album's calling card but also an absolute fixture of our live set for decades thereafter.

We'd been playing a version of that song, in one form or another, since the days at Holy Joe's, long before Rob or Glenn joined the band. At that time, it was called "Whiskey Woman." It was archetypal early Judas Priest and I absolutely loved getting lost in my head while playing the solo.

Why Rodger left it off *Rocka Rolla*, I'm not too sure. The only explanation I can think of is that, being essentially a fusion of two pieces ("Whiskey Woman" and "Red Light Lady," the latter a song from Rob's Hiroshima days), possibly it wasn't ready in time to record. These things happen.

As honed as we were as songwriters and as much as we had learned with Rodger, when it came to actually recording these new songs, we found that the same problems we'd encountered previously in the studio were still there.

When we played live (and we'd been doing so a hell of a lot from 1972 onward) we felt relaxed and full of energy. We could play the set list with one figurative arm tied behind our backs, to the extent that we were willing to sacrifice a little accuracy for the sake of putting on a great live spectacle. Even then, that seemed like a good trade-off to make.

But for some reason, as soon as we stepped into a recording studio, we became a bit green and directionless, perhaps self-conscious of the fact that the tape was running—and the meter in a monetary sense.

I thought, *I need to find a way to replicate what I do onstage in the studio.*

As it turned out, Chris Tsangirides, who was employed at Morgan Studios in London as a tape operator/tea boy at that time, was the first to witness my plan. He tells a great story about when we were mixing the record.

Chris was always mad about guitars and one day he was walking down the corridor past the studio where I was laying down the overdubbed solo for "Victim of Changes."

He could hear me vaguely from outside the studio but could see nothing. Curious, he opened the door to reveal me, standing up, foot on the wah pedal and headbanging with my arms waving around everywhere like a madman.

"What the hell are you doing?" he said. He'd never seen anything like it before.

Apparently, I didn't answer. I must have been too deep in the moment.

What I was doing was executing a plan.

The way I saw it, the only way I could ever hope to replicate the energy I generated when I was playing live onstage was to play in the studio as if I actually *was* onstage. Movements, expressions, gyrations, expressions of sexual arousal and sonic ecstasy, time travel—all of that stuff—as opposed to just sitting there on a stool with a guitar between my legs.

And the results spoke for themselves.

Although we still didn't quite capture every aspect of what we were able to do onstage, *Sad Wings of Destiny* nevertheless was a huge forward step in songwriting maturity.

As proud as I was of *Sad Wings of Destiny*—and I still am because it's a part of my life and the band's legacy—I could see the influence of other bands slowly creeping into our songwriting on what was a very important album. As such, I felt that I owed it to myself and the band to question things by saying things like, "Hang on, where are we going?" or "Is this right for us?"

I felt that tracks like "Epitaph" were totally out of place even though Rob and Glenn liked them. In a perfect world at the time I'd have erased it in a millisecond and replaced it with something else. That said, with the passage of time I became fine with it. I learned that no matter what a song is, it will eventually stick, become familiar, and then take its place as part of the masterpiece. I fully accept that to be true.

At the time, I think there was an element of "Look how clever we are as a band. We can also do this . . . " about some of *Sad Wings of*

Destiny. And on reflection that was OK. But, as that old saying goes, "It wasn't us."

That's exactly how I felt and I probably said it—"It's great . . . but is it us?"

I could not, however, have any issue with the artwork, which was commissioned by Gull to the artist Patrick Woodroffe and was derived from his gothic-looking image, *Fallen Angel.*

Yes. That's exactly what we want—this is more what Judas Priest is all about.

After the slight dissatisfaction I felt with *Rocka Rolla*, the combined effect of *Sad Wings of Destiny*'s sound, image, and art got us firmly back on track.

✦

We signed to Sony at the end of 1976—and thank God we did. Even with two albums out there in the world and with *Sad Wings of Destiny* landing on charts worldwide, still we were sinking. Despite the sales and accolades, we still had absolutely no money. I was still getting around on a bicycle.

Staring at the wall one day in Corky's flat, with no food in the fridge, I remember thinking, *What the hell are we doing here?*

I suppose Gull had done the best they could for us, with very little in the way of resources. Their intentions were good, but that wasn't helping us day to day. We needed to survive.

"Any chance of a weekly salary of twenty-five quid a week?" we asked them.

"Not possible, guys. We just don't have it."

Faced with such grim news, we looked at each other and said, "We've *got* to leave Gull."

At that point, shitty record deal or not, we needed to make a clean break, regardless of the legal implications of bailing on a contract. Offers to tour were coming in daily, but we hardly had any money for petrol, far less for a basic stage show or a road crew. Had we not elected to jump, the Judas Priest story might have ended right there in 1976, before it properly began.

As it turned out, at least one major record company, Sony/CBS, recognized our worth. For us it was an absolute no-brainer to go with them when they came knocking. We signed, and as we did we went from £2000 record advances at Gull to a £60,000 advance for our first record. It wasn't an immediate financial fix but we were at least moving in the right direction.

On reflection, we were perhaps a little naïve in that we gave little or no thought to our publishing rights for *Rocka Rolla* and our second album, *Sad Wings of Destiny*. Because we'd effectively walked away from our contract, those rights reverted to Gull. We had no other choice but to let it all go.

The sad part is that, to this day, none of us has ever received a single penny from either of those two albums. Many reissues have popped up in various territories over the years and seeing them always used to piss me off because I knew someone was making something—but that someone was never Rob nor Glenn nor me.

In the end, you can only weigh up the pros and the cons of making a decision. And leaving the Gull contract was definitely the right one for Judas Priest at that time

Predictably, Sony's involvement immediately felt like a shot of adrenaline and not only because of the welcome injection into our bank accounts. I'm not 100 percent certain about how much they knew about us, but they always, always treated us well from the first dealings we had with them.

There's a great story that may just be an urban myth. While we waited in Sony's London offices, someone came out to the waiting room and asked, "At what time can we expect Mr. Priest to arrive?"

That may be true—or just apocryphal; it's hard to remember the details so long after the event. Either way, it made me laugh when I thought about it again.

As much as £60,000 was in 1976, it was sobering to think that we still had to finance an album and cover all the related costs. After we did the calculations, it didn't leave a lot.

What it did leave was enough for me to buy my first car.

Oh yes, 1977 was the beginning of my many years as an aspiring petrolhead, crazy about the best and fastest cars around, but seemingly always limited by a lack of cash to buy them. If I needed to get around, I had to make do with a bicycle or my own two feet.

One of the few things I noticed as a youngster when my dad dragged me around the various horse-racing tracks were the flash cars the bookmakers drove. While my dad was literally throwing money away, I was thinking the opposite. *One day, when I get some money, I'll buy one of these . . .*

As it turned out, my first car was no beauty. Nevertheless, the band's cast-off vehicle—a 1969 white Austin 1800 with some rust and the big ends knocking—has the honorable but dubious accolade of being my first ever set of wheels.

I seem to recall that after a bit of haggling with Rob and Glenn, I paid them fifty quid for it. That seemed quite a lot in those days. And it seemed even more when, with catastrophic engine failure seemingly always imminent because of those dodgy big ends, I probably spent close to fifty quid a month keeping the thing in heavy-duty oil. I had only recently learned to drive and, other than tootling around Walsall and Bloxwich, I never went much farther afield.

Meanwhile, the band had upgraded to a horrible orange Volvo to ferry us around, while our gear was lugged in a Ford van bought for that purpose.

As I recall, a trip to London to play the Apollo Victoria was to be the Volvo's maiden voyage. The morning after the show, after we'd just finished a meeting with the label reps, we found ourselves driving down Wardour Street in Soho. We stopped for some food from a bakery.

Then someone, I can't remember exactly who, got this meat pie, took the pastry top off it, and then whanged it straight out the car window. Then we all sat there watching while, as if in slow motion, this pie flew through the air in the direction of this big rough-looking bloke, before landing, meat side down, on the back of his neck.

We all laughed—"Did you see *that*?!"

Thinking nothing other than how much of a good laugh it was to have smacked this guy with a pie, we kept driving. Next thing I know there's this almighty whack and when I look back, this big hairy fucker is chasing us on a motorbike while smashing the car to bits with this great big chain.

It was very scary, particularly trying to navigate London traffic to get away. We supposedly rufty-tufty Judas Priest boys weren't for sticking around to talk it through with the chain-wielding hairy guy. We just put pedal to the metal and hoped he'd never catch up. You should have seen the mess he made of the car, though.

◆

Getting Roger Glover on board to produce our third album, *Sin After Sin,* was our record company's idea. I can only think that Sony, given that it was our first release for them, thought, "Let's give the guys a bit of a leg up by engaging a name producer" in a Deep Purple-guy-produces-Judas Priest way.

We were fine with that. It made some sense, I suppose, even though none of us had a comprehensive idea what Roger's credentials as a producer were.

Nevertheless, Roger was a lovely guy and great to work with. We split the process between rehearsals at Pinewood Studios in London and recording at Ramport Studios in Battersea, owned by the Who.

Because we—Rob, Glenn, and I—were developing as a songwriting team, I'm sure we thought that we didn't really need Roger. We were still quite naïve in those days.

There was, however, a festering niggle.

It had become quite apparent that. because I'd generously let Glenn in on the first album, most of which Al Atkins and I had written, the songwriting was eventually going to become a three-way split among Rob, Glenn, and me. (The arrangement was formalized in 1980.) I just thought that if we agreed to evenly split the songwriting duties, that would in turn guarantee the financial side of things going forward. Nobody could argue with that logic; it meant that, hopefully, the best ideas would always rise to the top. I just didn't want weaknesses to start creeping in.

However, on *Sad Wings of Destiny*, I started to find myself in a position whereby I'd be coming to the table with what I thought were solid ideas, only to have them rejected and replaced with something of Glenn's instead.

At the time, I thought, *I'm totally pissed off with this . . .*

At the time, what I actually said was, "OK then. . . . "

Speaking of weaknesses, I thought "Last Rose of Summer" was exactly that.

It felt to me that Glenn and Rob were on the Queen bandwagon, and so Glenn had this idea to compose a ballad-type song on the piano, knowing full well that if he could carve out something to take to Rob, Rob would probably jump on it because ballads often appeal to singers.

"Yes, this is great!" Rob would say.

Meanwhile, I thought, *This sucks. We sound too much like Queen.*

Of course, I totally recognize that lots of similar bands went down a comparable path. Sabbath did "Changes," which I thought was a great song—far better than "Last Rose of Summer," in my opinion. I thought they got away with it—and lots of bands did.

Speaking of getting away with it, I was told that it was Roger Glover's idea that we record Joan Baez's "Diamonds and Rust" for *Sin After Sin*, the reasoning being that, by covering a well-known song, we'd be giving our debut for a major label a commercial leg up.

I actually think that this was the label's idea and that they were just using the man on the ground, Roger, as their spokesperson. In those days, labels were looking for radio play for their bands. And radio stations were more apt to play a known song by a new band than one that wasn't.

Initially, given my feeling about not covering other people's stuff entrenched in my mind, I thought, *No, we should leave it alone.*

But, after a bit of experimentation we found that if we put that Judas Priest stamp on a song—whatever that song was—instead of us becoming part of it, it would become part of us. That emphasis was important, and the fact that the song has been a regular in our sets ever since 1976 just confirms it. In fact, I've met many people over the years who thought that "Diamonds and Rust" was a Judas Priest original!

Of the others, "Dissident Aggressor" was always a favorite of mine: great riff, a fantastic vocal from Rob—and I loved playing the solo even though I don't think I ever played it the same way twice onstage. Little did we know that the song would be nominated for a Grammy—albeit many years later when it was covered by Slayer.

It's quite possible that the idea for the title *Sin After Sin* came about as a result of the lyric from the track "Genocide" from *Sad Wings of Destiny.* However we came up with it, it has always been one of my favorite Judas Priest album titles.

I always wanted titles and imagery to tie back in some way, even if a little cryptically, to the core concepts of the priest and the church in general. From that perspective, *Sin After Sin* did that with bells on, in my opinion at least.

The imagery and feel of what Judas Priest was all about was always much more at the forefront of my mind than anyone else's, I think. I thought that we should have always kept the band name in the Gothic font that first appeared on *Sad Wings.* I just liked that obliquely religious reference.

At the same time as we signed with Sony/CBS, we hooked up with the management company Arnakarta. Whether the label suggested them or whether they actively sought us out, I was never sure. They just sort of appeared.

The main guys, Mike Dolan and Jim Dawson, were two brothers with different surnames. That alone seemed a bit odd. When we came along they were already looking after The Tourists (later to become Eurythmics) and Dollar. They really were just two businessmen turned managers who perhaps had too many other business interests to be totally dedicated to Judas Priest.

Having said that, it wasn't that the Arnakarta guys didn't try to do the best they could with us in the beginning. It was more a case of them not really understanding what the best way was to market us. Even though they had an office in New York, I never got the feeling that they understood that market well enough to make the most of our initial breakthrough in America. As such, this business relationship started on a precarious footing and would, by and large, continue like that.

✦

I don't remember exactly when the thought first entered my head, but I can remember thinking on more than a few occasions, *You know, I'm really not sure about our image . . .*

On reflection, I think Judas Priest had a bit of an identity crisis from the beginning. There was *always* a bit of a question mark about the band's look. To me it never seemed to *say* anything—and in the earliest days of our career I suppose I actually saw that as a good thing.

In those days I prowed a lone and rather bewildering furrow myself. I was very much into a flamboyant style from the beginning. After I'd seen Hendrix that first time in '67, I thought nothing of wearing a big, white, camel-hair fedora and multi-colored shirts with big, wide sleeves. I don't mind saying that I always quite liked how I looked! If you can find footage of us playing "Dreamer Deceiver" on *Old Grey Whistle Test*, you'll see what I mean. I looked like a hippy wizard.

Looking back, I'm sure this taste came from really disliking the uniformed look, a la the Beatles. As I said, the Stones appealed to me much more—not least because, from a style perspective, they seemed much more like individual dudes, with different looks. They all performed with their own individual style, too, while still managing, somehow, to appear as if they were a cohesive band. For them, it worked. For us, it was a complete shambles!

I remember one particular gig at Birmingham Town Hall very clearly. We, just a four-piece at the time, were supporting Budgie in 1974. I was on my side of the stage, minding my own business, and then, for some reason I felt compelled to look across the stage at Rob. It suddenly dawned on me that he was wearing a knitted, mustard-colored Harvard sweater with letters on the front! *Arrr-rggggh! He must be going through a David Bowie phase! What next?*

But we carried on for a couple more years after Glenn joined the band and the fact that there were now five of us onstage only made things worse. There were now five people who had absolutely no clue about what image they were trying to project.

Then, sometime in '77, two things happened after we returned from that first US tour.

First, my need to be flamboyant disappeared overnight. It was as if I went to bed one night one person and woke up another. I put the crazy clothes in the wardrobe and they never came out again. I've never really understood the sudden change of heart. All I know is that I thought, *I don't want to look like that anymore.*

This, depending on how you look at it, created either a problem or an opportunity for Judas Priest.

Maybe this was supposed to happen?

Maybe we actually did need a focused image?

A uniform, I thought.

Even though this concept flew directly in the face of everything I'd previously believed, I let it revolve in my head before discussing it with the other guys. These kinds of conversations never happened—not because they'd have been awkward or difficult. We had just never discussed it. We'd been touring, playing music, living life, without ever taking a step back to say, "What's the long game here?"

I can remember a specific occasion around the time we went into the studio to record *Stained Class* when I started considering the whole image issue while on the tour bus. The idea of leather, studs, and a look immediately identifiable as "us" was egging me on. But I never had the conversation with the other guys; the opportunity just never came up.

What was motivating me was the toughness that this new image would project. The fact that I was contradicting everything I'd believed when I was a teenager wasn't lost on me either. It was a U-turn on a grand scale, but I justified it by telling myself, *Relax, Ken. We're hardly going to look like the Beatles!*

All I knew was that to reach the next level commercially, something had to change. I just wanted what might be best for the band—and I could imagine the fans getting behind the uniformed look I had in mind. I could see it all in my head: us, and the fans, suited up in the same leather battle gear, like some kind of heavy metal army.

It all sounded great, but only to me.

Suddenly, on one hand I felt like the odd one out—because I was the odd one out. But when I thought about it more, I felt more strongly that it wasn't me who was the anomaly. It was the others.

I just sensed a lack of motivation from the others on the subject of dress and image, although I knew that Glenn would adopt the image if he felt he had in some way thought of it. Les and Ian didn't have strong opinions either way. They'd go with whatever came along. Rob was different. I knew him well enough to suspect that, if I could turn his head somehow on a specific image, he'd then take it and run with it forever and a day—to the extent that people would think it had been his idea all along! And then the others would follow suit. And that's exactly how it would play out, given a little time.

✦

Stained Class came at a time, 1978, when we felt like we were among the only bands playing heavy music in the UK with any success or enthusiasm. And for metal-minded people, it certainly wasn't easy navigating the mid- to late-'70s while sitting and watching punk from the sidelines.

For a few years, it really was all about survival for rock and metal bands. I know that for a fact because I knew plenty of lads who'd been in rock bands who eventually just thought, "Let's go where the money is." And if that meant turning their back on everything that they stood for, so be it.

When punk and, later, new wave music arrived, a lot of these musicians just jumped on the bandwagon without ever considering where it might be going. And because of how new and untapped these genres were, and the degree of artistic latitude they offered, it must have seemed like there was plenty of room on this particular bandwagon for anyone that wanted to ride.

It had all culminated in 1977, when I was shocked to realize that it was really only UFO and us who were even touring in the UK. Nobody else was out there—all the venues seemed to be handed over to punk and new wave nights.

There was lots of toxic talk going around at the time, too, whispers about who's breaking up, who's done for. It got so bad that I even have some recollection of some acts, Ritchie Blackmore being one that springs to mind, being labeled as old farts whose time had come and gone.

Of course, the people who liked the kind of music we or bands like Scorpions or Led Zeppelin played were all still there. But they were underground, in hiding for a few years, in this awkward time when it seemed that nobody was being prolific.

The Priest machine just carried on regardless. We'd been out in the States touring for the first time there, with Foreigner and REO Speedwagon. It had been a tough baptism, learning the rules of what a support band could and could not have.

"Don't expect anything," someone told us before we left, "because whatever it is—lights, room onstage, monitors—you won't get any of it."

"Oh, fine . . . "

And by and large, that was the case. This was an era where everything was geared toward making the headline act look as good as possible. And if that meant suppressing the support act's sound and lights, then so be it.

I remember playing one gig with Foreigner on that 1977 tour when all we had for the whole show was one puny Super Trouper light on Rob. Everyone else was in darkness.

"What happened?" we said afterward.

"Oh, the equipment went down. Blah blah blah."

Oddly, the equipment seemed fine when Foreigner went on.

That's just the way it was and we accepted it. We never complained; we just did exactly what we were told.

But after that tour I made a vow—one that I stuck to for all the years I was in the band—that I wouldn't ever be party to treating a support band of ours in that way. If a support band ever came to us with a complaint about something or other, the shit would hit the fan. I didn't want any of that. Thereafter, we always prided ourselves in treating support acts well.

✦

Regardless, touring represented a positive learning step for us, although, having said that, I wouldn't necessarily say that playing with Zeppelin in '77 on the West Coast did anything particularly for our profile. While we were there, and the fans that were there liked us, the West Coast was still an incredibly hard nut to crack. A lot of this was governed by what the radio stations were playing. And so, if a lot of the DJs were into stuff like Crosby, Stills, Nash, and Young and the Steve Miller Band—as was still the case on that side of the country—then that was it. Music like ours had to sit on the sidelines until a few years later. Outside of specific towns like San Antonio, only select parts of the East Coast and the Midwest were receptive to our kind of music at that time.

Regardless of the divisions in the US, the States were still a completely different kettle of fish from the UK. America would be waiting for us in the future now that we had established a foothold. It was gratifying that we could travel so far away and have some people know our music.

The same applied to continental Europe. It was just the UK that had an infestation of "ugly stuff" as far as we were concerned. And nobody knew at that time how long it might all last, particularly when you started to see these bands on *Top of the Pops* and playing the same venues that we'd once played—and in some cases even bigger places. It became a real concern. I remember thinking, *This punk thing might just hang around . . .*

And it *did* hang around.

For all these reasons, *Stained Class* was a very important album for us. At the outset, we had to ask ourselves, even if it was just on a subconscious level: Were we going to make any concession whatsoever to the music industry trends of the time?

Would we waver at all?

Or was Judas Priest going to steam on the only way we knew how?

The answer was simple: the latter.

From memory—and I don't have much of the *Stained Class* era for some reason—we came up with many more ideas than ended up on the record. In the buildup Rob and I slipped into an agreeable routine for sharing ideas. I'd go to his place, we'd write, have some beans on toast, and then keep going.

Other days he'd come to where I was living at that time, a rented terraced house in Bloxwich with holes in the roof. "Saints in Hell" and "Savage" were borne of these relaxed liaisons.

I certainly have no recollection of why Dennis MacKay was chosen to produce the record. By that time, Rob, Glenn, and I were a pretty damned efficient songwriting trio. We were at the beginning of what would be a very long and successful roll. We just needed guidance and that important outside ear. I recall having a conversation about who might fill the role and the record company suggested Dennis.

"Sounds fine," we agreed.

He was brought in by the label, did what he did, and the results speak for themselves. It was all quite simple.

One odd incident, completely unrelated to music, has stayed with me about those sessions at Chipping Norton, the town in Oxfordshire where we cut the record.

"Ken, you'll need to come home."

My girlfriend Carol was on the phone.

"Why? What's happened?"

"It's the dog," she said. "He's trying to eat me."

"Christ! I'll be there as soon as I can."

I drove all the way back to Bloxwich right then. Carol had a pet Alsatian that, for one reason or another, needed various medications. If he didn't have them, he became belligerent at best, nasty at worst. The latter is what happened; he probably was trying to eat her. I got home, sorted the dog's drugs out, calmed Carol down, and drove back to Chipping Norton that night.

Of the tracks that stand out most in my mind, "Exciter" would definitely be one of them. I remember Glenn and I hearing Les Binks playing this distinctive double bass drum pattern at a sound check in the States on the *Sin After Sin* tour.

"Hold on. Play that again . . ."

"You mean this?"

"Yes!"

When we got into songwriting in Birmingham before going to Chipping Norton Studios, we asked him to revisit it. We then joined in with a fast guitar riff to fit it and "Exciter" was born. I'm not surprised that many people consider it to be a precursor to some of the speed or thrash metal styles that would come later. It's a uniquely energetic track—even by today's standards.

I should say that Les Binks was a really good addition to Judas Priest after Simon Phillips—who had essentially done *Sin After Sin* as a session job, I believe at Roger Glover's behest—left us before the US tour. I believe it also was Roger who suggested Les, and we were lucky to get him.

As good as Simon was, he was never going to stay. He was one of those musicians who didn't really enjoy the band life or, more specifically, the touring life. The idea of sex and drugs maybe wasn't his thing. He preferred to be a hired gun, working in the London scene where he was free to pick and choose his projects while wearing that "top session drummer" tag like a badge of honor. Guys like him got off on that role and that's absolutely fine.

Les Binks, who came from the same session-musician world as Simon, was a top player; rooted in jazz, he could play absolutely anything. He was a good guy, too: Irish, reserved, a vegetarian— a really top bloke who was with us for a couple of significant albums.

Funnily enough, the other track that I remember most clearly is "Beyond the Realms of Death"—not least because it came about as a result of Les Binks. One day he picked up one of our guitars, turned it upside down, and started playing it left-handed. The riff he came up with formed the basis of a Judas Priest classic.

As with *Sin After Sin*, Sony was keen to float the idea of a cover track, presumably for the same reason: to attract listeners who might not have been Judas Priest fans to our new record. Also, given the generally dark and moody tone of the album we'd made, I think that the label saw Spooky Tooth's "Better by You, Better than Me" as a way to liven things up.

We weren't particularly open to that idea at first; the album was intentionally dark and sinister. But we weren't in a position to argue. All we could do was put our spin on the song to make it fit. And that's what we did.

As I recall, this was a last-minute request from the company. Dennis MacKay had moved on to another project, leaving just his assistant, James Guthrie, to record the track at a different studio. James did a great job. If anything, he made the song sound as good if not better than the rest of the album to the extent that it came to feel like an actual Judas Priest track. But little did we know how that would become a double-edged sword.

Speaking of double-edged swords, 1978 was when my studio issues with Glenn first began in earnest. As much as Glenn's and my playing was an integral part of Priest's sound, our relationship pretty much existed on permanent, extra-fragile eggshells—for the reasons I've mentioned.

Personality schisms are one thing—they happen all the time in every workplace. But when differences start causing fundamental shifts in how an entity—in this case Judas Priest—functions, then only problems lie ahead.

I was never sure what the catalyst was, but I always wondered whether a guitar poll that came out in Japan around this time had something to do with it. As I remember it, I was ranked number three, and Glenn was down the list at eighteen. I paid no heed whatsoever to guitar polls; I pretty much laughed this one off. To me it appeared as if Glenn didn't like it at all, and that could well have caused the problems.

It seemed to me that being number eighteen riled Glenn into taking subtle control of aspects of the band. By this time, it seemed to me as if he thought that he might not face much in the way of strong resistance. There was certainly no formal band decision or debate. I just felt that Glenn started to pre-emptively decide what he wanted to do and what he didn't, right at the beginning of each album cycle. Then, when we sat down to share out the guitar solos, he'd say, "I'll do this and you do that. Then I'll do this and you take that."

And as he did this, there was no doubt that I was more than capable of doing much more than I was allocated.

At the time, this division of labor probably sounded fine. But when it came down to it, his solo time on the record ended up being five times more than mine. I always felt that Glenn chose flashy solos for himself. At least that's how it appeared to me. I probably thought that it might work against him someday but it never did. I suspected that he was trying to become popular on the back of mass production, and that's what happened: the more his playing overshadowed mine on our albums in terms of sheer airtime, the more people thought he was the main guy.

Was it to the benefit of Judas Priest as a band? I didn't think so, simply because we had two guitar players with distinctive styles that worked together to create diverse songs. To limit one of those guitarists' input meant that the songs sometimes didn't reach their peak potential.

Did this piss me off? Yes, I suppose it did.

But because Glenn was taking on the workload, I probably just let it go at the time. But even then, I can remember the occasional night when, as my head hit the pillow, I'd think, *Why are you putting up with this, Ken? You're a total mug.*

✦

Above and beyond the music, *Stained Class* was significant for where it sat in the evolution of Judas Priest's image progression. As we were bandying titles around, I think it was Rob who said, "How about 'Stained Glass'?"

"That could be cool," I replied.

In my head, the idea of stained glass, with its obvious religious connotations, offered scope for imagery that fit well with the tracks themselves and what I thought was Judas Priest's identity: darkness, religious doubt, betrayal.

I also liked the title because I saw the possibilities for an album cover—obviously, a stained-glass image in a religious sense, but also one that played on the many qualities of glass as a substance: something that could shatter, be looked through, could refract light. The possibilities were endless.

But sadly, that opportunity never came.

Glenn said, "Would *Stained Class* sound better?"

"Wouldn't people read it as 'Stained Glass' anyway?" I offered.

Other than thinking that people would (and did) mistakenly call the album "Stained Glass," I really did like the title and, ultimately, the image that accompanied *Stained Class*.

As it turned out, Rozlav Szaybo's cover image for the record was fabulous in its futuristic appeal. He perfectly captured, with that single image of the strange glass-and-copper head, where I thought we were at that time, but he also left scope, intentionally or otherwise, for something to build on.

✦

We went out on tour in the UK with a band called the English Assassin, kicking off at the Royal Links Pavilion in Cromer in January of 1978. It was to be a short run, followed by an equally brief US leg supporting Mahogany Rush.

Sony wanted us back in the studio.

What's funny is that I can distinctly recall making a mental note while sitting in the van one night that we now seemed to be the recipients of more blow jobs than at any time previously.

No matter where we played, Scotland, Wales, or England, there were more and more girls turning up at the shows—many of them ready and willing to pleasure us.

Even then, we were getting attention. Who were we to turn it down?

In fact, the offers of oral sex became so frequent that Rob used to get really pissed off because he had to sit in the van, waiting for us to leave venues after the gig.

"Will you guys get a move on?" he'd shout out the window.

"But Rob . . . "

"Yeah, yeah, come on."

On another night on that tour, we pulled into a motorway service station somewhere in the north of England. We all got out, went inside for whatever we needed, and then Glenn, Ian, Les, and I went back in the van.

"Where's Rob?" I asked.

"I left him in the gents' toilets," Les replied.

Half an hour passed.

And then another half hour . . .

"Where the hell is he?" I moaned, keen to get on the road.

"He must still be in there," Les said. "Who's volunteering to go and get him?"

"I'm not, that's for sure," I said.

"No chance," Ian added.

"Yeah, me neither." Les wanted no part of it.

"Oh, for fuck sake, I'll go," Glenn eventually conceded.

So off he went, into the gents' toilets, whereupon he returned a few minutes later with Rob, who was smiling from ear to ear.

"Sorry to keep you, lads," he said with a cheeky wink.

✦

"They'd be hesitant to release it as *Killing Machine* in the US," I remember being told by Arnakarta as we sat looking at Rozlav Szaybo's fabulous cover art for the first time.

With the gun culture and mass-killing history America had even in the late 1970s, I suppose our US record label, Columbia/CBS, didn't think that we should be giving people any ideas. (In 1979, eight children were injured in a shooting in a public elementary school in San Diego; the principal and a custodian were killed.) They had a point, I suppose.

To my eyes, that cover image, while not in any way controversial itself, was a logical extension of *Stained Class*: dark, futuristic, with an androgynous face that used the sunglasses lenses in a similarly ambiguous way that the *Stained Class* cover art had. It was just tremendous.

More importantly, if you look at the back cover of the album, at least three of us, me included, are dressed in leather. When I saw that, I realized that my plan to mold our image and toughen things up seemed to be working.

As we discussed it, we all agreed pretty quickly that, given the modest inroads into the US market we'd made on the two previous tours, it made no sense to undo all the hard work by having radio stations distance themselves from the album because of its name.

"What do we call it, though?" Glenn asked.

By this point in late 1978, I was absolutely hell bent for the leather image. What's more, Les, Rob, and Glenn were catching on, too. Only Ian was lagging behind then, with his white satin shirt.

Meanwhile, I was already quite accustomed to jumping on a train to London, getting on the Underground's Central line to Shepherd's Bush and then walking the five-minute journey to Andy's, a leather boot manufacturer with a small shop at 61 Goldhawk Road.

Andy was open to making anything on request, including a pair of white knee-length boots that I wore onstage a few times in the late '70s—including at the Day on the Green Festival at Oakland in 1977.

From there, I later found about another brand called Mr. S that made leather and other assorted bondage gear. I believe it was imported from San Francisco.

Sometime that year, I said to Rob, "Let's get on a train. I want to show you this place I know in London."

In my mind, I'd always known that if Rob specifically got on board with the tough, leather image I'd been working toward everyone else would likely follow. So, we got on a train down to London and we both had some leather clothes custom-made by a couple of gay guys. It seemed to me that after Rob had had his inside leg measurement taken, he was sold! It was a memorable moment.

"How about we release *Killing Machine* in the US as *Hell Bent for Leather* then?" the company suggested. I remember thinking that it was the perfect alternative. It played right into our hands. Furthermore, given that there was a track on the record with that very name, I didn't think that the title would be too confusing.

Everyone said, "We like it."

And that's how it went.

On balance, *Killing Machine* aka *Hell Bent for Leather* was one of our most important albums. Everything was still up in the air; I thought we could have gone down the pan if we hadn't gotten it dead right. As it transpired, the songs showed no sign of the pressure we might have been feeling. Instead, the album was the sound of Judas Priest simplifying, probably unconsciously, our songwriting style. It wasn't that we elected to move away from the longer, fantasy-based progressive pieces that had characterized previous albums. It was much more a case of us maturing, becoming more confident in what we could do, and therefore loosening the feel up a little. Consequently, many of the tracks were shorter and more direct. When I hear the record now, I feel that we had achieved something sonically that hadn't existed before . . . and never existed afterward either.

The overall result was a pivotal album, produced by James Guthrie at Utopia Studios in London, that verged on exhibiting a bit of sassy, confident swagger at times, particularly on tracks like "Burnin' Up," "Evil Fantasies," and "Killing Machine."

There were frustrations for me, too, though, as Glenn continued to exert subtle influence. I remember that the original solo on

"Before the Dawn" was much longer. After all, as a guitarist, when presented with great chord changes, there's so much room to create great solos. So, you can imagine what the solo was originally like. Glenn though, somehow thinking that "Before the Dawn" might be a potential single, moved to have my solo radically cut down. In my eyes, it was only because the song was entirely my composition that he let me do the solo at all!

✦

Of great surprise to us was the fact that "Take On the World" was picked up as a single. Not just that, it was the song that ended up getting us on *Top of the Pops* for the first time. I think the company thought that the cover of Fleetwood Mac's "Green Manalishi" we cut for the album might have fit the bill as a single. And as cover versions go, I think it's one of the best we've done. But it wasn't the single that was released.

"Your plan to make a hit record certainly worked!" people used to say in interviews.

"Sorry to disappoint you! We had no idea it was a single!"

And we didn't. "Take On the World" was just another song that came about through the usual process of throwing ideas at the wall to see which would stick. And it stuck resolutely—to the tune of 400,000 copies, I believe. I love the song.

Not just that, Wolverhampton Wanderers football club caught wind of it and started using it as their club song, giving it a shelf life that extended long after January 1979, when it was released.

✦

Our live record, *Unleashed in the East,* mixed and produced by Tom Allom, captured us at roughly the intersection of what we called the X Certificate tour, which had covered UK venues in October and November 1978, and the *Hell Bent for Leather* tour, which would continue through North America and Europe through much of 1979.

It has been suggested over the years by metal fans that the album isn't exactly what it appears to be. I'd like to put the whole debate to rest.

The truth of the matter is that, in all the years I've known Rob, I'm not aware of him ever having blown a gig because of a sore throat or any such ailment. Rob was like the Duracell bunny. He just kept going and going; he was amazing in that respect.

That aside, other than naturally having a strong vocal constitution, Rob was always someone who took great care of his voice when he had to. When you're touring for months at a time, doing interviews and sound checks during the day, it all gets pretty wearing. He knew that better than anyone. So, sometimes when he'd been pushing himself particularly hard and felt that his voice was on the edge, Rob just wouldn't speak at all for a while, leaving us to take care of the interviews.

By and large, that worked for him, and us. It was all part and parcel of the tight Judas Priest unit—and hopefully it led to some interesting variety in our interviews.

But when we got to Japan to play a couple of gigs at the Sunplaza Hall and the Kosei Nenkin Hall, Rob's voice was absolutely stripped bare. It really was in awful shape.

"What are we going to do here, Rob?"

"We'll do what we always do. We'll play."

So, knowing that the gigs were to be recorded for a live release, like the pro that he is, Rob battled on and did them to the best of his ability. But needless to say, his voice was far from top form. It was the worst problem he'd ever had with it. I remember looking across a few times after songs like "Ripper" and "Tyrant" and thinking, *God, he's really struggling here . . .*

He was visibly wincing, but Rob would never even consider throwing in the towel.

When it came to mixing the album, we had the benefit of having two sets of vocals from the two gigs to work with. That gave us, even in those early days, the luxury of being able to "fly" vocal recordings in or out if we felt we had to—to mix and match and find the best single track. And that's what we did.

How much was used from each and how much wasn't, I can't really recall. From memory, most of his midrange and low range would have been intact on both. But when he was going for the higher notes . . . I doubt the voice would have been there.

Because some of the notes just weren't there on either recording, if my memory serves me well, Rob had to do a fair bit of patching up of some of his vocals. For Tom Allom, it wasn't much of a challenge to match the vocal sound and, also, the truth was, to respect the many fans who would doubtless be spending hard-earned cash on our first live record, we just couldn't have put the vocals out as they sounded on those nights. Nobody would have thanked us for releasing a poor-quality recording with Rob's voice not at its brilliant best.

And that was how it happened, really.

The criticism? I didn't really mind. All I knew was that I hadn't needed to re-record any of my guitar parts!

Playing live when you know it's being recorded is an interesting discipline. I liked to improvise onstage, so I never felt any real pressure to be any more accurate than usual. Songs like "Running Wild," "Sinner," and "Victim of Changes" were always my favorites to switch up a little, depending on how I felt. On other tracks like "Dissident Aggressor" or, later, "The Rage," which I could never exactly remember how I'd played in the studio, I'd just try to play something that resembled the original, if it wasn't exactly the same. It always worked.

Amusingly, playing "Sinner" live in the early days made me feel like I was running the gauntlet from a tuning perspective—particularly before string locking systems became available. I did incredible things with a Fender Strat and a floating bridge, starting with "Sinner," with all that bending, then having to play the crazy solo in the middle, while always expecting the guitar to come back into tune afterward!

✦

As strained as Rob's voice was in Japan, there was no letup. It was the beginning of a pretty hellishly busy year of tour dates that took us straight to North America and then back to Europe again. We ended what seemed like a never-ending touring cycle for *Killing Machine/Hell Bent for Leather* by joining AC/DC on their European tour to promote *Highway to Hell* in November and December of 1979.

The American leg was memorable simply because we were partnered for a string of dates in March and April with UFO—some of the most notorious rock 'n' roll hell-raisers ever to have walked the planet.

They were promoting their live album, *Strangers in the Night*, which had been released to great acclaim at the beginning of 1979. They were absolutely flying. Suffice to say, they did not disappoint when it came to delivering the madness.

I wouldn't be the first to say that their bass player, Pete Way, was quite a man. He was gentle as a kitten, really, a truly lovely guy, but, hell, did he know how to live the rock star life. Every day was lived as if it was his last.

One night when we all had a night off, we went to see Blue Öyster Cult supported by UFO. That gig seemed like it was a magnet to any Hells Angels in the area; Blue Öyster Cult had that type of following. Afterward we all went backstage whereupon we then found ourselves being taken to what appeared to be quite an elaborate Hells Angel den across town somewhere, where the guy that seemed to be the leader not only had a big bowie knife in each boot, but he also had a daughter with him who, I kid you not, was no older than twelve! It was bizarre—but he seemed to think it was all OK.

He then pulled both knives out and started chopping a mountain of coke in front of us. Thereafter the entire Hells Angels troupe insisted on escorting UFO and us back to our hotel while stopping all the traffic on the freeway so that we could turn into the hotel's car park. That was their way of showing that they carried a bit of clout in town by escorting an international rock band. Some of us were the worse for wear, to put it mildly, by the time we got back to our hotel. Then, in the middle of the same night the fire alarm went off and everyone, including UFO and us, ended up out in the hotel car park half asleep.

Er, what's happening?!

That was just another UFO night.

◆

For many reasons, I remember these couple of months with AC/DC more fondly than almost any tour that I ever went on with Judas Priest. AC/DC had absolutely no arrogant side to them whatsoever. Everything was very chill; they couldn't have been nicer to us. As people they were absolutely salt of the earth—as I've always found Australians to be over the years. And at no point did they pull any of that "headline act suppressing the support band" bullshit.

Consequently, I enjoyed touring with them a lot and got on very well with those guys. As I recall, they had a big super-duper tour bus and we just had a little white van. Occasionally they invited us to ride with them for some of the longer daytime journeys and I used to sit there discussing guitars, guitar strings, and all kinds of other shit with Angus Young.

As big as they were in 1979, for a number of reasons I thought that, like for like, we weren't behind them as a band. The way I saw it, we were comparable guitar players, had good songs, and a very able singer. There didn't seem to be an ingredient that we didn't have.

But the significant difference was that AC/DC had all the stage, all the lights and the sound, plus, on top of all that, they did what they do, which is to kick arse wonderfully, every single night.

Being on a bill with them only reminded me how impossible it was to blow them offstage. What they deliver is impossible to challenge or question, but I still thought that Judas Priest was a comparable band on a few levels! I suppose it just depends what your cup of tea is. We were in the same genre . . . yet we were so far apart.

Funnily enough, playing with them reminded me of the first time we ever supported Status Quo at a venue called Quaintways in Chester, where the dressing rooms were underneath the stage. It must have been only 1972.

We went onstage, in our opinion, a comparable band to Status Quo at the time.

"Follow *that*, lads . . . "

Then they went on, played those simple twelve-bars, and the roof fell off the place. They were a serious force to be reckoned with in those early days.

Watching from the side of the stage I just thought, *Fucking hell . . .*

No matter what you did or how hard you tried, you *could not* blow that band offstage at that time. They were established, the fans knew every word of all the songs—and they just pogoed all night long. There was absolutely nothing we could do about it. You could play intricate solos; you could do whatever you wanted. It made no difference.

AC/DC and Status Quo are the only bands I've ever played with that have made me feel that way. I have absolutely the highest respect for everything they've both done. They do the same thing year in and year out and their fans absolutely love it. And as much as we might have, in my opinion, eclipsed both of them in a number of areas, they were better than us in a couple of *really key* ones. They had intangible ingredients that we simply did not have.

The biggest shame of all was that we never really ran into the AC/DC lads after that tour. Bon Scott, as much as it was obvious that he liked a dram of whiskey now and again, was an absolute gentleman.

We flew between a few of the dates and I remember showing up at the airport bar at nine thirty in the morning and Bon would always be there without fail, showered, shaved, and immaculately dressed. He wasn't just cleaned up; he was genuinely dapper.

All of this was a massive shock given how he'd usually been the previous night. He was a completely different person onstage. When he was chugging bottles of Jack Daniel's and throwing up in towels between songs as he sometimes did, it was hard to believe you were speaking to the same guy when you met him the next morning.

Conversely, Angus and Malcolm, although they were both habitual cigarette smokers, didn't drink much alcohol. They were dyed-in-the-wool tea drinkers.

"What can I get you, Angus?"

"A cup of tea, please, mate."

"Malcolm?"

"Ah, just a cup of tea, please."

"Are you sure?"

"Yeah. Cup of tea."

That was their thing, all day long. Both of them were so small and needed so much energy to perform like they did, they couldn't possibly have gotten away with being hard drinkers.

It was so sad to hear that Malcolm had passed away while I was finishing this book. Unlike Angus who was always smiling and outgoing, Malcolm was hard to get to know. Although always very friendly, he was extremely serious and self-conscious.

The news that Bon had died just a month after we'd been enjoying his company came as a huge shock, too. For some reason we were in London at the time, staying in a hotel in Swiss Cottage, when we heard of his death on the television. As much as Bon's death hurt us on a personal level, his passing left a huge void in heavy music at that time. I'll always treasure the memories of those four weeks with my Aussie friends.

CHAPTER SEVEN

THE RECEPTION TO *UNLEASHED IN THE EAST*—AN ALBUM that I've heard people refer to as the best heavy metal live album of all time—made the choice of producer for our next record a simple one. There was only one name in the running: Tom Allom.

Considering his background, Tom was much more rock 'n' roll than you'd ever imagine. Although he looked like a politician, or even a colonel, and spoke the best Queen's English, Tom Allom was always one of the lads as far as Judas Priest was concerned. If there was ever a party, you could always count on Tom being there.

As good a musician as he was (and Tom was a very fine pianist), Tom knew exactly how to work with us. By and large he let us do what we wanted to do while he sat in and made sure we kept it in time and kept things in tune. After each take he'd either say, "Are you happy with that?" or "Do you want to do it again?" Usually, it was the latter. We were always the kind of band who wanted perfection.

It was no coincidence therefore that many people consider *British Steel*, our sixth studio album, to actually *be* perfection as far as heavy metal music is concerned. As I've said, throughout the '70s, Judas Priest had been on a meandering path, trying to find our sweet spot. Most bands do the same.

At times, I don't doubt that the destination might have been unclear to the fans—certainly from an image perspective. But as *Stained Class* turned into *Killing Machine* and the entire Judas Priest vision started revealing itself, it was also clear to me that whatever we did next was going to be the culmination of everything we'd done since *Rocka Rolla*, rolled into one digestible package that essentially said, "Welcome to the 1980s. We're Judas Priest, and this is heavy metal."

We didn't approach the actual songs any differently. They were just what we happened to have at the time—although Dave Holland joining the band certainly gave us a new dimension after Les Binks left following a row about his fee for *Unleashed in the East*.

Apparently Arnakarta came to him afterward and wanted to cut his money. Les apparently just said, "Fuck them" and walked away.

I don't think I saw him again after that—at least not until I got together again with him in 2017 and we spent a good night having a few pints discussing old times.

In truth, Les Binks always viewed the idea of being in a rock band through something of a jaundiced eye. He just did not buy into the idea of fame one bit. He often would say, "Come on then, let's go and be rock stars" before we went onstage.

"What exactly do you mean, Les?" we used to say.

"You know what I mean. That's all we're doing," he'd answer—and always in a way that made it sound as if there was something wrong with it. I always felt that there was a strange kind of resentment lurking in Les.

"But this is *real*, Les," we used to say to him, "you really *can* be an adored rock musician . . ."

Even playing with Led Zeppelin in '77 at The Day on the Green Festival at the Oakland Coliseum couldn't convince Les.

Incidentally, that was an odd series of events—not least because we were on the East Coast, about to return home, when the idea was first suggested. We'd had a satisfying first tour, essentially playing clubs in Boston, Chicago, and New York. We really tore it up.

Then someone called and said, "Can you go over to the West Coast and play with Zeppelin?"

We were over the moon and honored to be asked to be part of something so grand. And that's what we did. Other than in Oakland, although they'd played the same Midlands circuit that we had, our paths didn't cross very often.

We played two days at Oakland—there was a shitload of people there. The stadium alone held 60,000 people, and then there was the floor area. As gigs go, it was strange because I seem to recall that we went on at about eleven in the morning. Then Rick Derringer went on, followed by Led Zeppelin. To me it seemed like, because it was such an early show, the audience were knackered. Many of them had possibly traveled overnight to get there.

When Zeppelin were on, I went out front and remember being surprised to discover that it was pretty laid back. Everybody was comatose, really—until they came on for the encore and everyone woke up! Nevertheless, it was a fantastic event—and about as close to being rock stars as we'd gotten by then.

But it wasn't enough to appease Les.

Whether it was that session-guy mentality, wanting to shun the spotlight, who knows? But Les could never get his head around the idea that people could want to have heroes, and that he'd have to give interviews, sign autographs, and be lauded by fans that did want heroes. And, with us having recently gotten a foothold in the

US market, maybe he could see just too much of that rock star life down the line.

In the end, it just wasn't for him. And from what he was saying years later, I don't think he has ever had any regrets about leaving. He's lived a varied life, worked with all kinds of musicians since—all on his own terms. Les Binks was there for some important years with Priest and I'll always respect and value what he did with us.

Dave Holland, on the other hand, wasn't fazed by very much at all. He just showed up, made no fuss, and laid the beat down hard every night. Believe me, having someone like that behind you onstage night after night was such an empowering feeling. From the start, as straightforward as his playing style was in relation to Les Binks's jazz-influenced chops, Dave Holland was *on* it. He had power that could make a hall shake.

Although he grew up in the Northampton area, I always considered Dave to be very much a Midlands man in the way he acted and fit in with our group. Maybe that was because he hadn't landed from the London or Liverpool scene, but instead had spent several years playing in Midlands bands like Finders Keepers and Trapeze, both with Glenn Hughes. Either way, he was always like one of us.

Beyond that, Dave was the kind of guy who actually *wanted* the touring band life. He liked everything about it. Whether it was being stuck on an island recording, being out on tour playing hundreds of shows, Dave was always quite happy—and from that perspective he always felt like he was a real member of the band. We now had a solid, five-man unit—six if you included our recently hired producer extraordinaire.

Speaking of which, Tom Allom's primary role was to keep an eye on the mechanics of what we were doing in the studio. That aside, he more or less left us to our own devices from a creative perspective. We played while he sat and oversaw the process. If we needed advice, we'd just say: "Colonel? What do you think?"

The result was that *British Steel,* while not a long album in terms of playing time, was a very easy record to make, mainly because we never got stuck at any time.

Sometimes you can get hung up on something in a studio: trying to force something that isn't there or letting self-doubt creep in. Before you know it you're asking yourself questions like, *Is this as good as it should be? Do we need to strengthen this? Do we need another song?*

All of those questions just suck up time.

Thankfully—and it was probably just luck—that didn't happen. Everything just played out how we planned it.

Before creating *British Steel,* we had no preconceived ideas of what we wanted to achieve. The only thing that was certain when we all reassembled with whatever ideas we each had was that we had definite standards. That's always the exciting part: seeing what's there when you lay it all on the table. And then we were able to look at everything and each other very critically as if to say, "Is this good enough?"

And on this occasion, it was good enough. We just went and did it, and it came out how it came out.

As usual, I can't really recall why we ended up in Startling Studios at Tittenhurst Park to record—other than we had mixed *Unleashed in the East* there. We were never really involved in these conversations anyway. Someone at the record company would just come to us and say, "We're going here to record, lads," whereupon we'd all shrug and say, "All right."

All I knew about it beforehand was that John Lennon once owned Startling before selling it to Ringo Starr, who still owned it at that time. Then, when we actually got there, we realized it was a hell of an impressive place: seventy-odd acres in the middle of Ascot, a fishing lake, a church on the grounds that we used for a photo shoot, cottages dotted around; it all seemed vast.

Above and beyond its aesthetic appeal as an old-school country pile in the style of the kind of place that big, moneyed rock bands of that era liked to use as a retreat, Tittenhurst was genuinely a great place to record an album. The house, specifically the shape and scale of the rooms, offered such incredible scope for the creation of sounds.

From the off, we were absolutely spoiled for choice.

Early on, I decided that I'd record my guitars in the library because it had wooden floors and paneled walls, all of which was great for creating the best guitar sounds. Wood is such a fantastic conductor of sound. Without ever sounding harsh, it always permits such incredible resonance. All guitarists love that kind of room.

Drums need something different. In conversation with Dave Holland, Tom elected to record the drums in the hall area at the foot of the stairwell. I remember hearing that Led Zeppelin had done something similar when they recorded John Bonham's drums at Headley Grange. Tittenhurst's stairwell offered a similarly great ambience and also allowed Tom to both close-mic and place extra microphones in positions whereby they were hung over the banisters to capture the monstrous scale of Dave's drum tracks.

From memory, Glenn was in the drawing room, which, again, had wooden floors and shutters. In this room we also set up our little rehearsal situation so that, when we needed to, we could play live on the floor in order to write songs that we didn't have before going in.

This was the very room in which John Lennon played the piano in the video for "Imagine," where Yoko Ono could be seen opening the curtains. By this point though, the room's rather minimalist aesthetic had been enhanced by the addition of a large television and table-foosball game that we almost wore out with excessive playing.

In fact, I seem to remember sitting in that room one night watching "Imagine" on *Top of the Pops* on the television. I think it had been re-released; viewing it there was the weirdest feeling.

Odder still, in the bedroom I slept in upstairs, the plug sockets were still labeled "John" and "Yoko." It's horrible to think that just a few months later, John Lennon would be dead.

As I recall, evidence of the Beatles was all around us, even down in the cellars.

"Look what I've found here!" Ian said, holding up handfuls of reels of tape above his head.

"What are they?" I replied.

"Looks like they're Beatles master tapes," he said.

They'd just been dumped there, *piles* of them—along with all kinds of other memorabilia: gold singles, gold albums—there was stuff lying everywhere.

One of the houses on the estate was used by Ringo's son Zak's band as a rehearsal space. We knocked on the door one afternoon on the way to fish the lake (they'd specifically requested that we not) and they were in there playing UFO covers and a whole bunch of other songs.

"All right? How's it going?"

"Not bad. How about you?"

"Yeah, pretty good."

And off we went. We never saw Zak Starkey again.

✦

I don't specifically remember which of the tracks came about while we were at Tittenhurst, but I'm pretty certain that "Living After Midnight" and "The Rage" were two that we conceived after our initial writing sessions.

Rob likes to tell a story about how he heard Glenn banging away on a riff downstairs while he was trying to sleep in the room above. The next morning Rob said, "What was that you were playing last night?"

Glenn repeated the riff that would become "Living After Midnight." Rob then came up with some lyrics about being kept awake all night—after midnight—and that's how easy it was to conceive a Priest classic!

"The Rage" is one of those anomalies that crop up all over our catalog. At the time, it started out as a vague idea. Then, as we added the layers—not least the funky bass intro that Ian played first—we started looking at each other in the same way as we did when we recorded songs like "Last Rose of Summer" and, later on, "You've Got Another Thing Comin'" and "Love Bites."

As much confidence as we had in our songwriting abilities, there was nevertheless a moment, albeit a fleeting one, where we all thought, *Does this work?*

We knew "The Rage" was completely unlike anything we'd ever done. Again, that wasn't intentional. It was just one of the ideas that got thrown on the table during the process.

Soon we began to realize that pretty much *everything* could work. Even by 1980, there was no formula for what a Judas Priest song could be. By virtue of the fact that we were open to a certain song or idea—that alone made it a Judas Priest track. Maybe we were one of the only heavy metal bands that thought that way.

I remember that "Rapid Fire" came together very easily. When we conceived it, we didn't do so with the thought of it being the opening track. Although a good few Priest albums start with a fast, energetic song to get the fans' blood pumping, we only made that decision once we looked at everything and weighed up each track's pros and cons from a sequencing point of view.

And only then would we say, "That sounds like a contender for the opening track, you know . . . "

That's what we decided with "Rapid Fire."

Other tracks needed a bit more in the way of lateral thought.

At that time, it was considered very outré for producers to create their own sounds in the recording studio. Sampling didn't yet exist; there was no alternative to approaching things organically.

Tom Allom was all about that kind of thinking; he loved it. Consequently, seemingly stupid things like dropping gongs into baths of water and big doors being slammed were committed to tape.

In general, there was a lot of experimentation with sound going on throughout the process of recording *British Steel*. The two best-known examples are the cutlery sounds in "Metal Gods." (Tom suggested someone go and get a big tray of cutlery from a drawer in the kitchen to shake at a predetermined moment to mimic the sound of lumbering, prehistoric footsteps.) For the same song, we used a billiards cue to make the whip-crack sound you hear. It was all great fun at the time.

And then there's that infamous sound of breaking glass during the sirens at the end of "Breaking the Law," which really was Rob and me smashing beer bottles against a wall outside!

All in all, Tom really enjoyed what we were doing, and that's one of the best relationships a band can have with a producer. As I said, it always felt like he was the sixth member of the band in the sense that, when we partied, he partied with us. There was no distance or boundary at all—not that we ever really did much in the way of wild stuff when we were making *British Steel*, which I'm sure will come as a surprise.

Really, we were all business. The most we ever did was go down to the local pub to have a few pints and a game of darts. Then we'd come back and have another session. Occasionally something good would come out after these impromptu après-pub sessions. But generally speaking we'd stagger into the drawing room, plug in the guitars, and have a bit of a jam session before calling it a night.

As with every album, the first and most important acid test is your own critical ear. I have a great picture of Ian, Rob, and Tom Allom standing outside at Tittenhurst with a giant barrel of beer in our midst during a playback. While having a few beers, we listened to every second of the album, looking out for even the slightest issues—technical or aesthetic—that might reveal themselves as we endeavored to remove ourselves from the role of creators and put ourselves in the role of our audience instead.

Sometimes thoughts crossed my mind—*Is that section too long and boring?* Or, *Is the sequencing wrong between those two tracks?*

If that happened (and it usually did), we'd just pull all our observations together and go back into the studio with Tom to address them one by one. Then, when that was done, we'd listen all over again. It was a laborious process, but we were the kind of band that was striving for perfection whenever possible.

Fortunately, by the time 1980 came around, technology had moved on to the extent that multitrack editing was possible. That was a huge help. Tom would have bits of tape stuck all over the back wall, ready to be used when they were needed. All of this was in stark contrast to how it had been when we first started, when the only way to remember songs was to keep playing them, over and over again, in the hope that we'd still remember how to play them after we'd been to sleep or had a few beers.

At some point during the final overdubs, Tom Allom said, "There's a young band outside. Can they come in and watch what you're doing?"

It was Def Leppard. They marched in and sat quietly. In contrast to Iron Maiden (more on them later), they were friendly and respectful. Tom had produced their first album and they were just delighted to meet us. The brief meeting paved the way for a good relationship.

At the end, I looked at *British Steel* as a record that had almost no faults. If I'm being hypercritical, I'd say that, as fantastic as it sounds, it still doesn't quite capture every aspect of how fantastic those sessions were. What's missing? I have no idea. All I know is that the songs we made sounded incredible when we were recording them.

Young me, probably
age four or five.

A seven-year-old me.

(*above*) My first ever passport, age sixteen.

(*facing page, top*) An impromptu photo shoot in a park in Wednesbury in 1972 with a war veteran we persuaded to join us. From left, Ian Hill, Chris "Congo" Campbell, the old man, me, and Al Atkins.

(*facing page, bottom*) A second, moodier picture from the same day.

Onstage in 1972, probably at a venue called JB's in Dudley.
That's the SG Special I got after the SG Junior.

In a car during the *Rocka Rolla* era.

above) With Les Binks sometime in 1976. He was never the snappiest of dressers. That's our dressing room for the day behind us.

facing page, top) In my girlfriend's father's garden in 1978, wearing a hat I had acquired from somewhere!

facing page, bottom) Carol's dad's house—drying my clothes in the garden.

Judas Priest in 1977 in stage clothes. Note how the image hasn't quite come together.

On tour in Japan, holding a fanzine that
someone had given me

Rob and I arriving in Japan on tour sometime in 1978.

Carol and I on the bonnet of a Mini I bought at a scrap yard for ninety pounds. We're outside my house in Bloxwich in 1980. Nice slippers!

With my Rolls-Royce Silver Shadow. Note how I'm still riding my bike!

Rob, me, and my guitar tech in the house we rented in Spain while we were writing songs for Turbo. I had definitely had a few drinks!

My car collection, shortly after moving into Astbury Hall.
The Porsche Turbo would later inspire the *Turbo* album title.

A dressing room somewhere in America with no showers
while we were touring *Ram It Down*.

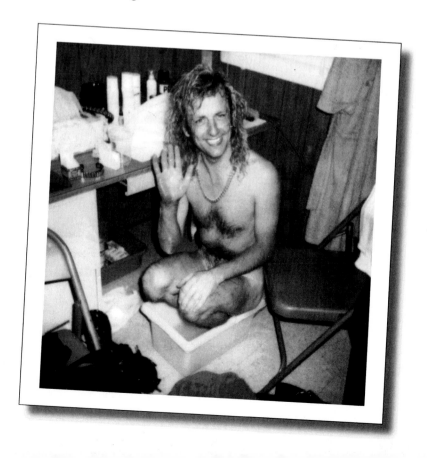

(*above*) In full flight on stage with Judas Priest at Wembley Arena in 2009. (*Ross Halfin*)

(*facing page, top*) Outside Graceland while on tour in the America while touring *Painkiller*.

(*facing page, bottom*) The same day at Graceland with Scott Travis and Kenny Silva our tour accountant.

Out on the
golf course at
Astbury Hall.
(*Today's Golfer*)

Throwing myself into
the golf course design
process at Astbury Hall.
(*Today's Golfer*)

As significant as the songs were, the iconic *British Steel* cover art was every bit as important in concretizing this whirlwind five-year journey of self-discovery we'd been on since *Rocka Rolla*. With the music, the leather-and-studs image all in place, the uniquely British image of the Wilkinson Sword razor blade clasped between fingers was just the icing on the cake.

Rozlaw Szaybo had been responsible for both the *Stained Class* and *Killing Machine* album art. As I've said, both, in their own ways, contributed key steps to an important final reveal. When I saw his final draft of the *British Steel* cover, I remember thinking, *That's it . . .*

In a sense, with its clear reference to an instantly recognizable brand like the *Rocka Rolla* cover five years prior, Szaybo's cover not only created something new, it also served to nicely perpetuate a distinct theme from the past. As such, *British Steel* was a cheeky nod to *Rocka Rolla*, which I think all our fans understood and appreciated.

The first version we saw actually had the razor blade cutting into the fingers slightly. I think there was even blood visible. When we saw it, we all vetoed it at once because we were worried our American record company wouldn't swallow it, after our experience with *Killing Machine*. As much as we liked the edginess, it just wasn't worth the risk.

"Tone it down," we said. "Let's suggest, but not actually show . . . "

"You mean like this?"

"Yes . . . *exactly* like that."

The next version we saw—the final one—worked better anyway. The blade still seemed to be going into the fingers, but there was no blood. Somehow it was more effective. We made that decision fairly quickly, and that was that.

✦

Going out on the road with *British Steel* really should have catapulted Priest into the stratosphere.

We had the music and the look; it was the happiest we'd ever been. But what we never quite had was effective management from the guys at Arnakarta.

Let's face it, in 1980/1981 we were so ripe to take America that it wasn't even funny. There were very few bands doing what we were doing in America at that time. Van Halen were cool—but in my mind they never really were heavy metal. All the rest at that time were much more focused on more of a hair-metal thing.

Really, apart from us, only Scorpions and perhaps a band like Dokken were doing what we were doing. As such, we should have taken America on that *British Steel* tour in May 1980, but our domination would end up taking somewhat longer to achieve.

Meanwhile, back in the UK, we had a tour to focus on that was due to kick off in Cardiff at the beginning of March. Before going out, we rehearsed at a venue in London—possibly at what is now called the Shepherd's Bush Empire.

By this time, we knew that we'd be taking out Iron Maiden as our support act. They'd just released their self-titled debut record and, honestly, we didn't know much about them. As far as we were concerned, we were helping them. We were the main act, with an established following and a solid track record of albums behind us; they were starting out.

However, it soon became apparent that they saw themselves as something more than a support band. In fact, while we were finishing *British Steel* at Ringo's place, I remember being in the kitchen and picking up a copy of one of the weekly music papers where I read an interview with Iron Maiden who were saying that they were going to be touring with Judas Priest and, as such, planned to blow our bollocks off! It was the last thing I wanted to read. Looking back now it was a bit of youthful mouthing off which the press understandably made a meal of. But at the time I remember thinking,

Right. That's it. I don't care who they are. I'm not putting up with that shit. We'll get somebody else.

I was outvoted.

Worse still, the tension soon heightened further.

As we were rehearsing onstage prior to the tour, I remember seeing these guys sitting ten rows back in the auditorium, watching our every move and absorbing every sound. These were brand new tracks we were playing; *British Steel* wasn't even out.

"Who are these guys?" I remember saying to my guitar tech, when we'd almost finished an entire rehearsal set.

"That's our support band," he told me.

"If it's Iron Maiden, tell them to fuck off," I said.

Ten minutes later, we jumped off stage and went over to where these lads were standing. They all looked like they didn't care that they were stepping on our toes. If anything, it looked like they were studying us: our clothes, our stage set, our songs. Don't get me wrong: it wasn't a pride issue for me to be playing in front of a support band. That wasn't my gripe. My issue was that they just walked in there like they owned the place, blatantly ignoring accepted protocol as they did so. The incident set a bad tone for the tour that followed.

Not surprisingly, the tour was tense on the back of the rehearsal standoff. Furthermore, Paul Di'Anno wouldn't keep his mouth shut in the press and kept implying that Iron Maiden were going to blow the bollocks off Judas Priest every night—something that never, ever happened.

I watched Maiden's set on a few of these nights and in fact saw that they didn't always go down very well. And the reason for that was that these audiences were very much Judas Priest fans. They were there specifically to see us. It all left a bit of a sour taste in our mouths. Even worse, it always felt to me that they were copying our clothes. I remember seeing a picture of Dave Murray around that time, with his long blond hair and his leathers, and thinking, *Is that him? Or is that me in disguise?*

Coincidentally, we didn't particularly help ourselves on that tour by almost not making it to one of two hometown shows at the Birmingham Odeon in March. A few weeks before, one of the guys at Arnakarta called.

"You've been asked to go on *Top of the Pops* on March 27 to play 'Living After Midnight,'" he told us.

"That's great news," we all thought.

"But it's the same day as the Birmingham gig," he added.

"Oh. Well, maybe we could do both?"

And that's what was agreed.

Bad decision!

We thought that a second appearance on Top of The Pops was too good an opportunity to turn down. We'd already appeared there to showcase "Take On the World" on the *Killing Machine* cycle a year earlier. It had done us no harm at all—particularly since we were always wary of alienating British audiences with our obvious focus on the US market.

"Living After Midnight" and "Take On the World" weren't entirely unrelated in a stylistic sense, but it was purely by coincidence. Both featured a kind of sing-along chorus that British audiences seemed to relate to. But neither had been intended as singles when we wrote them. Yet, those were the songs that people seemed to identify most with. "United" would be the same, a few months later.

Anyway, we did *Top of the Pops* and the day soon descended into total chaos. The performance ran over, and the weather that day was really horrendous. On reflection, we were never going to get from London to Birmingham in time for the gig, no matter how hard we tried. Someone even commissioned a plane to get us there but the thick fog soon scuppered that idea. We even had a police escort from the airport—we tried everything.

And we didn't make it.

I remember that we turned up an hour or so late, by which time a large number of fans, *our* hometown fans, had left. It was a huge own-goal on our behalf—particularly with the Iron Maiden guys there probably reveling in our misfortune. Given the choice now, I would have definitely said "Forget *Top of the Pops*" and focused on turning up for that hometown gig.

◆

There was something radically different, not just about how we looked from 1980 onward, but also how we felt about the look.

That glance across the stage at Rob in 1974 had brought us here, with the unified black-leather look. No more was one of us wearing a satin shirt or a sweater. In general, we all looked like a slight variation on a very carefully developed theme—one that I'd instigated several years earlier with a view to taking on the metal world. As we toured in 1980 with *British Steel*, I wanted audiences to look at us up there and think, "That's what Judas Priest looks like"—in the same way as they might look at a soldier wearing camouflage and say: "He's in the army." I'd spent the previous few years specifically trying to create a set of conditions that would foster an association that would forever be synonymous with us.

By 1980, we'd done that—and then other bands followed our lead to the point that the black-leather-and studs look became not only synonymous with Judas Priest but with heavy metal music in general. Not only did I want heavy metal to be an empowering place where people could feel strong and safe—a religion of sorts—I also wanted to add a defined dress code to the tenets of the religion. We were the genesis of it all, and that felt extremely gratifying at the time.

Without ever asking each other how it felt to walk out there in leather every night, I don't doubt that it meant different things to each of us. For me personally, there was a feeling of power when I first started wearing leather onstage. I felt like I was part of something—a small army maybe—and that made me somehow invincible. It really was an extraordinary feeling, particularly for someone who, ever since I saw the Thames van on the Yew Tree Estate, craved not only the comfort and familiarity of a group, but also the protection and sense of strength.

Other than the fact that it was really hot and sweaty to wear on-stage, especially in America on account of the generally warmer climate, there were simply no downsides to black-leather stage wear. No longer would anyone have to search around for something new to wear; instead it quickly became as automatic as putting on a pair of shoes.

Better still, there was a limitless flexibility to the leather look that extended far beyond the *British Steel* era. Outfits could be enhanced to fit whatever theme we were presenting at any given time (we would later have bespoke leather jackets made for the Fuel for Life tour to support the *Turbo* album)

Rob, of course, was particularly legitimized by the leather-and-studs look from the outset. All he needed was a green light and he was off and running. As time passed, he went far beyond what any of the rest of us had in a full stage wardrobe, by adding leather hats, a vast array of boots, and, of course, the leather bullwhip, which he wielded from atop a Harley-Davidson motorcycle. But *British Steel* and 1980 was the beginning of it all.

CHAPTER EIGHT

WAS NEVER REALLY AWARE OF WHAT FANS AND CRITICS thought about *Point of Entry* at the time. I was never one to sit and read album reviews and there was no Internet in 1981 to force such information into your world, whether you wanted it or not.

As an artist, you never really know what you're creating at the time anyway. There's no doubt that you can get too close to what you're working on to the point that you completely lose perspective on what's good and what isn't. And that's when you need outside ears, someone to come along and say, "Look, guys, this sounds a bit wet compared to what you've done in the past."

I now know this because I've played that role for a couple of bands that I've produced over the years. I've listened with those outsider's ears and then gone back and stripped out anything that I thought was weak and replaced it with strengths. That's what a producer is there for.

But sometimes even that's not enough, and that's not a criticism of Tom Allom, who was there with us the whole time in the studio in Ibiza. As always, Tom worked with the ideas we had at the time, but at the end of the day, if a band doesn't have the material, a producer can't put what's not there on the record. It's that simple.

Anyway, we did the bulk of the writing and recording for *Point of Entry* at Ibiza Sound Studios. As far as I know, the reason for that was twofold. One, my understanding was that if you manufacture a product in another country, everyone gets tax relief. I think that's the gist of it. Two, I think our record company liked to put us places where they could contain and keep an eye on us while we made a record.

So, what did they do?

They put us on an island in the Mediterranean.

They probably thought, "What could possibly go wrong?"

The answer? Well, initially not a lot. We arrived, drove the ten-minute ride to the studio where we met the owner, Fritz Ehrentraut, a German with wispy, long blond hair with more than a hint of rock 'n' roll about him.

"How do you do, Fritz," we said. "Nice place you've got here!"

"You boys make a great rock record, ya?"

"We'll try, Fritz—thank you."

And we could tell, right there, that this was an amazing place where we could probably focus, work hard, shut ourselves away, meditate, be enlightened and free of spirit, bond as metal brothers—and of course follow up *British Steel* with a belter of an album.

Then we went into town later that evening.

Immediately, the whole thinking changed in an instant.

We've got no chance here, I thought.

As I looked across the bar, Glenn and Ian were already surrounded by scantily clad females—all young and free of spirit—not to mention sexually titillated by the incessant heat of the Mediterranean sun and whatever alcoholic refreshments they'd already had that day.

No, we were in deep shit in Ibiza, right from the start. There were far too many distractions: too many late-night bars ready to receive our money and too many young girls ready and willing to receive our manhood. These distractions, in combination but not necessarily in that order, would be just too tempting for us to resist.

And we didn't even try.

When we finished recording each day, usually around midnight, we'd just walk out the studio door, head down to the bars and clubs—and then the real fun began. It was like a holiday camp, night after night, for the couple of months we were on the island.

There was this place in San Antonio at the north of the island where they used to put sprinklers on at five in the morning to sober everybody up. Then they kicked everyone out. We'd jump on motorbikes and ride out to this place in the hills for breakfast where we'd be greeted with the not unpleasant sight of numerous young, hungover girls drying off while sitting in the sun around long wooden tables. The worst part of it all was that we then had to go back the recording studio.

✦

Nevertheless, by some miracle, we got the record done—albeit with a subconscious desire to not just churn out the same stuff time and time again. I'd be lying if I said that I loved every song on *Point of Entry* (or indeed on any album of ours).

As was often the case, I'd sometimes walk into the studio to find Glenn and Rob getting into something of their own, jamming out on an idea and getting off on it. All I could do was just go with it, even if I didn't particularly like the track.

Unless I had a very strong opinion about one of my own compositions, mostly I was happy to go whichever way the creative wind happened to be blowing at the time. Everything about making music is so subjective anyway, then, when you're stuck on an island, just the band and a producer, it's even harder to assess what's in front of you. At the time, we thought the songs were as good as anything we'd done.

The same applies to the *Point of Entry* cover image (both of them). They might seem a little vague and unfocused to the casual observer, but they were the best ideas we had at that time.

And time has done nothing to change that view. When I put the CD of *Point of Entry* on in the car now, I enjoy listening to it. And really, few could argue with the claim that "Hot Rockin'", "Desert Plains," and "Heading Out to the Highway" are absolutely seminal Judas Priest tracks, no matter what kind of listener you are. For me, I feel the same way about our albums as I imagine I might about children: I won't have one slighted over another!

✦

Unbelievably, to me at least, after we'd toured the UK with Saxon on the World Wide Blitz tour, somebody told me that Iron Maiden would be taking over from Savoy Brown on the US dates from May of 1981 onward.

I just thought that they were trouble.

Maiden's manager Rod Smallwood is no fool, though. They were promoting their second album, *Killers*. Nobody really knew or cared about Iron Maiden in the States in 1981 and nobody was more aware of that than Rod.

We, on the other hand, had an established and growing audience and I'm sure Rod could see that. Looking at tour options to get Maiden to the next level, maybe he thought something along the lines of, "Let's see if we can hitch a ride on Priest's coattails here."

As far as I was concerned, given how petty and unpleasant the Maiden guys had been on the UK dates of the *British Steel* tour, I didn't see any reason why we should give them an opportunity to undermine us again.

Unlike us when we first went out as a support act, Iron Maiden, to me, seemed to think that the world owed them a living from the get-go—a living I wasn't prepared to give them at our expense. We were the main act. I thought they should accept that and get on with it. As I recall, the US tour passed with an undercurrent of discomfort between the Iron Maiden guys and us.

◆

A couple of months after returning from the States, we were back out again for the UK leg of the tour with the German heavy metal band Accept, which was due to begin at Hull City Hall on November 6, 1981.

By this time, we'd upgraded the band car from the orange Volvo to a Granada GXL. That was a great car: big, solid, comfortable, tons of grunt—but it was destined to have a short life.

As we left the Midlands on the way to Hull, it was starting to snow pretty heavily. As we got farther up the road, it began to lie thick on the ground—Glenn was driving, it was dark; I was half asleep in the back as usual.

Suddenly the car must have hit some black ice under the freshfallen snow. It glided—quite gracefully, really—off the road and smashed into one of those retaining barriers.

From my position in the backseat, I actually thought we'd crashed clean through this barrier because of the speed we were going. Then the car went into a spin and for a split second I thought we were spinning in midair! I thought, *This is it. We're dead here.*

I was certain we'd driven off a bridge or something. I was just waiting for the smash.

There was no terminal impact.

Instead, what had actually occurred was that the car had hit the barrier, bounced off it, and then been propelled back onto the road, whereupon it continued to spin, out of control, down the motorway on black ice, before coming to a gentle stop.

When it did, we all looked at each other and said, "What the hell happened there?"

Meanwhile, there was enough smoke and steam pouring out from below the Granada's hood to suggest that the car wasn't going anywhere, much less the remaining distance to Hull City Hall.

"Great, now what?"

Luckily for us, some elderly farmer showed up and helped us tow the car to the side of the road to be repaired, before loading us all into the back of his old Land Rover.

We were very grateful. That was the only way we could have gotten to the gig that night. I doubt anyone in the audience at Hull that night has any idea what we went through to play that night!

When we finished the UK leg, Europe beckoned just three days later, with Sheffield lads Def Leppard opening for us. They had previously joined us for a few shows on the US leg of the *British Steel* tour. We'd struck up a good relationship with them. One night in the bar somewhere, after a few pints, their singer, Joe Elliot, issued a challenge.

"Me and Sav will beat whoever is your best golf pair tomorrow."

"You reckon?" Glenn said.

"Guaranteed," Joe replied.

"You're on. It'll be me and K.K. Losers buy everyone pints that night."

We played the next day, and they gave us a good thrashing.

"Fine . . . what about tennis?" I said, that evening.

"Yeah, we can do that, too," they said.

We thrashed them.

As this happened, I remember thinking, *This could be something great to do on days off instead of propping up a bar!*

And we played and did so many times thereafter. I wouldn't go as far as to say we structured our US tours around where good golf courses were, but there were many occasions when, on spotting a sign for a driving range on the road somewhere, one of us would shout, "Driver, please take us to that driving range!"

We'd jump out, get the clubs from the luggage hold, and go and hit a few buckets of balls. It was great—we did that for years, all thanks to Def Leppard.

Anyway, back to Europe...

My first thought after about the second night in Germany was, *Damn, can some of these guys drink...*

From a drinking sense, Def Leppard was a band that consisted of two distinct factions. Joe, Rick Allen, and Sav were "everything in moderation" guys: a few beers here and a few there—nothing too serious.

The other two—the guitarists Steve Clark and Pete Willis—were guys who loved the rock lifestyle. Don't get me wrong, they were both fit and healthy lads but they always had a bottle of vodka in hand. And by that, I mean one *each.*

The two of them had known each other since school, and that's where all their partying ways had started. And they just kept going thereafter, and they certainly managed to kick ass every night.

Sometime on that relatively short tour in Europe I remember thinking, *I don't know if I can keep up here!*

Sadly, it was devastating to hear that poor Steve passed away. But I'm glad to know that little Pete is still with us and doing well in life.

✦

"You've Got Another Thing Comin'" was without doubt the song that broke Judas Priest in America. By the summer of 1982, it wasn't just getting heavy rotation in our stronghold areas of St. Louis and San Antonio. That song was everywhere. You couldn't turn on a rock radio station anywhere in North America without hearing it.

Bizarrely, it almost didn't make it onto the album *Screaming for Vengeance*. It was only when we'd reached Florida for the final mixing of the album that the pieces of a track that we'd had lying around without ever committing to fully finally fell into our laps.

And when it did, the song's appeal seemed like the most obvious thing ever.

"How did we miss it?" Tom Allom said.

"I don't know. But you could just imagine putting this on, getting in the car with the sun shining, and then blasting down a freeway," Rob replied.

"That's it!" we all agreed. "It's got all the elements of *driving song.*"

We hadn't been aware of that intangible ingredient when we wrote it, of course. But there's no doubt that it had the kind of beat and tempo that, even if you were driving and going just thirty miles per hour, when you heard that *duh-duh-duh-duh* intro, you'd be simply compelled to accelerate. On top of that it gave you a happy, carefree feeling that was just so undeniable.

Better still, everything about America at that time seemed to revolve around the ethos of "get in the car, turn up the stereo, and drive." It was the ideal song for the time.

That track aside, *Screaming for Vengeance* was a very complete and balanced album, right from the intro piece, "The Hellion," about which I remember saying to Glenn at the time, "This is just *made* for the house lights dimming, dry ice . . . and two guitars."

There were energetic tracks like "Electric Eye" and the title track, and there were slow-burners like "Pain and Pleasure" and the Bob Halligan, Jr–written "Take These Chains."

I don't know who made the decision to collaborate with Bob. Somebody at the time said that idea had been presented to us by the song-plugger May Pang, a former girlfriend of John Lennon's. Either way, as they'd done previously, Sony sought to elevate the album's profile even higher by setting their sights on a radio smash with "Take These Chains." As it turned out, we didn't need their help—as good as this particular Bob Halligan, Jr. song was and is.

With *Screaming for Vengeance,* we demonstrated that we were on an absolute roll from a songwriting perspective. Ideas were pouring out of us. Not just that, America was finally ready for the complete Judas Priest package, primarily because the LA metal scene was just igniting, with bands like Quiet Riot getting signed to our label to release their debut LP, *Metal Health.* Thereafter, the floodgates just opened for American metal bands.

Meanwhile, we had the benefit of having had a five-year head start on all these bands. In 1982, we weren't a no-name band releasing a tentative, awkward debut record. We were established—and we were dropping the heavy metal mother lode on America.

Again, the package was a complete one: twelve great songs and the first of Doug Johnson's three iconic album covers that somehow fuse the futuristic with the deco to give the art a sleek look reminiscent of a video game. When I saw *Screaming's* cover, I thought, *Oh boy . . . that's killer.*

We finished recording the album in Ibiza at Fritz's place, and then, with Tom Allom living in Florida and having made a few industry connections there, we mixed it at Beejay Studios in Orlando and Bayshore Studios in Coconut Grove Miami, the latter owned by Bill Szymczyk and famous for having hosted bands like the Eagles, the Who, and Santana.

With the finished album in the bag, the road loomed.

With our focus on the US market, the World Vengeance tour began not in the UK but in the States in late August of 1982.

Notably, other than the Dortmund Rock Pop Festival in December of 1983 (technically the initial part of the next album cycle tour), we played no other European dates in support of *Screaming for Vengeance.*

As a side note, I always considered that Rock Pop festival performance at the Westfalenhalle stadium to be one of our best-ever live gigs. Everything was right: the sound, the performance, the energy, and to top it all, Rob's voice was incredible. Everything clicked for that hour-plus set.

I'd like to be able to say that the fact that we were so heavily invested in America in 1982 and 1983 gave me pause at the time. But it really didn't. If I'm being really honest, maybe there was part of me that was thinking, *US audiences have been much kinder to us than British ever have been. Let's focus on delivering the goods there.*

Was that a mistake?

In retrospect, it probably was.

Did our absence open the door for other British bands to wrest the top spot away from us because of that?

Possibly.

But you can't take these decisions back. You can only do what you think is best for the band at the time. And to us, *Screaming for Vengeance*'s success in the States vindicated us, as have its cumulative sales. I guess we all thought, *We'll get back to the UK before too long . . .*

✦

Speaking of bands that benefitted from our absence, to my surprise, Iron Maiden had been booked for some of the US dates of the World Vengeance tour.

"No, no, no!" I said. "Whose idea was it to take *them* out again?"

The deal was, the Rods and Krokus would start the tour; Iron Maiden would join in mid-September in St. Louis. That start date was intentional: St. Louis was a Priest stronghold. I remember thinking, *Aha! Let's see how you get on here, lads!*

As it turned out, by the time 1982 came around, Maiden had gone through a major line-up reshuffle—Paul Di'Anno had been replaced by Bruce Dickinson, formerly of the band Samson.

That could have been a good thing.

But when Bruce went onstage one night in Illinois, bold as you like, and announced to what was primarily a Priest crowd that Maiden wouldn't be playing the following night because Judas Priest had screwed them over on this, that, and the other, I quickly realized that not much had changed.

What he said wasn't even true. What had actually happened was an illustration of how good Rod was as a manager and how less effective Arnakarta were on our behalf.

Before the tour, Rod Smallwood had put forward proposals for Maiden's contract rider: stage sizes, this and that to be available in the dressing room, and all the rest of it. Somebody on our end signed it, as we had to—but the reality was that in some of these places, *we* didn't even have the stage space that Maiden's management had stipulated for them.

Certain places just weren't big enough, but some local promoter had probably signed it all off anyway, saying, "Oh yeah, we've got that much height. Sure, we've got that much width. Oh yeah, the load-in is great . . . "

Then, when you get there, nothing is as it's meant to be, but . . . you should still all pull together to put the show on as best you can with the resources that are available. That's the unwritten code of the road.

But Iron Maiden didn't think like that at all.

They just created problems by saying, "It's in our contract." And because somebody had signed it on our behalf agreeing that they had to have a stage size of thirty by forty or whatever, then what happened was that our backline had to take all that stuff off to put on our show afterward. It was much more work—and there was almost no time to install our stage set between bands. Nobody was trying to restrict them in any way, shape, or form. We were just trying to put the show on with what we had. Instead of being reasonable and making things work, Iron Maiden seemed intent on being arseholes.

Anyway, I went totally apeshit that night in Illinois. I immediately went flying into their dressing room after they'd come offstage. Rod Smallwood was there; it was an ugly scene. I was ready to punch someone, anyone really, and not specifically Bruce Dickinson either, who I knew was probably just a mouthpiece in the same way as Paul Di'Anno had been. Even then, most people knew that Iron Maiden was Steve Harris's band—not that Steve ever said a word himself. He just sat there smirking!

As it happened, the next night, somebody had to come in and build a stage on top of the stage that was already there, all to give Iron Maiden the room that they wanted. We were in a situation where the support band was dictating to *us*. Worse still, we had to pay dearly for it because we ran into overtime with the unions.

As far as I can recall, the tour continued with a simmering undercurrent of tension that never receded until it ended for Maiden at Rochester at the end of October. They complained, they moaned; they always seemed to be creating an upset. I just thought, *How ungrateful can you possibly be?*

Unsurprisingly, we never toured with Iron Maiden again. I don't think our paths ever crossed again with the exception that I did later run into Paul Di'Anno in the States, while he was doing something on one of his solo projects.

"You had some balls back then," I told him, perhaps emboldened by a couple of beers, "talking all that crap about us knowing that Rob Halford was going to follow you onstage!"

To his credit, Paul laughed and then apologized for what he'd said in the press at the time. I thought, *That's a pretty decent thing to say.*

I doubt he could have disagreed anyway. Paul is basically a good guy, as are all the Maiden lads. What you had back then was just two groups of young, ambitious musicians from a similar scene, vying for bragging rights. With the passage of time, I understand that.

What Maiden maybe forgot at the time was that we, because we were many steps ahead of them, were actually doing them a favor. Any other band would have given their right arm to be offered those two tours at such a pivotal time in their career. For some reason they overlooked that, but I don't hold any grudge now.

In fact, nowadays, if I saw any of them, I'd be the first one to sit down and have a beer and a laugh—as long as they were buying, of course! Although Maiden's music hasn't always been to my specific taste, I couldn't for a second deny the incredible influence they've had on heavy metal and music generally.

Being British, I'm incredibly proud of what Iron Maiden has done over the years and the distinct niche they've created for themselves. Not just that, I've always admired how well they've positioned themselves commercially via the merchandising side of things.

After all, their longtime manager Rod Smallwood, as tightly as he grips the purse strings, has done the kind of job with Iron Maiden that all bands, including Judas Priest, can only dream of. On many occasions I thought, *If only someone would manage us like that . . .*

✦

The World Vengeance tour ended in Honolulu, leaving a three-month gap before we were due to appear at the US Festival Heavy Metal Day on June 29, 1983.

Glenn and I had a plan.

With so little time before US Festival, it made no sense whatsoever to go back to the UK or to Spain.

"Let's stay and play golf for a few weeks," I said to Glenn.

"You're on," he replied.

And that's exactly what we did.

We drove our rental car directly to the reception of the Royal Hawaiian Golf Club resort office.

"Do you have any houses to rent for a month?" I asked.

"How about that one?" the girl said, pointing to a smart-looking villa overlooking the first fairway.

"We'll take it," I said.

And that was that.

As much as Glenn and I did not always see eye-to-eye in the band, when we were alone together like we were in Hawaii, it was easier for both of us to remember the things—even if there weren't many—that we liked about each other. In that sense we were more like an old married couple. We rubbed along pretty well when we were doing things we enjoyed doing, when the stresses of touring, live shows, and politics were off the table.

So, for an entire month we did very little else but drive and play golf somewhere, drive, eat dinner, drive, have a few beers, drive, play golf somewhere else. Looking back, those were some of the best times I ever spent with Glenn—even if he still mostly dictated the day-to-day schedule. Somehow, in Hawaii, that didn't bother me.

But the feel-good time had to end.

The US Festival was an extraordinary spectacle, however. Never in my life have I seen so many people in one place. The official estimate (and I've no idea who came up with it) was 300,000 people. To me, it looked like there might have been a lot more.

"What time is the car picking us up?" I remember asking in the hotel that morning.

"It isn't," Rob said. "We're going in and out in a helicopter!"

Finally, a helicopter rescue!

Later that day I remember being up in the helicopter in a bright blue California sky, gazing out of the window at a sea of people that just never seemed to end. For a second, the scale of the event was hard to fathom: *All these people are here to see heavy metal bands. And we're one of them.*

More than any other single moment, being in that helicopter was the one that really brought it home to me that we really had made it to the top table—and that there was no going back. The album was flying, our single was all over the radio, and we all looked great.

In the context of heavy music, we had reached the Promised Land. And that meant no more sleeping in the van, no more beans on toast, and no more scratching around to find the Lodge Road rent.

Curiously—despite the vast audience—the gig itself was unremarkable. In some ways, the sheer scale of the crowd made things more impersonal and therefore easier to navigate. Instead of being in any way overawed, we just went out there, focused on the first fifty rows, and laid the show down tight.

✦

In the background, during the final months of the tour, we'd been having issues with our management partners Arnakarta. I really don't know the precise reasons for these issues but our management was becoming increasingly detached and nonresponsive. I heard through the grapevine that they were mired in financial complications. Whether that's true, I'm not sure.

What I do know is that our success by that time owed as much to our tireless work ethic, backed by our always-enthusiastic label partners at CBS/Sony, than it necessarily ever did to management. They weren't by any means useless, however, and at least they'd had the courage to take us on. But they were a stepping-stone, and the relationship with Jim and Mike came to an anticlimactic end: no screaming and shouting, no desks upturned. We all just went our separate ways. We finished the tour playing arenas, but we did it with no management.

And then, in stepped "Wild" Bill Curbishley.

At this point in our trajectory, I thought we could have picked almost any manager in the business to look after our affairs. Indeed, several prominent managers had been looking at us. James "Herbie" Herbert was one that I remember. At the time he was big—he had a lot of clout. He'd started out as a roadie for Santana, whereupon he'd met Neal Schon and Gregg Rolie, with whom he'd later reappear as the manager of Journey, among several other high-profile bands.

We'd had conversations with his company on the World Vengeance tour; they even came and filmed a couple of nights of us playing live, one of which later appeared in its first incarnation as the concert video entitled, simply, *Judas Priest Live.*

At the same time, we were also in informal talks with Bruce Allen, who managed Bryan Adams and Bachman-Turner Overdrive.

We were undoubtedly hot property.

However, at some point on the World Vengeance tour, one of the UK's most successful managers, Bill Curbishley, came to one of our arena shows—I think it might have been in Augusta, Georgia. Seemingly, he'd looked at Eric Clapton as a potential client. I think Bill had seen him play the same arena on some previous night where there weren't too many people. We, on the other hand, had completely sold it out. Undoubtedly this turned Bill's head and we were very pleased that he offered to manage us

We agreed to go with Bill for a few reasons. One, he had an office in New York and was very au fait with the States in general. I only found out later that he shared the office with Mick Jagger. Secondly, he managed mega-bands like The Who and Plant and Page. Honestly, we went with him because he had great credentials and a fantastic reputation in the industry.

On a personal level, Bill was and is a great guy with a terrific sense of humor. That said, you wouldn't want to cross him, really. In his early life he seemingly got connected in a rough, tough London world, even knowing guys like the Kray brothers, etc. When Reggie Kray died, someone said that Bill was a pallbearer. Over the years, we'd meet quite a few of these characters in person. I remember meeting Mickey Green, one of the notorious "Wembley Mob." Mickey was in the helicopter with us when we flew to US festival in 1983. It was all very exciting, to be honest, and great to hear Mickey and Bill chatting away. These guys were genuinely Bill's friends, and you couldn't help respecting that.

Bill had obviously had a very tough start in life—something which I can certainly relate to. He must therefore have worked very hard to rise so high up the ranks of the music business, but not before he served his dues as a crewmember then a tour manager for The Who. From there I guess he built his career in management and film production until everything finally took off for him in a big way. Consequently, by the time Bill arrived in our world, he knew everybody of any importance in the industry.

Initially, Bill focused on us entirely, and his first decision after taking over toward the end of the World Vengeance tour was to say, "Look at the crowds you're pulling. You need to get back in the studio as soon as possible."

Who were we to disagree with "Wild" Bill?

CHAPTER NINE

W E ALL FLEW STRAIGHT TO IBIZA, AGAIN, AFTER THE US Festival at the end of May 1983. The island that never sleeps would be our home again for several months.

When we arrived on the island and went straight to the studio for the first time, we soon realized that there was a problem.

"There's no gear here," Ian said.

"What do you mean there's no gear?" we all replied.

"There's nothing. No desk, no microphones!"

Christ, what's happened?

As it turned out, what had happened was that the wheels of our mercurial studio-owner's business had come off sometime in our absence. In a nutshell, Fritz had run out of cash. Like most studio owners in those days, he certainly had the opportunity to make quite a comfortable living—but only if he had a steady stream of bands going through his studio

Seemingly, a dry spell in that respect, in combination with quickly evolving technological advances pushing up the cost of gear, meant that the people who supplied him with his equipment knocked on the door one day and said something to the effect of, "If you can't pay, we'll take it away."

Because he was awaiting a first installment from us three weeks before we were due to get there, they took all of Fritz's gear away.

"What do we do?" we asked him.

"If you pay me, I'll ask to get the gear back. But it'll take a few days, ya?" he told us.

"All right, we'll take it easy until you call us," we said. We instructed the record company to make payment of our first installment.

For a few days, we hit the beach until the call came.

"Err, yes, I have the desk," Fritz said. "But it's not in the studio yet."

"Where is it?"

"It's in the road, down the hill from the studio."

"Christ!"

Anyway, we went around there and this enormous desk was indeed sitting in the road. At that point it would have been easy to say something like, "Excuse me. We're platinum-selling rock stars. We don't move heavy objects for anybody."

But we didn't say that.

We said, "All right lads, let's get this thing up the road."

With the assistance of a few nicely rounded logs, we rolled this desk up the road in the Ibiza sun and maneuvered it into the main room. All the other stuff we reassembled. It took us four days to get it all into shape. We just wanted to record an album.

As distracting as that place was, recording the record that would become *Defenders of the Faith* was one of the most enjoyable processes I've ever been involved with. Buoyed by sales, accolades, and the security of some welcome cash in the bank, we had so much confidence. Pretty quickly, we rolled out the big guns—*bang! bang! bang! bang!*—one after the other.

Within weeks we had "Freewheel Burning," "Jawbreaker," "Rock Hard Ride Free," and "The Sentinel" in the can.

When we played them back in that order, Glenn said, "Does it get any better than this?"

He was right. If there are four better opening songs on any metal or rock album, I'll happily listen to what they are. In my opinion, those four are untouchable.

As easy as they came together, we had to push Rob a little with his vocals on *Defenders of the Faith*. I would never for a moment suggest that Rob was ever lazy with his takes. Quite the opposite: he was a hard worker in the studio, in quality of delivery and basic musical accuracy in pitch.

It was more a case of Glenn and I being annoying perfectionists who by that time knew Rob as well as he knew himself. This was an area where Glenn and I always backed each other up, simply because we both knew very well what Rob's capabilities were. Not just that, we also knew that vocals weren't just related to the physical state of the singer at any given time. There were other factors also that influenced how good the takes were at any given moment: mood, sleep, etc. The voice is such a finely tuned beast.

From that perspective we were always certain that whatever Rob thought was his best take, probably wasn't. The amazing man always had it in him to nail that absolutely magical take—especially if we gave him a nudge.

"Rob, that was great. But, have you got any more on that bridge section?" I remember we asked him when we were working on "Rock Hard Ride Free."

If someone had instead said, "Fine, that's a take," he'd have probably gone with it.

"Lads, I don't know . . . " he'd say, peering at us wearily from behind the glass.

"We *know* you do. Come on, Rob—make this last one The One."

And the rest is metal history. What you hear on *Defenders of the Faith* is the matured, fully realized Rob Halford, soaring and snarling at the absolute limits of his ability. It was humbling to watch; I got goose bumps when he was in the booth.

And then there was "Love Bites."

This was one of those songs that just appears from somewhere, with no precursor whatsoever. Rob just started with an odd idea while we were in the studio. I added the bass intro from an idea of mine, and then it all morphed from there. It's not about who came up with what; it's that, together, one way or another, we made these songs. That's what was so important about Judas Priest: it was a team.

"What *is* this song?" we all said when it was finished.

Many years later, I remember reading an interview by a member of a popular American metal band who seemed to think that, on account of songs like "Love Bites," Judas Priest couldn't really be called a heavy metal band.

I laughed out loud when I read it.

I wasn't offended at all; he'd just misunderstood us. The fact is, as with other songs in our catalog that some people might say "aren't metal" (and there's a good few), the act of committing to songs like "Love Bites" at all, and with absolute confidence that they *could* be Judas Priest songs, didn't devalue us in any way. In fact, it made us stronger and, by extension, even *more* "heavy metal"— simply because, with such tracks, we were willing to challenge the boundaries of the genre. For us there was no formula—and that's what made us so diverse, for want of a better word.

As such, "Love Bites" sits very well in the catalog for me. If anything, it does so more comfortably than "Some Heads Are Gonna Roll" ever has, which for me never really felt like a Judas Priest song—probably because it isn't a Judas Priest song!

Again, the label came to us with a song idea brought in by Bob Halligan, Jr. Again, I suspect that that they did so with a potential hit song in mind—and on this occasion they achieved just that. I'm probably doing myself few favors by saying so, but I always felt that it was the odd track out on *Defenders,* both stylistically and in its production. But, just like every song we've ever done that I've had fleeting doubts about, I'll take it!

Finally, no mention of *Defenders* would be complete without a nod to "Eat Me Alive." In a uniquely British way, Rob's S&M lyrics were intended to be tongue in cheek—and certainly not "corrupting," as Tipper Gore and the Parents Music Resource Center (PMRC) took them to be. They certainly didn't warrant being included on the PMRC's "Filthy 15" list a few months after the album was released.

For us, the song was a bit of fun—but I won't deny that we included it with full knowledge that it would get media attention. Little did we know at that time that its inclusion on the "Filthy 15" would be the precursor to a far more disturbing predicament for us.

✦

As with other sessions on Ibiza, the good times (and the heads) rolled. We worked until late, got the job done, and then, wearing just T-shirts and beach shorts at midnight, we sought out whatever the bright lights of the town could offer five young guys.

A particular favorite by that time was the Zoo Club, a locals' place on the edge of the town that had become the most powerful of magnets for not just us, but also for seemingly every pretty, suntanned girl north of the equator. Needless to say, we were there often, long after the sun had gone from the sky. There was plenty of sport.

On one such night, our engineer Mark Dodson and I had left the studio after the others. Mark, by the way, is top man. He'd worked with us on *Sin After Sin.*

Anyway, if I recall accurately, I was driving that night, so Mark and I went for something to eat and had a couple of drinks before going to catch up with Ian and Glenn—and whoever else—at the Zoo Club.

We finished our meal, jumped in the car, and I drove across town. I parked the car opposite the bar. As we stepped out into the balmy evening air, it was like a scene from a spaghetti western. There was nothing anywhere. The only thing missing was the odd bit of tumbleweed blowing by.

Mark and I walked across this deserted road, with him to my right, and then he suddenly went, "Watch out!"

Mark jumped back to avoid whatever he'd seen from the corner of his eye, and a split second later a car hit me. Never heard anything, never saw lights—never saw a damned thing. It all happened so quickly.

The car hit me up the arse, basically. And from there I was tossed up in the air before coming down and smashing into the windshield on my back. The car stopped, with me lying prone in front of it on the road.

Meanwhile, the whole accident had been witnessed by the various patrons inside the Zoo Club, and this great big German guy called Dani—a friend of Glenn's, I believe—ran out, picked me up and carried me to the side of the road while simultaneously pouring a double scotch down my throat in what felt like one smooth motion.

At this point, however, there was blood pouring from my mouth. I immediately thought, *I've got internal bleeding here*, but, as it turned out, some small shards of shattered glass from the windshield had gotten under my tongue and cut me. It could have been a lot worse. But I did have a problem with my leg that clearly required hospital treatment.

I've no idea what time it was when we got there but it seemed like there weren't many doctors around when we reached Ibiza's main hospital. Instead, a guy who I initially thought was the hospital porter decided to wrap my leg in two-inch Elastoplast—to what avail I do not know. Honestly it was like being gaffer-taped—my whole leg and my foot.

The situation then got worse, because, as I mentioned earlier, I'm allergic to the adhesive glue in Elastoplast. And yet there I was, with my whole leg wrapped in the stuff. Despite lengthy protestations in my best Spanglish, they sent me away anyway.

After a couple of days, I started to break out in a horrible rash, so I went back.

This time a doctor told me to remove all the tape. He knew exactly what I'd have to go through. I healed very quickly once I had, but for as long as I live I'll never forget what the removal process felt like. First, I tried soaking the tape in the bath, then cutting it with scissors. Nothing worked. It just had to be pulled off, but I couldn't do it quickly because there was too much of it. The sweat was pouring down my forehead.

I found out later that the driver of the car that hit me—a taxi, it turned out—was just a young kid. Apparently, the guys in the club had been looking to beat the shit out of him, but thankfully they didn't. I genuinely don't think he meant to hit us. He'd probably just been thinking, "There are a couple of drunken foreigners. I'm going to scare them to death."

These things happen in Ibiza. But it was nevertheless a long time before my nervousness would allow to me to cross a road—not just in Ibiza, but anywhere. I just couldn't get over the fact that, even though I'd looked both ways to see that there was no traffic coming, I *still* got hit. That freaked me out for months!

◆

We were back at Bayshore Studios in Miami in September of 1983, to mix *Defenders of the Faith*. To illustrate the music industry circles in which we were mingling at the time, Julio Iglesias was in the studio next door and Miami Sound Machine were up the hall. While we were there one day, a car transporter pulled up outside.

"Whose is that?" Ian said, pointing to a brand-new Ferrari that was being lowered to the ground off the loader.

"That's for Julio," one of the studio staff replied, "a gift from Sony."

Julio went out, drove the thing around the block a couple of times, before coming back and saying, "No, no. This doesn't suit me. I'll give it to my son!"

And that's apparently what he did.

We returned to the UK at the end of 1983 to begin what was called The Metal Conqueror tour with Ted Nugent and Raven— and we did so with a bit of trepidation. I remember thinking, *Will they welcome us back?*

We had no issue; it was as if we'd never been away. Rather than reject us for our absence, the audiences seemed to respond positively to having been starved of live Judas Priest for a year.

The US tour support was Great White. We went out there with what I consider to be one of our best stage sets. The central feature was a large version of "Metallion," the figure that adorned the *Defenders of the Faith* album cover. We'd enter the stage either through Metallion's mouth or from under one of its legs. It was always quite the entrance.

As usual, the tour was eventful for a number of different reasons.

In Madison, Wisconsin, I think it was, the support band Great White were playing their show when a member of their road crew walked onstage, put his arm on the singer's shoulder, and started talking in his ear.

The singer listened while wearing an expression that said, "You better have a damn good reason for being here."

As it turned out, he did have a good reason: the police had just informed him, and us in the dressing room, that a large tornado had touched down a few miles away and was headed in our direction.

A few days earlier, in the nearby town of Barneveld, an F5 tornado had ripped the town apart, killing thirteen people in the process.

"We're stopping the show," an official said.

"OK, then what?" we all replied.

"Then we're evacuating the whole building into the parking lot for safety reasons."

"There's ten thousand people in here," Rob said, "and you're moving everyone outside into a parking lot? And that's safer?"

But that's what they did.

And by the time the tornado had passed by, there was only just enough time to get the fans back in and for us to play a shortened set.

A couple of weeks later, as the tour arrived in New York, it seemed like another tornado had hit a venue.

For some reason, the preshow MC was getting dog's abuse from the 20,000 people in Madison Square Garden. I think it was in some way related to the list of upcoming shows he was announcing—distinctly non–heavy metal acts like Neil Diamond and Helen Reddy.

As he continued his announcement, while occasionally trying to rebuff catcalls with barbed responses of his own, stuff started raining down on the stage.

Then firecrackers.

Then the cushions from the seats.

When all was said and done and it was time for us to play, the stage was so full of seat cushions that there was no room for us. I remember thinking, *This is like a trampoline!*

The crowd had done $250,000 worth of damage. We later got a message: *"Judas Priest are banned from Madison Square Garden for life. Don't come back."*

Sometime later, Glenn and I ignored the ban to go and watch John McEnroe and Jimmy Connors playing in an exhibition tennis match. To avoid detection, we went in wearing hoodies and baseball caps. But only half an hour after we'd arrived, this usher came down the steps.

Here we go.

"Excuse me, guys," he said. "Do you mind signing my program?"

Phew!

"And by the way," he added, "thanks for the new seats!"

To my knowledge, Judas Priest are *still* banned from the Garden!

Drama aside, the tour was invaluable from the perspective of discovering new technology that was becoming available in the recording industry. When the tour reached Illinois, we got a message from one of the artist reps that said, "Come into the factory tomorrow, I've got something to show you guys."

The morning after the gig, Glenn and I went to the factory in Wilmette and we were shown what was the earliest incarnation of a Roland synth "guitar."

Admittedly, this thing looked very odd, and not much like a traditional guitar at all. But on hearing what it could do—reproduce a huge variety of synthesized sounds—Glenn and I thought, *This could come in handy sometime in the future.*

While we were in Florida, we were introduced to two new other pieces of gear.

The first was the latest version of the LinnDrum programmable drum kit, which sampled real drum sounds. When Dave Holland saw what it could do, I remember him saying, "It's great. And I'll be out of a job soon if I'm not careful."

Less threatening was the Toro bass pedal that Ian was introduced to at the same time. If I haven't mentioned it already, Ian Hill is an incredible bass player who never, ever seeks the limelight in any way. The fact that he was never formally credited as a songwriter did not mean that Ian didn't have a lot to say about arrangements and performance.

As well as being incredibly reliable in terms of laying down the foundation of Priest's tight sound over the years, and in the most understated way, there was always a lot more going on with Ian's bass playing than he's ever been given credit for.

The Toro was a piece of bass gear that Ian really liked; it was like a mini-keyboard that could be controlled by his foot. Its most effective use was to create really deep, lustrous bass notes. Ian may have used one on that tour at some point, on "Love Bites."

"All this new technology," I remember commenting. "I hope we can keep up with it!"

✦

The Metal Conqueror tour in support of *Defenders of the Faith* ran from December 1983, when we played that mini UK pre-tour of half a dozen shows, until September of 1984, when we walked offstage in Japan and said, "That's *it* for a while."

Thereafter, we all went down to Marbella in Spain for a few weeks to a house that Glenn had rented at the beach. We played golf, relaxed, and started thinking of some ideas for whatever would be our next album.

Later, back home over Christmas of 1984, I caught a brief whiff of an ill wind. Carol's and my relationship had been fine—in my eyes, at least—but I was starting to get the sense that me being on the road, touring the world, playing in front of adoring fans, being lusted after by suntanned girls, wasn't exactly an ideal life for a young woman from Walsall who was living in a house that we shared. It was tough for me, too, being away from home for six months at a time.

I felt terribly conflicted.

I was very fond of Carol and the security of the relationship. I'd never really felt loved or wanted before. But I'd reached a point in my professional career where the band was successful and we were finally seeing the fruits of a fourteen-year-long struggle. I didn't want it to end, but I didn't want to lose Carol either. It was that familiar "have your cake and eat it" scenario.

The whole subject of girls on the road is so complex. And the truth is that I didn't put a metal band together to behave like a priest—or at least not that kind of priest.

Girls came with the territory, especially in America. I remember my first time with a girl on our first tour where I was sitting in a dressing room, tuning my guitar on my own, somewhere in Orange County.

The door opened, and in walked this absolutely killer girl wearing a white leather mini-skirt. Without saying a word, she came over, bent down, pulled her pants down, and that was it. In that situation, as a young guy in a band and regardless of the fact that you have a loyal girlfriend at home, what are you going to do? I remember thinking, *OK, Ken, you've got to take one for the team sometime . . .*

Despite these attractions common to the road, if someone had said, "You can do this, or you can be at home," I would have chosen to be at home.

As much as I was philandering out there on the road, I still missed most of the comforting aspects of being at home: Carol, and the dog, British food. The reality of the road is that it's a grind: girls, drugs, and alcohol are just the things that help some people get through it. You live with your bandmates, day in and day out, under each other's skin for months. You can go to the bar and have a drink with them as many times as you like and go over the old stories but the truth is that you always long for female company—even if you have someone you love at home. It's not that you're some pervert, rampaging around having sex with everyone just because you can. That's not it at all. It's escapism into intimate company with the opposite sex, even if it's superficial.

And the way I saw it, once I'd been with one girl on the road, I might as well be with a hundred—it made me no guiltier—not that that's any justification.

What's more, I suspect Carol knew all of this.

"What are we going to do?" she asked me as we sat and discussed our mid- to long-term future. It was an intentionally open-ended question, but deep down I knew what she was driving at.

"I don't really know what to tell you," I said. "This is my lifestyle—it's not going to end anytime soon."

I didn't want to sound callous and unsympathetic by adding, "And you knew very well when you met me that the life of a professional touring musician was what I wanted."

But that's more or less how I felt.

"I think I want to call it a day," she told me.

At the time, I don't think I took her suggestion too seriously. When somebody says "I want to split up," you often think, *Let's have a cup of tea and go to sleep.*

At those times you always suspect that they're half bluffing and that they'll eventually change their mind. With the benefit of some experience, I now think that it's silly to think that way because it's never the case. People have usually made up their mind long before they pluck up the courage to say something out loud.

Fortunately, the band's lack of touring commitments through the bulk of 1985 temporarily came to my rescue; I had several opportunities to try and reconcile the situation while we were in Spain and, later, Nassau in the Bahamas, recording the next album.

To this day I'm not sure why we didn't play live shows that summer. I don't doubt that Sony was keen to capitalize on the success of the previous two albums. But I suppose they also knew that if they were to get the best out of us as songwriters, they couldn't really ask us to keep on going to the well without a break. That could have been part of it.

The other, slightly more unnerving possibility was that Glenn had put the mockers on any tour dates because he now had a family. Jayne Andrews, one of Bill Curbishley's employees, had been assigned Judas Priest as her pet management project. While Bill was still our manager, Jayne became our day-to-day contact for all band matters: label liaison, expenses, press, and touring.

Right from the beginning, we all liked Jayne a great deal. She was clearly very efficient and good at her job. In many ways, with her extreme focus on everything we were doing, she was exactly what we had needed for many years.

It soon became obvious that Glenn got on better with Jayne than any of the rest us. Whether that was simply because of a basic good fit of personalities, who knows. But, over time I'd start seeing a slow erosion of any degree of democracy in the band, in favor of a more autocratic system that, to my eyes, was being driven by Glenn via Jayne.

None of this was ideal, of course, but at that point in 1985, it was what it was. As it stood, apart from being booked to appear at Live Aid in Philadelphia in the middle of July, we had no other live shows.

In early 1985, and for the first time in my adult life, I had time to reflect a little before we started writing again. Here I was at the age of thirty-three, arguably in my absolute prime of life. I'd not only ac-quired my first mortgaged property—that little semidetached place in Bloxwich that I lived in with Carol—but, in an act of what must seem like blatant rock star greed, I'd also owned a Rolls-Royce for quite some time.

Buying it was a rather rash move. I don't really know what I was thinking, but I guess, in my car life, I had always fostered a certain type of taste in cars—an *expensive* taste.

The ascension had started at a pretty low level.

After the Austin 1800 I'd bought off the band in 1977, I straight-away went for a fifty-pound Rover 2000—simply because that was the vehicle that I'd seen all the bookies and posh people driving at horse-racing tracks when I was a kid.

It wasn't pretty. It was a mustard color and was, in my eyes, what you might call an "Arse of Crockery" car—because it was almost always driven by people who thought they were well-off or high and mighty in some way.

But what was I going to do? With the chance to drive around in a posh car for fifty quid, I just thought, *I've got to do this!*

Of course, in an ideal world I would have wanted the 3.5 V8 derived from the really muscular, American Buick engine. Ian bought one around the same time and could never afford to put petrol in it. In the immortal words of AC/DC, he'd bought himself a Cadillac but couldn't afford the gasoline!

But in the end, I had to settle for the lesser, underpowered two-liter version, which shortly got written off when someone crashed into the back of me in the winter months, so I went straight out and bought another. It was a bad one—and at that point I started realizing that if you spent fifty quid on a car, lots of things are going to go wrong.

I then got a chance to pick up a Jaguar XJ6. It was the next rung up the ladder. As soon as I had the money together, I said, "I'm having one."

As much as it wasn't a great one either, I just loved driving that beast. And then, just like the first Rover, it got written off when someone drove into the back of it while it was parked on a main road. A big van just drove into the back of it while I wasn't in it. I wasn't having much luck to be fair. I was gutted to lose that car.

And then in 1983, I thought, *That's it—I'm having a Rolls.*

I seem to recall that a private seller who wanted something like sixteen grand was advertising it in the *Walsall Advertiser*. That was a hell of a lot of money in those days! By way of comparison, I'd paid about twelve hundred quid for the Jag—and that was about every penny I had at the time. But with the Rolls, I thought, *I've got to have it. I'm going to need one at some point so I may as well get one now!*

I haggled with the guy and got him down to fourteen grand cash and then drove this Rolls-Royce Silver Shadow back to my modest little Bloxwich semi. I wasn't living luxuriously by any means. But I was sure as hell driving in luxury. I just loved the feeling I got when I got in there and drove that machine.

Understandably I got some pretty shitty looks as I drove around Bloxwich. People would stick their middle fingers up when I was stopped at traffic lights. However, it was worth all the abuse to be driving around in what I thought was the ultimate status symbol.

While we had been playing the Rock Pop festival in late 1983, Glenn and I had been invited to take a tour of a Porsche factory. As we stood there watching these incredible cars being made, I remember being struck by the sheer precision and quality of the build. Everything fit perfectly; the panel gaps were even, the interiors were simple yet so incredibly ergonomic. Yet these Porsche 911 Turbo SEs we were looking at could still pump out in excess of 300 bhp. Ever the lifelong car nut, I thought, *I've got to have one of these.*

Some weeks later, back in the UK, I phoned Glenn up and said, "Let's go to that dealership in Stourbridge and order ourselves a Porsche each."

"You're on," Glenn said.

We went to Swinford Motors in Stourbridge, studied all the various spec levels, picked out a white one for Glenn and a black one for me, and the salesman said to us, "You could pick them up in a month if you want."

Not long after picking up the Porsche, I'd started thinking, *I'm not leaving this thing on the pavement outside a house in Bloxwich . . .*

Armed with quite considerable cash for 1984, I'd been thinking about investing money in a bigger, more private place to live, possibly with a bit of land attached.

I looked all around the broad local area: Shropshire, Worcestershire, and Staffordshire. I saw all kinds of different places, some large, some smaller, some with land, some without, some like new, others quite dilapidated. After a couple of months of looking at properties, I was discouraged that nothing had grabbed me.

Maybe the right house isn't out there.

And then I saw the brochure for Astbury Hall.

Immediately I was taken by the image of the house on the glossy brochure's front cover: big, Georgian, imposing, and well proportioned—it looked perfect.

On closer inspection in person, it was far from that.

"It certainly needs a bit of work!" I said to the estate agent as I was given the tour.

"It would indeed benefit from some renovation," he said, using well-known property industry terminology for "It's a barely habitable wreck."

"What's the history? Why is it for sale?" I inquired.

"Well, I'm not sure," he explained. "An industrialist lived here, but the building society took it back for some reason."

Aha! Maybe there's a deal to be had . . .

The asking price was in the region of two hundred and fifty grand, which was still a hell of a lot of money at that time. The house was not only sizeable and in structurally sound condition but it also came with a couple of small cottages and nine acres of land.

Factoring in that the entire place would need to be completely gutted and refurbished (and that there was the possibility of more of the surrounding land becoming available down the line), I then asked the agent if he or the building society was open to sensible offers.

"Depends what you call sensible!" was his response.

"OK, how about [X]," I said.

"I'll relay it and come back to you when I get a response," he said.

A week passed with no response.

Two weeks passed.

Thinking that, the building's financial status was possibly a little complex, I didn't push it.

Instead, I went to Spain again. This must have been late January of 1985.

✦

The band had rented another beautiful villa, right down at the beach in Marbella. Although it was technically winter, "winter" in southern Spain isn't like winter in West Bromwich. The sun was out most days, the bars were busy—in a nutshell, it was the perfect place to relax, forget about the relationship problems back in England, and start writing music.

Again, we had no idea how divisive the album we would ultimately call *Turbo* would end up becoming. We'd just come back from an expansive tour in America with the sights and sounds of the country fresh in our minds. By going about our day-to-day business as a touring rock band, we'd absorbed it all like anyone would have, with no fixed agenda for the future.

Certain things were unavoidable on that US tour, though. One was plentiful casual sex. The other was MTV. Things were changing by 1985—and it definitely seemed for the better. The atmosphere everywhere was upbeat, it seemed like the sun shone more than before, the girls were hotter, gigs were rammed to the rafters while, in the background, glossy music videos revolved 24/7.

So, when we arrived in Spain, it was inevitable that we did so with some of the flavor of the times embedded in our DNA.

That said, the process of accumulating ideas and material was exactly the same as it had always been, with one notable exception: the Roland synth guitars that Glenn and I had been sent from the Hamer factory in Illinois.

Initially we just experimented with them, possibly without even thinking that they could be of use. Then one day Glenn plugged it in and played us a sound that resembled an aircraft taking off.

Or maybe a turbocharger spooling up.

"Hold on. Play that again," Rob said.

"You mean this?

Whhhhaaaowwwwwoooossssssh!

"Yes, that . . . "

I wouldn't go as far as to say that the sound informed the whole writing process, but it was definitely significant. It was as if we'd been given an instrument—and we never for a moment questioned whether the guitar synth fit into Judas Priest.

Enlivened somewhat by the synth discovery, our generally good vibes, and the sunny climes, the ideas for songs flowed like water down there in Spain. Within weeks we had enough songs for two albums and at that point we were seriously considering releasing what he had as a double record that would be entitled *Twin Turbos*—after a combination of the synth's first sound and Glenn's and my recently acquired Porsche 911 Turbos. I always thought that was a great title.

By the time we arrived at Compass Point Studios in Nassau in the Bahamas in May or June of 1985, Sony/CBS had caught wind of our double-album plans.

Then we changed our minds. We decided to consolidate and focus on the songs that we felt would give the album the best continuity in the context of the very specific time period we were working in. This was the mid-'80s, there was a feel-good factor attached to working in the sun. Consequently, we were wise to the fact that certain tracks, as good as they were, just didn't belong together on one record.

"Focus on the best songs. Keep the rest," we all agreed.

And that's what we did.

"Turbo Lover" almost wrote itself on the back of the sound effect, and when Rob added some of his best lyrics about great sex, we all knew we had the song that defined the album. From there it was simply a case of building the layers on top, using the new technology to best effect but still retaining what we thought was the classic Judas Priest sound. "Locked In," "Private Property," and "Wild Nights, Hot and Crazy Days" followed quickly thereafter.

The last named was aptly titled.

Not dissimilar to Ibiza's, Nassau's nightlife presented us with all kinds of distractions. Again, that bars-open-all-night, easygoing island vibe just played havoc with us. Pretty soon, as much as we had the songs written in demo form, the recording work just wasn't getting done.

Again, there were too many girls around, all seemingly with nothing else to do but hang out with us. And if they weren't immediately on hand, I soon found a way to locate them.

Compass Point Studios itself was located on the west of the island down a smaller offshoot of the main drag, John F Kennedy Drive, called West Bay Street.

By night there wasn't much happening there—but there was always plenty going on in downtown Nassau, twenty-five minutes away by cab, and Paradise Island resort, another five minutes from there and attached to the main island by two bridges over Nassau harbor.

How do I know this, I hear you asking?

Well, on more than one night, after we'd finished recording and when everyone else was asleep, I'd call a cab and make my way down to Paradise Island where, within five seconds of our arrival on the island, news had traveled around that Judas Priest were in town.

Cue the mayhem.

Just the act of my setting one foot on Paradise Island immediately flushed the chicks out of wherever they were hiding: with husbands, with boyfriends, with other girlfriends. I wasn't fussy.

"I'm staying at Compass Point, where my friends and I are recording a HEAVY METAL album. Do you want to take this discussion back there?"

"Ooooh, sure—how do we get there?"

"You see that taxi with the engine still running? Jump in."

And that's how it went: lots of girls on multiple nights back in my lodge that was on the grounds at Compass Point. The casting couch was red-hot. Honestly, I felt like I was in the absolute prime of life in Nassau. I guess on some level I felt as if I was enjoying myself again in the capacity of being a single man.

Not everyone was feeling that way, however.

As the summer of 1985 passed, in the background it became clear that Rob was having serious issues, the extent or nature of which we had no idea at that time. All we knew was that he was having relationship problems and, as a result, he was uncharacteristically distracted, moody, and at times seemed completely unmotivated to work—not that you'd ever know as much from his vocal takes.

And he wasn't the only one having relationship strife.

Although Carol had told me she wanted to break up, I'd spent much of 1985 trying to—quite selfishly, in retrospect—reconcile things from my remote position in either Spain or the Bahamas. I suppose I wanted to know she was still there without ever really having to do much more than pick up a telephone receiver.

So, we spoke on the phone on numerous occasions—stilted, awkward conversations with lots of dead air. I was hoping that absence would indeed make the heart grow fonder. Meanwhile I was still seeing a tall, blonde croupier and various other girls on the island.

"Your offer has been accepted on Astbury Hall," the voice on the end of the phone said. "You'll need to sign the paperwork to complete the sale."

"I'll be over as soon as I can."

I flew back to Birmingham from the Bahamas with one duffle bag and two things on my mind. One was to buy a house, the other was to try and talk Carol round.

First, I drove to the estate agent, parked my Rolls-Royce outside, and went in.

I signed the papers and paid in cash.

As I did so, I caught a glimpse of my suntanned face and blond, teased hair in the mirror in the office.

Suddenly, a big part of me felt as if I was taking part in the biggest of all rock star clichés: jetting in from the Bahamas, turning up in a Rolls with mirrored shades on, and slapping down cash for a Georgian mansion.

Instead of disowning myself on the spot in shame for playing "the game," I distanced myself from the thought while also reassuring myself: *You're investing in bricks and mortar, Ken. It's not like you're squandering it.*

Carol, on the other hand, was much harder to reassure. In fact, if anything, she seemed even more adamant that our relationship was over. Absence had not made her heart fonder; it had made her indifferent to my existence, it seemed. But that only made me plead harder for reconciliation.

Now, of course, I fully see the comically deluded contradiction in my whole immature approach. There I was, begging my long-time girlfriend for a second chance when, not three days prior, I'd been sneaking out in the dead of night on a tropical island to corral as many females as humanly possible for my sexual gratification.

This disconnect just didn't register at the time, and I reasoned it away with the justification that extensive touring wears you down to the point that you start craving company other than that of your fellow band members. But even without knowing the specifics of my nocturnal activities, Carol still wasn't having any of the idea of us getting back together.

I then retrieved what I considered to be my ace card from up my sleeve, with a view to playing it at the opportune moment.

"It's just not working, Ken. You're not here. You're *never* here," Carol said.

Long pause.

"Would you marry me?" I replied.

It's hard to know if, when I uttered these enormously profound words, I meant them. Looking back, part of me thinks I did—and knows that if we'd gone ahead with it, life might have been very different.

The other part of me is much more realistic. I was young and clueless and ill equipped for what marriage entailed. I think I was only doing what any other desperate man would do when the longest relationship of his adult life was slipping away before his eyes. It was a last throw of the dice.

And I rolled a one.

As it turned out, Carol didn't want me to marry her anyway.

"You've never asked me up until now. Why should I say yes now? she asked.

And she had a valid point.

Also, there was another reason why she was turning away my last-ditch effort.

Although I didn't find this out at the time, it turned out that she'd been sleeping with a local lad while I was away. I should have known. A bird rarely flies the nest until it has feathered another, as they say.

Looking back now, I don't blame Carol for anything she did. I was out there, doing the Priest thing, treading the boards, looking as good as a guy like me was ever going to look. And in 1985, the truth was that I was still much closer to the beginning of that life-style than the end of it. I can't blame her for sitting there, night after night, in cold, rainy Bloxwich, feeling increasingly insecure.

In the end, I'm sure she knew all that and just wanted some-body local, who'd be there for her day in and day out—and who also might want kids one day.

And that person wasn't me.

As sad as I was when we parted for the last time, I was forced to analyze exactly *why* I was feeling sad. Was it because I really wanted to marry Carol and she'd turned me down? Or was it simply because I was resistant to losing someone with whom I'd been intimately fa-miliar for many years, and all the feelings of loss and insecurity that came with that?

The answer, clearly, was the latter.

I simply had to let Carol go and live her own life, one that didn't involve waiting around for me. As shaken as I was by the thought of another man in the equation already, I still also wanted her to have a chance in life. With a heavy heart, I let go, and as I did I signed the semidetached house in Bloxwich over to her and gave her a car and my eternal best wishes. To me, that was the absolute least I could do. Regardless of how things turned out between us, Carol was there for me through thick and thin when I was aspiring to be in a band.

The sad aftermath to Carol's and my relationship breakup was that, for one reason or another, things didn't go very well for her thereafter. At some later point she had to sell the house, I assume to release capital. Meanwhile, I heard that she was living in rented accommodation and drinking to excess. Some years later, someone said to me, "If you want to see Carol, you'll need to do so in the hospital."

Seemingly she'd been admitted to hospital for treatment for her drink problems. I saw her, and then later heard that she got herself sorted. I haven't seen her since.

✦

Prior to returning to Nassau, I took one bag of belongings I'd collected from the semi in Bloxwich and transferred them to the front hall at my new home. At some unknown point in the future, I would be starting a new life there with basically nothing. I then locked the door, backed the Rolls-Royce into the garage, and jumped in a taxi to the airport.

A chapter in my young life had closed.

✦

When I arrived back in Nassau, Tom Allom came over to my lodgings with an uncharacteristically stony looking expression on his face.

"We're leaving, Ken. There's not enough getting done here."

"Where are we going?" I inquired.

"Miami—and then the Record Plant in LA."

In fairness, at this point, December of 1985, we pretty much had the album recorded and we already thought it was exceptionally strong and well balanced. The hard work was done. We just had to make sure we got it across the line with mixing and overdubs.

Turbo's aura was lighter, no doubt, and not just in a sonic sense with the addition of the synth, most obviously on "Turbo Lover," "Out in the Cold," "Locked In," and "Private Property." Rob's lyrics were more positive, too, with talk of partying, love, and sex replacing the dark sci-fi leanings he'd been focused on while recording both *Screaming for Vengeance* and *Defenders of the Faith*.

Curiously, throughout our whole career, I don't think I ever had a conversation with Rob about the inspirations for his lyrics. We just left him to it—and when the time came to present him with song ideas, he'd then start trying to fit words and syllables into whatever the music called for.

Time and time again, he unearthed these deep and meaningful lyrics about all manner of subjects. Looking back now with more knowledge than I had at the time, I see that a lot of these lyrics of Rob's must have been inspired by some of his own feelings at the time—that he couldn't be open about his sexuality.

Otherwise Rob was always a reader and a watcher of the world generally; he has a naturally very inquisitive nature about all things. Consequently, I don't think Rob will ever run short of lyrical ideas. And the better the musical ideas we had, the better Rob's lyrics seemed to be. The upbeat, good-time tracks on *Turbo* were just another example of Rob's incredible versatility.

◆

As a package then, *Turbo* was taking shape as a record that was, in several senses, born of a specific place and time. Furthermore, *Turbo*'s distinctive "joystick," video-game artwork, Doug Johnson's third cover for us, was entirely in keeping with the music contained therein: less dark and brooding, and more of a celebration of everything that America was at that time.

In Miami, we'd focus on *Turbo*'s overdubs and vocals. At the Record Plant, we'd mix. With such an innovative record, both were very important stages given that *Turbo*'s music needed an appropriately smooth production sheen.

When we arrived in Los Angeles, I remember hearing talk of a movie deal in a conversation with Bill. Seemingly Sony had been approached by those responsible for the soundtrack of a movie called *Top Gun*, which was due for release sometime in 1986.

"They want a song," Bill said.

"Which one?" Glenn asked.

"'Reckless.'"

"What do you think?" Glenn asked.

"What's the film all about?" I replied.

We researched what information was available about the film. It was a romantic, military-action drama.

"I don't know," someone who shall remain nameless said. "Sounds like a potential flop to me."

In addition to our misgivings about whether the film represented good use of our music given that, as we thought, it was likely to be a turkey, we also questioned whether we'd be doing *Turbo* a disservice by altering its flow and sequencing by removing a strong track which was intentionally positioned toward the end of the album to give it a lasting finish.

We deliberated about these two issues for several days before, finally, Bill Curbishley made the decision for us.

"Leave 'Reckless' where it is."

"OK," we all agreed.

"I'm sure there'll be other soundtrack opportunities," Bill added.

Now, obviously, whoever predicted that *Top Gun* would flop clearly misjudged things just a little. Not only did it not flop, it became the highest-grossing film of the year and one of the most popular films of all time, with an iconic rocking soundtrack to boot.

Furthermore, when we saw the film, as most people did, we all said: "Shit. 'Reckless' would have been perfect for that."

Looking back, I think we should have been given more detailed information about the film. In the absence of that, all you can do is make an educated decision and hope it's the right one. We got that one horribly wrong. It was definitely an opportunity missed.

✦

With the mixing under way and Rob's vocals finished, Glenn and I were left alone in the studio in Los Angeles with Tom Allom.

One morning, sometime in December, Glenn walked in and said, "Rob's gone into rehab."

"Rehab?" I shot back. "For what?"

"Alcohol and drugs, apparently," Glenn replied.

"I can't believe that," I said. "Rob? Drugs? Drink?"

Initially I thought, *This sounds like a publicity stunt.*

Up until that moment, at no point in my life had I ever seen or been aware of Rob Halford taking drugs. Furthermore, I had never, ever seen Rob buy a drink at a bar, much less seen him drunk. These were things he just did not do. The most extreme thing I'd ever seen Rob do was, at a gig in Arizona once, shotgun a whole beer for a joke. Sometimes he and Dave Holland would get together and have a large vodka and tonic before they went onstage. But that was it. And it never affected the performance for either one of them.

Incidentally, drugs were not something that was ever prevalent in Judas Priest. Because I'd tried LSD and uppers and downers on a couple of occasions as a teenager and hadn't liked them, I was pretty much anti-drugs.

I certainly never did cocaine when everyone else was in the '80s, or at any other time. On account of my bad hay fever, my mucous membranes would have never tolerated me putting powder up my nose all the time anyway. I'd have been out of action for a year!

These were the days when promoters would come in and throw a couple of bags of cocaine on the table, naturally expecting that everyone did it.

It got to the stage where I'd say to our tour manager, "What are they going to give me?"

Some nights I'd see Glenn turn around and stamp his foot at Dave Holland onstage as if to say, "Come on! Speed it up!"

Meanwhile, I'd be standing there on the other side of the stage thinking, *We're playing this at three times the speed it is on the record!*

Because, for the twin-guitar rhythm section to work at its best, Glenn and I had to be locked right into Dave Holland's tempo, I'd find myself with no option other to just speed up and up. It was messed up; I went through hell with it. If you listen to some of these live performances from the '80s, you'll hear how much faster they are than the studio versions.

Beyond that, I always thought that the whole image that surrounded cocaine in the '80s was amusing: people with their runny noses, trying to walk around looking innocent as if to say, "Cocaine? Not me . . . " It's not meant as a knock on any friends of mine who enjoyed it, but it was just never for me. Just a personal choice.

I was further turned off cocaine by an incident that happened in Miami while we were finishing *Screaming for Vengeance*. We went to a club; various people were there, some girls. I was chatting to girls, having a beer. Then, when I turned around, people had a bunch of drugs on the table.

I'm in this room doing nothing wrong. But if we get busted, I'll go down with them.

And, what do you know, the very next night the place was busted. We got away with it but it was a close call. I was so off because these people were roping me in, often without my knowledge.

Other times we'd be in a limo, driving down the freeway. Then the cocaine would come out and certain people would be chopping it up in the backseat. *If we get pulled over, we're all in deep trouble.*

I really started to resent it.

And there was the incident with Dave Holland. I don't remember what year it was but we were traveling to Berlin, through the corridors, with tanks and machine guns pointing at us. Meanwhile, Dave had a bunch of marijuana on him. I flew off the handle—got in his face.

"What's the problem?" he said.

"If you'd told me you'd had that on you, I'd have said 'you're not taking that through the corridors,'" I told him.

"Why?" he asked.

"Because if you get caught with it, we're all in deep shit."

These were the kind of issues I always had with people who used drugs of any kind: they didn't care who else got unwittingly involved. Similarly, I always found that people who smoked cigarettes never really cared where they flicked their cigarette butts, because they thought they had a divine right to do it wherever they felt like it.

So, with all of that said, drugs were absolutely off the agenda for me throughout my time in the band. Furthermore, I never at any time drank before going onstage either—not even one beer. I barely ate a meal because playing in Judas Priest was always a really physical workout. I wanted to be as fit as humanly possible for the performance. I used to see people scoffing down full dinners before going onstage and I used to think, *You've got to be kidding!*

By and large, Ian and I were the beer drinkers in the band, and we always used to look forward to a pint after the gig when the work was done. Don't get me wrong, we'd get tanked up on a good few nights, but we'd never be rolling about and belligerent; we weren't that kind of drinker. In the early days, Glenn wasn't much of a drinker at all, really.

But as I was saying, the mid-'80s was an era when everyone seemed to be going into rehab for something. You weren't really considered to be living a rock star life until you did. I thought Rob might have been playing that game—until I found out that his cry for professional help was a genuine one.

Consequently, I was shocked and also a little confused about what had happened to force this change of habit in Rob. As I said, I knew, vaguely, that he was having relationship issues, but I also knew that that could mean almost anything. What I certainly was aware of from experience was that gay relationships always seemed to end with more of a "may you eternally rot in hell" sign-off than heterosexual relationships. Why that was, I don't know. Any gay relationships that I'd seen come to an end—like some of my friend Nick Bowbanks's, for example—seemed to do so in a nasty, bitter, and vindictive way that I simply couldn't relate to.

Sadly, several years later, in 1992, a failed relationship would cost my old school friend Nick his life. While Judas Priest had taken off, Nick's own career also had been on an upward path. He worked in a hospital as an assistant but he managed to elevate himself, via sheer determination, to the position of an anesthetist, traveling back and forth between a roundhouse that he owned in West Bromwich and the Middle East.

One thing about Nick that never changed over the years was his temper. As a young man, if things didn't go his way, he didn't just get angry. Nick Bowbanks foamed at the mouth with rage. Whether that was his way of expressing the residual pain of his horrible childhood, who knows.

Anyway, by the late '80s, Nick was in a stable relationship with a guy in the West Bromwich area who either had been, or still was, married with children. In those days, it was not in any way uncommon for gay men, conflicted about their sexuality and society's likely reaction to it, to endure seemingly normal heterosexual relationships. It was a sad reflection of the intolerant times.

From what I've been told, Nick's relationship with this man turned sour. I have no idea why. Whether the guy had found someone else, I don't know that either. Either way, Nick seemingly went to the guy's house to attempt to talk him round and was rebuffed. Furious, Nick left in his car and ended up speeding away before crashing into a tree on a country road. No other vehicles were involved. Nick Bowbanks died at the scene, aged just forty-two.

We all returned to the UK, from wherever we were at the time, for his funeral. It was an awful day to see a chapter of my childhood being closed so prematurely. The only consolation was that we all knew that Nick lived every second of his life to the absolute maximum.

✦

As we'd later discover, Rob had been in a strained relationship and it, too, had ended tragically, in a way that must have been very difficult for Rob to process. Out of absolute respect for Rob, no more details are necessary.

Perfectly understandably, this had obviously pushed Rob into behaving in a way that was completely out of character, to the extent that he needed professional help.

I really felt for him.

"I'm assuming he'll be fit to tour?" I asked Glenn.

"I hope so," he replied. "We can't exactly do it without him."

I thought about that for a second. *What would we do without Rob?*

CHAPTER TEN

AS IT TURNED OUT, APPROXIMATELY ONE MONTH LATER, Rob walked back into the Record Plant in LA as we were finishing the mix, poker-faced as usual, as if nothing significant had happened in the month during which he had basically disappeared.

"How's everything going?"

"Good, Rob. Great to see you."

That was it.

Rob never discussed the details of his drug and alcohol problems and we never asked him about them. We respected him enough to know that he wouldn't have sought help if he hadn't needed to. Equally, we knew him well enough to understand that he wouldn't have been back with us if he hadn't completely overcome his issues.

As far as everyone was concerned, it was business as usual. *Turbo* was ready. A huge tour cycle under the moniker Fuel for Life was ready to roll in Albuquerque at the beginning of May with Dokken and Bon Jovi as support.

Meanwhile, Sony had thrown the proverbial kitchen sink into their investment in the album, including slapping down considerable money for two state-of-the-art videos, first for lead single "Turbo Lover" and second for "Locked In." Both were designed to sit perfectly on MTV.

The video for "Locked In," shot at the disused Los Angeles Zoo, was memorable in that it was, at that time at least, the epitome of mid-'80s excess, with Rob hung upside down by his ankles in a cave amid a twenty-plus-strong harem of scantily clad female, mud-wrestling cannibals, and us.

As we were creeping around amid all these animalized females at the zoo I remember thinking, *This is why you're in a band!*

Three hundred sixty thousand dollars was the figure that I heard at the time. Whether that was for just that video or for both it and the slightly lower tech video for "Turbo Lover," I'm not sure. Either way, Sony, to their immense credit, were right behind us in every sense. We loved the album, and not for a moment did we suspect it would end up dividing our fan base. We just needed to repay them and Sony with a fantastic tour to drive sales further.

One thing we had to consider before hitting the road was how to seamlessly integrate the *Turbo* tracks into a live Judas Priest set while still utilizing the guitar synth technology.

Thankfully, Hamer Guitars came to our rescue.

"Things have moved on," they told us. "Instead of the Roland synth guitar we initially gave you, we now have individual pickups that can be integrated with standard Hamer guitars."

This news was music to our ears, and especially Glenn's, since he was the one who'd be tasked with having to create these synth sounds onstage. Instead of having to switch back and forth between guitars when playing tracks like "Turbo Lover" and "Out in the Cold," all he'd have to do was flick a switch on his guitar, which would in turn engage what was essentially a synth pickup. In this way, Glenn had the flexibility to switch sounds onstage whenever he needed to.

In May of 1986, with a fit and healthy Rob Halford back in the band and a state-of-the-art stage set behind us, we held each other closer as we shifted to overdrive.

Fuel for Life was ready to take on America.

And what an experience it was.

Everything about that tour seemed to sum up the mood of the summer of '86. Not only were we flying high on an album that, while raising a few eyebrows with our die-hard fans, was nevertheless selling by the barrow load because it was attracting lots of new fans, many of whom probably had never heard of Judas Priest before 1986. But the heavy music business was exploding, too, driven by the MTV video revolution.

Everyone who mattered seemed to be out on tour: Ozzy was out there, Scorpions were out there, Van Halen were out there, and Metallica was just breaking through. Regardless of what was happening, it seemed to us, that we, for that never-to-be-repeated summer, sat at the top of that whole pile. The documentary *Heavy Metal Parking Lot*, filmed in Maryland during Fuel for Life, really did encapsulate what was going on out there. As mad as it was, it really wasn't a parody. Those people in the film—and many like them—were there every night.

"Have you ever seen so many girls before?" I remember Ian saying after one of the early gigs in Sacramento.

"You know, I don't think I have," I replied.

Our audience demographic had certainly changed a little since the previous tour. Now, not only did we have the die-hard metalhead men who had always come out for Priest in the US, it also seemed as if we'd lured their wives, girlfriends, daughters, and even mothers with the radio-friendly sounds of *Turbo*. The audiences were a sea of blonde, big hair, and tits.

"Can you sign these?" lines of girls would say, lifting up their tops and unleashing their ample breasts while handing us a Sharpie.

"Sure!"

Sometimes it was hard to focus on spelling my name.

We signed programs, T-shirts, arms, legs, tits, and ass cheeks—whatever was requested.

"Could you guys sign *these*?" some girl said to us at a signing in a record store in Indianapolis.

Glenn, who was first in line at the table, looked over at us and said, "Can you believe this!?"

This girl had with her two blankets and rolled up in each of them was a baby that could only have been weeks old. Twins, apparently.

She placed them on the table, side by side.

"Could you guys sign my newborns?" she repeated.

I thought, *I've seen it all now . . .*

We had a brief impromptu conference at the table.

"We *can't* sign babies," Rob said. "It's just not right."

We agreed.

"Sorry. We can't sign your babies' skin. How about we sign the blanket or some clothes instead?"

"Well, OK."

She was genuinely surprised—as if other bands had signed them previously and we were letting the side down! I still find it hard to believe that somebody wanted Judas Priest signatures on her children. The world had gone crazy. It had gone from boobies to babies—Fuel for Life was like that. It was epic from day one.

✦

The tour rolled relentlessly on through that summer. Venues were mostly sold out; the new material, and particularly "Turbo Lover," seemed to be going down a storm. There were, however, a couple of hitches along the way.

At one gig, I can't recall where, as we were playing "Heading Out to the Highway," I recall feeling a great rush of wind go past my head. Given that it was an indoor arena, I thought, *What the hell was that?*

When I turned around toward center stage, I saw what the problem was. The lighting rig, which was suspended above the stage and revolved and tilted at moments that were sequenced with the music, had somehow slipped one of its block-and-tackle fastenings at one side. When that happened, the whole rig detached, swinging like a wrecking ball straight down the middle of the stage as we played.

Whooooooosh!

How none of us were killed on the spot, I have no idea. It gently brushed Dave Holland's cymbals as it went by. That was the only contact. We were lucky to make it through the tour alive!

In Dallas, at a show that was recorded and filmed for the *Priest . . . Live!* album and concert video that would be released the following year, I had another narrow escape.

People always said to me in later years, "Ah, K.K., you looked so cool back then, wearing those dark shades onstage."

"Are you kidding?" I'd say. "I wasn't wearing them to look cool. It was to hide the fact that I couldn't see a thing!"

Just before hitting the stage in Dallas, I noticed that my mainstay Hamer guitar—the red Mini V—needed a quick re-string.

"Could you give this a quick changeover, please?" I asked Tom Calcaterra, my guitar tech at the time. "But you'll need to be quick."

He did the re-string quickly and handed the guitar back to me. But what he hadn't done was trim the string ends, which I only became aware of when Rob did one of his pirouettes. As he did so, he unintentionally knocked the neck of my guitar, forcing the headstock toward my face. The end of one of the strings embedded itself deep in my right eyeball.

Immediately, the pain was searing. I was sure it had done major damage; I genuinely thought that I might have been blinded. The eye was closing fast. There was blood, too. *How the hell am I going to carry on with this?*

I had no choice but to grit my teeth, grab a pair of sunglasses, and walk back onto the Reunion Arena stage where, it's worth pointing out, there was no sun at the time.

Pretty soon, even though I had one functioning eye, I understood what Stevie Wonder has been going through all these years.

As hard as I tried, I just couldn't help myself from bobbing my head around, looking upward, in a way that felt completely unnatural, while all the time trying to compensate for my total lack of vision in my right eye.

Fortunately, while I wouldn't quite say that I was able to play these songs with my eyes closed, I did know them well enough that I was able to get through the show, in great pain, with sweat pouring down my face as a result, so that nobody would have noticed what was going on.

Nowadays, whenever I hear songs from those live shows or see the footage, I can feel that burning pain in my right eye. I never blamed my guitar tech at the time; he was a good guy. But I probably should have!

✦

Whether it was a reflection of how very America-centric the whole *Turbo* process was or not, we didn't play any gigs at all in the UK on the Fuel for Life tour in 1986.

What we did do was finish in Canada at the end of August, before swinging back through continental Europe, then through Japan, before returning to the US to milk every last drop out of *Turbo*—while the chicks on the road milked every last drop from our testicles. The mammoth tour ended in Honolulu in December of 1986.

One thing I neglected to mention was that, during that tour, as we passed through Los Angeles, I met a girl. Her name was Kyme and she was leggy, confident, and half-Vietnamese, half-French. She was born in Alabama but had grown up in California.

As soon as I saw her I thought, *Jeezus. This girl has a hell of a lot going on.*

Very quickly, Kyme and I fell into a relationship. On reflection, it was probably a rebound from Carol. But it was different in that she had her own business ideas and was very confident. I suppose you could say that she was quite low maintenance in that respect. She wouldn't be chasing me around—I knew that much.

After Fuel for Life, Kyme and I came back to Astbury with not much other than an alarm clock and a couple of toothbrushes. We'd be starting from ground zero together and we immediately set up home in one of the cottages while the main house was being refurbished.

By this point I'd also bought a house in Spain so we'd go back and forth. Given that we recorded abroad, toured abroad, and all had houses in Spain by that time, it was a perfectly logical decision that we should take the opportunity to gain some tax relief given that we were already away from the UK for so much of each year. In any case it was no hardship whatsoever to stay out of the country while only being liable for national insurance contributions. This scheme was responsible for preserving a good proportion of our hard-earned money during the lucrative years between 1984 and 1991. It was one of the better pieces of business advice our manager Bill gave us over the years.

✦

When we went into the studio in Ibiza in December 1987 to do the album that would become *Ram It Down*, I was at a point where I really felt that we needed to stabilize everything for the sake of our image by doing an honest-to-goodness heavy metal album. As much as we always like to think that Judas Priest more than any band had pushed the boundaries of acceptable metal in every way possible, I thought that for the sake of our audience retention we needed to consolidate what we did best.

As enjoyable as the years prior had been, there was no doubt that we'd subjected our fans to something of a stylistic roller-coaster ride by going from *Point of Entry* to *Screaming for Vengeance*, back to *Defenders of the Faith*, and then all the way to *Turbo*. It felt like we were standing at a crossroads.

Let's just pull back a little here . . .

I felt that we needed to refocus on our core listeners to secure our commercial future, because the harsh reality was that as effective as *Turbo* had been in attracting a new audience, it hadn't sold five million albums, or anywhere close to that. It always puzzled me why not.

Other bands, like Def Leppard, AC/DC, and Van Halen, released albums that grossed huge numbers, but we, for some reason, never quite got there.

In the end, I believe *Turbo* has sold 2.5 million copies to date. These numbers, while not to be scoffed at, are nowhere close to those that we envisaged at the time of release. And the only explanation that I could come up with was that by attracting new fans who maybe had never heard of Judas Priest before *Turbo*, we had lost as many if not more of the fans who had been with us *before* 1986.

That was very discouraging to me. Frustrated, I thought, *If we couldn't hit a sales home run with* Turbo *in 1986, what will it take for us to become something more than a very good journeyman band?*

Then, whether it was because we came to *Ram It Down* with some overspill from *Turbo* (namely "Ram It Down," "Hard as Iron," "Monsters of Rock," and "Love You to Death"), or whether we just didn't hit the right tone with the record as a package, I wasn't entirely satisfied with the album.

I suppose, with retrospect, that I was probably looking for a darker, moodier feel overall. "Ram It Down" and "Blood Red Skies" definitely fit that bill. But the other tracks, as much as I absolutely love them all, were anything but moody and dark. They were kickass, without doubt—"Heavy Metal," "I'm A Rocker," "Love Zone." But they were upbeat, positive numbers, not the dark and sinister beasts I was hoping for.

Regardless, in Ibiza, I just rolled with what we were doing. It would be our last record with Tom Allom and, as he always did, he invested all his blood, sweat, and tears into making sure that the sound of Judas Priest in 1987, whatever that was, was committed to the recording.

As usual, the songs sounded great in the studio after we'd worked them out and gone through our usual self-checking process over a period of several weeks. When we put them up through the big Cadac speakers in the studio, I remember thinking, *Christ, these songs are absolutely massive!!*

And I still feel that way. "Johnny B. Goode" (more on this song shortly) aside, I love all the individual tracks on *Ram It Down*, despite my various misgivings about the album's overall tone. I also really like the cover—the first of many for the band by the illustrator Mark Wilkinson—because I felt that, in a different way from all our other album artwork, it got that message across about what I like to call the religion of heavy metal, which, to my mind, we'd been preaching since we started. The powerful fist, pounding down on the earth, encapsulated the sense of freedom and power that believing in the religion of heavy metal could lend a person. It was strong and all-conquering—as we intended the music and the accompanying art to be.

Again, Ibiza didn't disappoint from a social-life perspective. The Zoo Club was still going great guns. It was our home away from home. This time, however, our recording was to be split between Ibiza and Puk studios in Denmark—probably because, again, Sony wanted to put us somewhere where they thought that we couldn't find any distractions. After what had gone down in Nassau, I'm sure they thought, "Let's send them to remote Denmark in the middle of winter. Surely there they'll get the work done."

They pitched it to us thus: "There is this great-looking studio out there. You'll really like it."

Like dummies we went, "Oh yeah? Sounds great!"

Then we got there to find that it was in the middle of nowhere—with nothing for miles in any direction.

"Now what?" Ian said.

"You know very well what happens next," I said, looking at a map on the wall.

There was one thing the label hadn't bargained on: no matter how far away the nearest pubs and girls are, we *will* find them. No ifs, no buts—if there's anything resembling a town, we *will* go there.

And we did.

The problem with Scandinavian countries generally is that if you go out in a town on any Friday or Saturday night, it's just a drink-fest. Those Scandinavians can really, really put it away, and it's so easy to get caught up in all that. The only difference between there and somewhere like Ibiza was that, for logistical reasons, we couldn't do it every night of the week in Denmark. We probably would have tried if the studio hadn't been so far away.

On the nights that we weren't out on the town, we were left with, and don't laugh, a solitary table tennis table for entertainment. It wasn't particularly rock 'n' roll. I readily acknowledge that. But everybody played table tennis in Denmark, it seemed. Even the cleaning ladies could kick our arses. They were superhuman on the table tennis table!

Midway through the sessions in Denmark, Bill showed up. His appearance was usually a precursor to a business suggestion of some kind.

"Two things," he began. "First, I might have an opportunity for you for a film soundtrack. Second, I've got some producer friends I'd like you to meet sometime."

The gist of it was that Bill had had an offer for us to contribute the title song to a movie called *Johnny Be Good*. When he told us, we had mixed emotions. Given how well *Top Gun* had done, we realized that we had probably missed a trick by not giving the producers "Reckless." But you always worry about backing the wrong horse, as it were.

We discussed it at length and decided to record Chuck Berry's classic song "Johnny B. Goode" for the movie *and* with a view to it being included on the *Ram It Down* album.

As it turned out, we backed the wrong horse.

Not only was the movie a huge flop, but also the song, in my opinion at least, just didn't sit right on the album at all. Even though as a cover version it was a typically energetic Judas Priest take, from a stylistic and sonic perspective I thought that it stood out like a sore thumb. I'd even go as far as to say that, despite the fact that it was ultimately released as the lead single, it devalued *Ram It Down* considerably.

And there was the offer of collaboration with Stock Aitken Waterman that Bill also was touting.

After we'd finished the majority of the recording and mixing of *Ram It Down*, Bill suggested we fly down to Paris for a couple of days to spend some time with these high-flying pop producers in a studio. They were lovely guys, very skilled in what they do, and they wanted to find out if we were open to recording a few demos and we all said, "OK, I suppose there's no harm in experimenting."

As I recall, three songs were recorded, and the one that surfaced on the Internet at some point is the cover version of The Stylistics' "You Are Everything."

"There's no way on earth this can work . . . "

"Actually, hold on . . . "

"OK, in a very strange way it does work, I suppose."

"This is great!"

"We're making an album of this stuff!"

This was more or less how our reactions progressed after they put the demo up and played it back. As polished and poppy as the track sounded, Judas Priest's stamp was all over this fluffy love song—that much was undeniable. Out of nowhere, it felt like Judas Priest were standing on the edge of the abyss, with career suicide staring back at us from the bottom.

"Now what?" I remember Rob saying.

These were *very* successful producers; everything they touched in the mid-'80s turned to gold. Meanwhile, we'd just put out our most commercially oriented album and, while sales had been solid, we hadn't completely crossed over into the mainstream as other bands seemed to have done.

"What have we got to lose?" I remember asking the guys.

"What have we got to gain?" Rob countered.

Both sides of the arguments were valid. For a good few moments I sensed that we were all tempted to see where it could go.

In the end, though, common sense prevailed. We put it all to bed in one quick conversation. And the reason it was so easy to pass on the idea was that, at that time, we all had an awareness of the fact that some other bands had gone down this commercial singles route, sold a few, but then watched as their album sales and credibility dropped off a cliff. We were never a singles band—we just happened to have albums that spawned singles. There was a distinct difference that we recognized.

Not just that, given that we already had "Johnny B. Goode" on the album, I think we all felt that there was no way we could add any more poppy fluff, as tempting as it might have been to see if we could come up with a huge crossover hit.

With the benefit of hindsight, the Stock Aitken Waterman collaboration was a fun experiment with great people. It was wonderful to meet them and I completely understand why they had so much success. But I really think that it would have been the kiss of death for us. It would have been a step too far for our fans, too—and for some fans *Turbo already* had represented a step too close to the edge.

As we finished *Ram It Down*, I clearly remember saying to the guys, "I'm not doing another song with the word 'love' in it after this!"

And I meant it!

CHAPTER ELEVEN

AFTER THE LAST SHOW OF THE MERCENARIES OF METAL tour in Vancouver at the end of 1988, I couldn't wait to get home to take a break. As I usually did after touring, I felt the need to disconnect from everything Judas Priest—to not think about traveling on a bus where toilets overflowed with waste products, arguments about set lists, guitars going out of tune in cold arenas that are normally ice hockey rinks, and the complex business of locking Glenn and I tight into that kick-drum every single night as if our lives depended on it—before I even started to try and come up with some new ideas for whatever we were planning next.

We'd been on the road promoting *Ram It Down* for almost an entire year. It was our longest tour of the decade. Toward the end, as we made our way up the West Coast through LA, I was feeling weariness kick in. As much as you can run on the adrenaline of playing to sold-out arenas and the titillating thought of having the world's most beautiful women pawing at your pelvic regions at every spare moment, there's only so long you can keep it going, the act of delivering a heavy metal show, night after night.

The 1980s had undoubtedly been very kind to us. We got on a roll with *British Steel* and it just kept going. Album, tour, girls, album, girls, tour, money. I could only look back and smile.

That decade was a defining one not only for the band, it was equally so for heavy metal music. For us, the moment we released *British Steel* in 1980, everything changed. The scale of the Judas Priest operation on every level—sales, venue size, album advances—steadily rose thereafter and a good few bands had followed in our slipstream.

Breaking into the American market on a small scale with that album was the key. Overnight, on the back of a lot of promotion, it seemed like we had acquired small pockets of fans all over the country, mostly driven by radio play. It felt like a symbiotic relationship and that inspired us to make better music. We weren't intentionally turning our back on our British roots—not at all. But there was this sense that America was where everything was happening, and it started to feel like a second home for us.

I remember one incident that really crystallized that feeling for me. Glenn and I were driving through San Antonio at lunchtime on a Tuesday while we were on a day off. San Antonio, as I've mentioned, is one of those cities that really helped Priest's cause. It was always a massive stronghold, mostly on the back of the KMAC radio station DJ Joe Anthony, who was one of the few guys unafraid to intersperse songs by Judas Priest or Scorpions or Budgie among the Allman Brothers and Grateful Dead.

That's all it takes, and the result in the *British Steel* era was that in San Antonio we'd sell out an arena, whereas in other places where metal was not played on the radio, we'd still be playing clubs or smaller venues.

So, Glenn and I are driving through town and we pull up at a stoplight. "Living After Midnight" is blaring from a car beside us as we wait for the light to change. Our paths crossed momentarily. Two regular guys in a car maybe heading to work . . . five feet away, us, the guys playing the riff. I thought, *Amazing. People are playing our record, here, in the middle of Texas.*

These kinds of incidents made it feel that finally we were getting bigger and the world was shrinking. And we *were* getting bigger— my bank balance would confirm it as the 1980s went on.

During these halcyon mid-'80s days, sometime in the spring of 1985, I made that decision to buy Astbury Hall.

When I saw it I thought, *I have to buy this . . .*

As I've mentioned, the decision came at a point when the serious money had started coming in, the eventual filter-down of proceeds from *Defenders of the Faith* and *Screaming for Vengeance,* the latter still the album of ours that sold the most copies.

I remember thinking, *Christ, Ken, you've worked hard for a good few years. I hope you see some cash sometime soon. I hope that it's all been worth it.*

The thing is—and nobody tells you this at first—it takes a while for the money to reach the guys who make the music. Yeah, you're signed to a big label and, yes, you're playing to a lot of people and selling what you think are lots of albums, but there are a lot of wheels to oil and a few mouths to feed before the band sees anything.

Despite the prevalent public perception of being in a rock band, it took us much longer than most bands of our stature to start making reasonable money. I wouldn't say I worried about money a lot, even in the early years. Not having much was hardly a new concept for any of us. I was always too focused on just writing and playing, writing and touring, and then one day, out of nowhere, a big check arrives with your name on it. And if you're anything like me, you hold it up to the light to make sure it's real and think, *What the hell am I going to do with all this?!*

As much as it might seem like it, I definitely didn't buy Astbury to fit that cliché of "rock star makes money and buys large mansion"—although I did consider it for a moment about as I handed over two hundred and fifty grand in the estate agent's office, my Rolls-Royce parked outside. *How's this going to look?*

But that thought passed.

In truth, the purchase came more from self-preservation and not knowing what else to do with the proceeds of my life's work. Because I'd never had any money to speak of up until that point, it was a new kind of decision to make. One thing I did not want to do was waste it all. I'd seen far too many people in other bands squander what they made, so if anything, it seemed like more of a cliché to blow it all and have nothing to show for it instead of making what I still think was a shrewd investment.

And that's what it was.

The choice to sink what I had into this piece of property in the Shropshire countryside with some acreage on a neighboring farm potentially available to buy and develop at a later date was calculated with my long-term survival in mind, even though at the time it seemed like an overtly mature thing to do for a so-called rock star. Beyond that I also fantasized, *I'd like a little piece of England of my own . . .*

And Astbury would become the refuge that I desperately needed. As well as the ten bedrooms—eight of which lay empty for almost five years—and the fields and woodland, there was a tennis court in the walled garden at the back of the house.

As much as I'd always enjoyed golf on tour with the band, particularly with the access to great courses we increasingly got in the States, I'd always fancied myself as a bit of a tennis player. The problem was that I'd never had anyone to play with at home.

Then one Saturday afternoon, down in the Bellman's pub between Bridgnorth and Kidderminster, I was standing at the bar having a pint, staring at myself in the mirror that covered the entire wall behind all the spirit optics.

"Oi, Kenny!" the voice from somewhere behind me said. "Somebody saw your old man at the dog track the other night."

I didn't even look up at first. I just glared into the bottom of my pint glass. The mere mention of the words "your old man" made me want to sink through the pub's carpet into the beer cellar beneath it.

Instead of turning around, I allowed my eyes to pan across the mirror to where I sensed that the voice had come from, and there I saw a figure at the end of the bar, slightly refracted, with his pint of bitter halfway to his mouth. The mouth was grinning.

It was Robert Plant.

I'd known Robert slightly for years. We'd grown up in broadly the same area and our careers had overlapped somewhat, most notably at Oakland Coliseum in 1977 when we supported Zeppelin at the Day on the Green. There I wore what I considered, at that time, to be the coolest outfit I could ever own: white, knee-length leather boots over red trousers. I might have worn a fedora, too. I loved that look at the time.

My first Led Zeppelin exposure was an amusing one. Robert married a lady called Maureen, who I believe was from an Indian family. She had two younger brothers, Glenn and Bruce. Bruce, who was younger than me, and I used to hang out in a coffee shop in West Bromwich called the Casa Bamboo. One day he said, "Come up to my house. My brother-in-law is in a band and they're about to release an album."

I went to this terraced house, into the family home, and Bruce put an acetate record onto the Dansette record player. It was a promo copy of *Led Zeppelin*. It was all crackly; it had obviously been played to death!

"Check this out," he said. And that was the first time I ever heard Led Zeppelin.

Anyway, Robert knew my dad, as most people in the area seemed to. But he didn't know that I didn't want to hear about him. So, after

I had told him, "Thanks, but I don't want to hear about that man," we ended up chatting about life like two regular Black Country geezers. This kind of impromptu social interaction entertained me while I was at home.

◆

Eventually as the rock 'n' roll cycle goes around, it gets to the point where you get up in the morning itching to do something. There's only so many games of tennis you can play, so many times you can play golf, and so many days that you don't think about making music.

Fortunately, for me, even when I wasn't engaged in writing music, I always picked a guitar up at some point in every day. It might not have been for long; I could just see a particular guitar as I walked past the room I used as a makeshift home studio, play a lick or a solo, and then put it down again. Pick one up, play the solo from "Before the Dawn," put it down. Go to the bathroom, come out of the bathroom, and on the way back downstairs pick up another guitar and play the opening riff to "Electric Eye" and put it down.

Anyone watching all of this would have thought I was nuts! But it was enough to keep the hands moving and the rust from setting in. And then as that inevitable day approached when Glenn or Ian would call and say, "All right, mate, want to start writing a few things?" I would always be ready technically, if not exactly in the songwriting headspace.

I've heard it said that *Painkiller*'s sound—at least when compared with *Ram It Down* and *Turbo*—was a reaction to trends in the metal scene at the time. The truth is, we never at any time in our careers reacted to anything. Anything that happened, I always considered to be a natural progression (with the exception of *Nostradamus* a few years later, which was obviously a different kind of record with a clear concept that needed music to suit). The rest of the time we always waited to see what the songwriting process would throw up and then took it from there.

True to form, *Painkiller* was just like that.

There was no agenda whatsoever and the process was the same. Restarting work generally followed that period of time during which we'd be apart, with little contact between us at all. Then, the next stage would be phone calls followed by an interim period where Glenn would be off working on some song ideas, I'd work on song-writing, and then Rob would be somewhere else putting together some themes for lyrics.

And then, and *only* then, when we thought we had a decent amount of material between us, would we get together to see what we had.

Once in the same room, a purging occurred. We'd literally play everything to each other, riffs, drum patterns, any ideas that had come to us, no matter how basic they might have been. It was just like that. No magic formula, and sometimes hit and miss.

Occasionally, my ideas would be nearly complete by the time we all convened and some of Glenn's might have been more ad-vanced, too. Some days we'd come out of these group sessions having achieved a lot, maybe even a couple of close-to-finished songs. Other days might be frustrating, with nothing at all com-ing together. But the latter was rare; we were prolific songwriters, really. When we got together, songs that fit the Priest template usually came quickly. That was one of the many strengths of the group.

At that time, we all had houses in Spain down on the Costa del Sol. As you know, we'd rented this huge place on the beach when we were writing the songs for *Turbo* and we liked the lifestyle. I got up one morning, looked around, and thought, *This'll do* . . .

Sun, golf, and a three-hour flight to the UK.

What wasn't there to like?

A few years later, we all had our own places down there, all within a couple of miles of each other. Glenn had this fancy house that he'd bought. It was a bit of a statement, really. Glenn, as we know, was partial to a bit of one-upmanship now and again. That was always his style.

He even did it with his hair.

That whole palaver all started months previously outside Irvine Meadows Amphitheatre on the Mercenaries of Metal tour in support of *Ram It Down*. As we were walking down the street on the day of a gig, in front of us, cruising toward us along the pavement on roller skates, were two of the most perfect all-American girls you've ever seen in your life: blonde hair, golden suntans, big tits—perfection on wheels.

Glenn and I looked at each other and smiled, the one that says, "We're in here."

We didn't need to *say* anything.

It was me they seemed to want. I was the lucky one on that occasion. And within a matter of minutes I was getting intimate with this pair back in my hotel room. And within a few more minutes I had a dozen more of their friends in there, too. It felt like the Playboy bunny mansion. In between moments of extreme intimacy, I remember thinking, *If only my school chums could see me now . . .*

I was spoiled for choice; all of these girls were stunning and very, very willing. And a lot of them seemed taken with my hair, which was blond and pretty big at that time.

Then, what do you know?

The first time I set eyes on Glenn down in Spain for the *Painkiller* writing sessions, he's got his hair all done—feathered up with even more blond and black highlights. I looked at him, and he looked back. He didn't mention the hair, and neither did I.

Anyway, Glenn had an eight-track in his place in Spain and it was here that we met to go through all the ideas we'd been working on in the months since we came off the tour. One problem was that, at that point in 1989 after the departure of Dave Holland, we didn't have a drummer.

Dave's end was a strange one.

All the time he was with us, he and Rob were very much the two with the poker faces. No matter what shit was going on round about them, Rob and Dave never said very much. They just focused on the job at hand.

Then, after a gig at the Nassau Coliseum in New York, Dave walked off and said he just wasn't happy with the show. Worse than that, he then said to Glenn, "I'll tell you this: you played like a man with no fucking arms tonight."

We all just sat there staring at the floor.

"And by the way, I'm quitting the band."

That was the end of Dave. He said he was quitting Priest when the tour ended. It was all so very out of character. Obviously, his frustrations had been building up and reached a point where he'd just had enough.

I never saw Dave Holland after 1989. Like everyone, I saw the news about the court case against him and his subsequent imprisonment in 2003, for acts that he vehemently denied committing.

All I'll say is that in all the years of working with Dave, I never witnessed any aspect of his character that would make me say, "Aha, I've caught you—that's what you're all about." That never, ever happened.

He turned up, never was a problem, and did his job very well. That said, I know from experience that there aren't many people walking the planet who don't have a skeleton of some kind in their closet. If that's his or her real personality and they don't want to disclose it, that's up to them.

What I'll also say is that nobody will ever condone illegal sexual activities with underage persons by anybody. And if Dave was guilty of that, he must face the consequences, just like anyone would.

Knowing very little about the case as I do, given that Dave had been out of the band for many years, I still think they seemed to throw the keys away on him very quickly. It seemed like a slam dunk.

In recent years I've been in situations with the press and have been in a few awkward legal corners also. Therefore, I know all too well how they can really, really twist things. But I've been in a lot of law courts over the years and have seen people blatantly lie under oath.

I've seen a lot of things go on over the years; I've seen how innocent men have been hung out to dry and how guilty men have gone free. It usually comes down to whoever has the best lawyer.

So, that all being said, if I saw Dave now I'd have no hesitation in treating him on face value, based on the guy I knew for all those years in the band. The jury is out on Dave. Best to leave it like that.

◆

So, there we were in 1989, a heavy metal band with no drummer! Although Dave had played on the tour, we'd recorded the bulk of *Ram It Down* with a programmed drum machine.

For some of the fans, that wasn't a popular decision. They thought it went against what Priest was all about but for me it made sense. There's something so relentless about a drum machine. To me it's like an unstoppable, robotic creature and that automated beat fit perfectly with those songs. In fact, I loved the energy of that album at the time and I still do. I couldn't have imagined recording a song like "Blood Red Skies" without that drum machine.

The result was that all of the *Painkiller* demos were guitar tracks with a basic accompanying drum track created by this little computerized unit we had. It was a complex thing and I got handy at programming it. In fact, we all had a go at doing it, which is a drummer's nightmare because guitarists just love to come up with the most complex drum patterns imaginable. We don't know anything about the technical aspects of drumming, so we put all kinds of complicated fills in strange places, most of which can't actually be played in reality.

The title track came first from a riff idea that Glenn and I worked up, and it immediately set the tone. Fast, direct—it was a powerful Priest statement in the tradition of openers like "Rapid Fire" or "Freewheel Burning," only even faster—to the extent that I'm sure some fans and critics thought, "Christ, where did *that* come from?"

It is sometimes forgotten that we had toured with some thrash metal bands in the late '80s. As I listened to these bands play every night I could see the appeal, not to mention the audience reaction, to very fast songs played in a speed metal style. And while that hadn't been our approach in recent years, it wasn't completely new to us. If you go back and listen to tracks like "Sinner" or "Exciter," you'll hear that although the guitars are less overdriven than some of those on thrash or speed metal records, the chugging riffs are exactly the same. From that perspective you could say that we were doing it before anyone even thought of thrash or speed metal.

Anyway, we urgently needed a real drummer. So, at some point during that time in southern Spain, Scott Travis, a bloke who'd been in the band Racer X, came down to Spain to audition. The origin of the connection was that Rob was a good mate with Racer X's Jeff Martin and it was he who had told Scott, "Apparently Judas Priest needs a drummer."

It all made perfect sense. Scott had been a huge fan for years; there's a story out there that he once waited backstage at a Priest show to hand us a demo tape of his playing. I have no recollection of ever hearing it but I knew that he could play.

Skilled or not, nothing could have prepared Scott for my programmed drum tracks.

I remember his face when I first played him some of the *Painkiller* demos—"Hell Patrol" is one that I seem to remember I'd done a particularly good hatchet job on. Well, when he first listened, Scott looked at me as if to say, "What the hell am I meant to do with *this*?"

But Scott was a pro. He was very capable. Unfazed, like any really good drummer might be, he'd just alter the drum tracks to suit how he wanted to play them—and always in a way that synced perfectly with the rest of the band. Nevertheless, I liked winding Scott up no end in his early days with us.

"Scott, I've sort of gotten used to hearing that drum track with this fill and that fill; can you play it like that?"

"No! Stop! Those fills aren't physically possible!"

He took it all in good humor, though. Scott was top man from the start.

After we'd assembled a decent set of demos, the *Painkiller* recording sessions shifted to the rather upmarket Studio Miraval in Correns near Brignoles in the South of France. It's a fantastic recording studio without doubt; the control room alone is sixty square meters. Also, there's a resident chef and three or four lodges. Not surprisingly many great musicians had preceded us there: AC/DC, Shirley Bassey, and Pink Floyd, who came there to record part of *The Wall* in 1979.

What was the drawback?

Well, Miraval is very remote. It sits in the middle of a huge vineyard, which itself is set in miles and miles of remote French countryside. When we pulled up in the car on that first night, I woke up, squinted into the interminable blackness, and thought, *Jesus. Where are we?*

You couldn't even see the light from the nearest place of habitation, far less those of the nearest nightclub. There just weren't any. So, in contrast to madhouses like Ibiza or the Bahamas, it was pretty clear that there was absolutely nothing to do apart from making music. We couldn't have found a distraction if we tried (we half-heartedly did) and maybe that was no bad thing.

One night after we'd finished early Ian said, "Let's go to the nearest big town to see what the nightlife is like."

"Sounds good to me!"

Aix-en-Provence was fifty or so miles away, so we jumped in a taxi that took us along the A8 road to Aix. When we got there I remember thinking, *Beautiful town . . . but where are the girls of questionable morals?*

It just wasn't that kind of place, so we had a bit of dinner and a few drinks and went back to Brignoles. All very grown -up, and not at all rock 'n' roll.

◆

Regardless of the extracurricular shortcomings of being miles from the nearest human being, there's no doubt that having Chris Tsangarides from the *Sad Wings of Destiny* days back on board helped make those weeks an extremely productive period.

Chris had learned a lot since we last worked with him; he'd assembled an impressive list of credits since he slummed it with us as a tape operator back in '76. Better still, we all shared a similar broad vision of not only what the record should sound like, but also the message it was trying to convey via its imagery, its sound, and its look. It was, after all, a record we absolutely had to get right. Chris, sad to say, passed away while I was working on this book. I was shocked to receive the news. He was such a lovely guy and an important part of Judas Priest history.

Fortunately, every component of *Painkiller* seemed to fit. It was undoubtedly a great bunch of heavy songs, and that album artwork, with the saw blades on the wheels and so on, seemed like ideal visual accompaniment. Although it was futuristic, I was always pleased to see that the prehistoric-looking Priest pitchfork symbol was planted right in the middle foreground.

Then there was the title, which was initially a bone of contention. From the beginning, *Painkiller* seemed to be the absolute icing on the cake for me. I often stuck my neck out when it came to decisions within the band, and I definitely did so with the *Painkiller* title.

But not everyone felt the way I did.

"We're not sure . . . "

"What's not to be sure about?"

"What other ideas does anyone have?"

"We don't need any other ideas. It's got to be *Painkiller!*"

This went on for a day or two before everyone eventually came around.

Thereafter, we did our usual self-critique in Holland where we ultimately mixed the record at Wisseloord Studios, this time by jumping in the minivan we had and driving around the Dutch countryside, listening to the album from start to finish. Then we'd drive back, have a few beers, and ask ourselves, "Did we enjoy it? Was there continuity? Was the running order right? Did anything jump out that was mechanically wrong, out of tune, or substandard?"

We'd have already grilled the thing to death by this stage, by the way. We'd have played it in the studio, slept on it, played it on a crap sound system, slept on it. We had to imagine that we were fans. Nothing could slip through the net—and *Painkiller* was one that was pretty much faultless.

✦

So, by early April 1990, everything in the world of Judas Priest was going to plan.

Then, a few weeks after recording was finished, out of the blue, we got a phone call to say that we were being taken to court.

The gist of it was that there had been some issue with lyrics but details were sketchy.

I remember thinking, *Not this again?*

In the past we had gone through a lot with the ultraconservative PMRC organization, as many musicians, not only metal musicians, had. But while we were finishing the *Turbo* record in '85, it felt as if the focus turned specifically toward heavy metal bands. These organizations were becoming aggressively and at times indiscriminately anti–heavy metal and they didn't seem willing to back off.

At that time Judas Priest had a target on its back. We were in the Bahamas, minding our own business. All we wanted to do was finish recording our album. We'd been given a significant advance from the record company to get it over the line. Meanwhile, back on the mainland, there we were on CNN every other night it seemed, where they played the song "Eat Me Alive" while flashing what they considered to be "dangerous" lyrics up on the screen for everyone to read. It didn't make us look good, but we carried on with what we had to do.

Although the track "Parental Guidance" appeared on *Turbo* and was specifically intended to be a playful but undeniably direct rebuttal to all the latent oppression we felt that we were being subjected to at various time (protests, warning stickers on album covers, and all of that shit), this wasn't the first pressure we'd felt from such groups.

As early as the *British Steel* tour in 1980, anytime we went through the Carolinas on tour, or through the so-called Bible Belt to places like Minneapolis, there would often be demonstrations from various groups opposed to what we did.

Or so we were told.

Because we normally went directly to the back of concert venues and all the people with banners would be out front, mostly we wouldn't actually see it. It was nothing too extreme, though, and I remember seeing far more dramatic scenes when we toured with KISS in '79 in the same geographic areas.

There were *massive* crowds demonstrating sometimes—and I don't think it was just because Judas Priest was on the bill. I really think it was just the beginning of a reaction to the whole genre. As time passed, it became obvious that these people were gunning for somebody, *anybody*.

A momentum was gathering that had to culminate somehow. Then when Ozzy got dumped into court because he was sued by the parents of a kid who claimed that his song "Suicide Solution" was responsible for their son killing himself, it seemed inevitable to me that at some point, a band or an individual was going to carry the can for everyone.

The funny thing is, by the time 1990 came around, we thought that we might have evaded any trouble. Nothing had been said; nothing had been done for a while.

Maybe it had blown over?

Or maybe it was a false sense of security because we were detached from it all, back in Europe, working hard for months?

Either way, as far as we were concerned, everything was going great. The album was all but finished; an extensive world tour was signed and sealed. And then we got the bombshell: "That's it, guys, you are in court."

✦

In the days that followed, more information filtered through via Jayne Andrews from our management's office in London. All she said was that they had received documentation that we'd been summoned to appear at a hearing in Reno because our music had been deemed to contain subliminal messages that had led to two suicide attempts, one of them successful. That was all anybody knew but that was enough. I can remember thinking, *This is ridiculous. We're going on trial for making music? How does that work?*

It was all so confusing; I wasn't even sure that I believed in the concept of subliminal messages anyway. It made me think about when I used to sit in the cinema as a kid and I'd see "Coca-Cola" being flashed up on the screen. Did it make me go and buy a coke? I doubt it. Did I care that the message was being flashed up there for me to see? Not particularly.

In any event, the suggestion that messages *could* even be conveyed via music, much less that they could be the reason some youth decided to kill himself, didn't make sense to me. And it wasn't until we flew to Chicago where we were shown the actual written deposition that the seriousness of the situation sank in properly. When I read those papers in the lawyer's office, I thought, *God, we're really up against it now.*

Further to the written documents, there was a filmed deposition of one of the youths—the one who survived but had shot most of his face off. It was just gruesome and disturbing to see that he had to wear a baby's bib because of his injuries. And because he now didn't have a nose, they had grown one upside down on his forehead and then turned it around. It was an awful sight, and one that made the gravity of the situation hit me.

Reading the official depositions from the court in greater depth, it was easy to see how it had all been skillfully worded to attract sympathy. When you thought about it a bit more, you could also see what the agenda was for people who wanted rock music outlawed or vilified and were willing to dedicate a lot of time and energy to achieving that.

And as is often the case with these things, money was at the heart of it all.

Think about it. If armies of teenagers were spending all that money on beer, T-shirts, petrol, albums, and concert tickets, then that's all money that could potentially be going other places—like the church. And it was no coincidence that areas of the US where we ran into the most opposition were the very areas where organized religion was most powerful.

When you put it in those terms, it actually seemed like the money of the youth of America was being contested and, as a means of laying out the battleground for that contest, the suggestion was that what we did was actually *harmful to* the youth of America. It sounds crazy, but that's where it was all going.

As I recall, as a band, we didn't discuss the details too much. I think we all just thought, *OK, we're going to have to go through with this.*

We were resigned to having to jump through legal hoops, but from a timing perspective it was frustrating because *Painkiller* was finished and we were ready to go on tour. But we had no choice; we would have to endure a month in Reno while the record company took the decision to delay *Painkiller*'s release until the dust settled.

Before the case even started, we flew to New York with the producer Eddie Kramer. The idea was to establish the basis on which the whole case was founded, with Eddie's technical know-how deemed to be the quickest and most reliable way of doing it. Eddie is a legend in production and engineering, having worked on records by Hendrix, KISS, and many others.

The process didn't take very long.

All he did was put up the multitrack of the song in question, "Better by You, Better than Me" from *Stained Class*, pull the faders down one by one, and listen to what was supposed to be there.

"You hear that, lads?"

"Yeah, and?"

We could hear it—and what we heard certainly wasn't a subliminal message. It actually was a complex combination of three things: a downbeat of a drum, Rob expelling air after delivering a note, and some other random sound that I can't recall. Because there actually is a human voice in there, you could hear, if you really, really tried, what they said was there, the words "do it." But it really took a massive stretch to get there.

When we realized what all the fuss was about, we just laughed and thought, *What a load of bollocks.*

Up until that moment, I had absolutely no idea that it was there. To our ears, we knew exactly what was on the record anyway. We knew it inside out and upside down so there was nothing to doubt. When you think about it logically, we put together *Stained Class* every single day for months, so if there had been anything untoward on the album, it would have stuck out a mile. These were just normal sounds that arose during the recording process. I've played it no end of times to people since and they can't hear the words at all.

The important thing was that, by the time we got to court in Reno, we understood the parameters of the case very well. But regardless of how silly it all seemed to us, we still had to convince a judge to rule in our favor. We'd done our homework, but to get the court to go into a recording studio to have it all explained in technical terms wasn't going to be quite so easy.

Ultimately, they agreed. What we had done ahead of time to reinforce our argument was to select records by artists from many different music genres—Donna Summer was one—and we played them backwards. By doing so, we were able to show that if you played a record backwards long enough and listened intently enough, it might sound as if actual words were being spoken. As they say, "If you want to find something badly enough, you'll find it."

When Rob took the stand (he was the only one of us who was required to), he went with a ghetto blaster and played these songs while the court documented what could be heard when certain passages in the tracks were played backward. Some of them were an entire sentence long. One of them was "I asked her to get me a peppermint," clear as you like. It was farcical, but it helped prove an important point.

I'd always known that these things could happen. In fact, when I was younger, I had taken a little mono tape recorder of mine to a guy in Walsall and asked him to reverse the motor so that I could play stuff backward. I wasn't doing it to hear subliminal messages; I just thought it might inspire me to come up with some better riffs!

The fact that we could come up with a variety of songs that, when played backwards, distinguishable words could be heard really helped our case. It was quite obvious to people in court, too. As each example was presented, you could hear them exclaiming, almost chuckling at times, I suppose because they thought it was amusing. It felt to me that they were thinking, "Oh yeah, isn't all this silly."

But we didn't do it to be clever or to trivialize the case; we were simply trying to illustrate what can actually happen, completely inadvertently, and it might just have tipped the balance in our favor. That was, as they say, a good day in court for us.

As far as the outcome was concerned, we were never really certain what might happen. We were confident because we knew exactly what we had done and had not done, but you know the way things work. You can never be too sure in a court of law because someone's always looking to get some money from somewhere to offset against costs and whatever else. And sadly, because the court was ordering up all these multireel tapes of ours, many of which had been lying around in storerooms for ten years or more, there were significant costs that somebody would have to pay—particularly when the judge decided to fine Sony $40,000 because they couldn't locate the multireel for one particular song. This is just my opinion, but I think the judge used Sony as a scapegoat to get some dollars back, by fining them money for not being able to find a reel that they weren't duty bound to be the keeper of. But somebody has to pay somewhere—not that Sony minded too much. That figure paled into insignificance when compared to the megabucks that lawyers would have sought from Sony had we been found guilty.

On reflection, I'm still not entirely sure what they could have found us guilty of. If they'd found us guilty of intentionally putting subliminal messages in our music, what would they have charged us with?

Murder?

Manslaughter?

Who knows?

The saddest thing about it all was that Judas Priest was probably the single most important thing in the lives of the two kids whose parents had decided to take us to court—and there were a lot of other factors that contributed to the events of that night in 1985 when they decided to shoot themselves.

The connection to us came about because it just so happened that, and even this is only hearsay, the album *Stained Class* was on the turntable in these kids' apartment when the investigator knocked on the door. That's what the lawyer said had been found at least.

But what if it wasn't on the turntable?

It always seemed like too convenient a coincidence for me. What if it had actually been someone else's album? Did they go through lots of other band's albums to find subliminal messages?

But, if two lads go out and do what they did and are obviously into heavy metal, then it stands to reason that some lawyer's going to think, "OK, let's go through their album collection to see what caused this." And when you look at it from their perspective, it was probably worth a shot.

I've always thought that the whole plan was something that some guy somewhere had probably been working on for quite a while, listening to the band's records, trying to find something. I wouldn't discount anything whatsoever. And the parents who brought the case against us definitely weren't down the straight and narrow. I had a difficult childhood myself. I could recognize that kind of parental behavior, and the only direct contact I had with them was when I saw them in court.

They'd racked up five divorces between them and there was testimony that one of the fathers used to lock his lad in the garage and beat the shit out of him with a leather belt. And there was another story that one of the lads had had a run-in with his boss at work at some point before the court case, and that his parents were gunning for him, too—trying to fabricate a situation to somehow claim some money.

The background was murky, but there's no doubt in my mind that they were out to make a fast, easy buck and it just so happened that we were, so to speak, the "ones." Sadly, there are lots of families in the world who would have done exactly the same thing. It seemed to me that it was done out of desperation, and from a need to divert blame from themselves and onto anyone or anything for what their kids had done rather than face up to their own shortcomings as parents. The whole episode was a sad situation—to see two young guys, fans, end their lives this way.

CHAPTER TWELVE

THE PERIOD LEADING UP TO ROB LEAVING THE BAND WAS such a complex one. That's the best way I can put it. The Reno trial unsettled us, no doubt about it. But beyond that there were many other forces pushing and pulling not just Rob, but all of us. However, although there were other more immediate triggers—like a fiasco in Toronto that I'll get to—I've always thought that Rob's reasons for leaving Judas Priest were in one way or another driven by his sexuality.

It wasn't that he was wrestling with the specifics of his sexuality as such; he'd have probably known where he stood since he was ten years old. And we knew it, too, right from the start. It was also never discussed. To me it had absolutely no relevance whatsoever. In the early days we had a black drummer. Then we had a gay singer.

If at some point we'd had a female bass player or if we'd had *whatever,* none of that would have mattered at all. Judas Priest was always all-inclusive.

Ironically, when Rob came into the band initially, I thought to myself, *He's here to stay.*

I felt that way because he *was* gay—which, regrettably, in those far less tolerant days, meant that he'd probably have difficulty holding down a normal job. Also, because he had such a great voice and so much to offer the world in general, I knew that he was unlikely to ever come to us and say that he was quitting the band because he was worried about losing his job or his girlfriend and all that complicated shit that causes bands so much grief.

Maybe it was a subconscious thing, who knows, but the reason I think I was perceptive in some way about Rob's needs was that my best friend at school, Nick, turned out to be gay—even though I didn't actually twig that until I was eighteen or so.

Up until that point, I had no clue (unlike with one of my other gay friends who engaged in sexual activities in his car outside his house). Nick wasn't outwardly gay; he was a pretty tough looking guy. But even if I had known, it would have been of no consequence at all.

Through Nick I got to know other gay people, and eventually, during the days when we were sleeping in the van, Rob and Nick moved into a council house, not as partners, together with a woman friend of theirs. To us it was all perfectly normal. We were round there all the time; we were all broke. Nothing mattered! Nick even ended up working for us as a roadie for a while and Rob's open homosexuality was absolutely part and parcel of daily life in the early years of Judas Priest.

And, by and large, Rob was always a hundred-percenter. Although, looking back now, there was this one instance where we played the Cromer Links Pavilion in East Anglia, probably in '74 or '75. There was this girl there that night that was really beautiful. She was hot.

I think Rob might have.

"That girl last night," we said to each other. "Did he?"

I can't be sure. That's the only time there was ever a shred of doubt.

But on the whole, when we were on tour, Rob departed into a different world from us in whatever town or city we happened to be in. We rarely saw what he was doing, and vice versa. Our worlds just magically reconvened onstage when the house lights dimmed.

Occasionally he'd have dalliances on the road that we couldn't ignore. He'd have longer relationships on tour and various people would tag along with us, and that worked for everyone. We were doing our thing and Rob was doing his. As long as everyone was happy, there was never a problem.

As time went on, it felt like Rob needed more from his life. And the big question was always going to be whether that latitude existed within the confines of Judas Priest, an environment he'd been immersed in since he was a teenager. The private aspect of being a gay man was one thing, but the public one was another.

On reflection, the leather, the studs, and that whole image Rob projected had done a good job of giving him some kind of release for many years. When I steered us down that path to cement the band's image, Rob really took it and ran with it.

I don't think Rob was ever happier than when he was pulling those leathers on. Not just that, he also got a bullwhip and a Harley, too! Consequently, I always felt that the onstage persona not only went a long way to appeasing him—it also served to acknowledge, with just a sly wink perhaps, the gay community to whom it must have been blatantly obvious that he was a gay man. After all, that "Village People" look was completely synonymous with gay men at that time. I for one was quite happy to encourage Rob in that direction because in the gay world he would be acknowledged, but in the world of rock and metal the image he went with worked, too.

To that end, Rob's image was dual purpose in that it fit Judas Priest's needs and formula while also giving him some safe ground to exist on from a personal perspective. For a good few years, everyone was happy . . .

But over time, things started to change.

In the period between *Turbo* and *Painkiller*, we all noticed small signs that maybe Rob wasn't going to be able to suppress things indefinitely. There were subtle methods of expression at first: the kinds of T-shirts he wore in interviews for example, with fairly explicit homosexually oriented images on them that were derived, I believe, from the gay art publication *Kake*.

He started wearing these all the time, including when we were doing interviews together. None of us batted an eyelid at the actual images. We just felt that Rob was diverting attention away from Judas Priest to whatever message he was trying to get across with his clothing choices. *Instead of listening to what we're saying, they'll be looking at Rob's T-shirt.*

I must be clear and say I thought that the nature of Rob's clothing didn't matter. If one of us had suddenly started turning up to press conferences wearing a gorilla suit, we'd have all viewed that as a similar diversion. No band can afford to have anything in the camp that diverts from the core message. All that does is create a situation of perceived weakness in the eyes of the fans and the media. And that's never good.

I even think that management via Jayne Andrews might have had a word with Rob in the background and it might be that that conversation triggered more in the way of pulling and tugging with Rob and the people he was mixing with outside of the band at the time.

For some reason, I never knew why, when he was getting more and more into the American vibe with his house in Phoenix, Rob seemed to start wanting more recognition for who he really was— as opposed to the figure he was within a metal band.

Also, as a part of this evolution, he was at a point where he had his own management, making his own decisions for him. He wanted to do whatever he wanted and go wherever he wanted. He craved total freedom. Also, he wasn't happy with a lot of the dynamics that I was never happy with and, really, when you thought about it, the timing was just about right for him to go out there and do everything that Ozzy had done when he quit Sabbath.

On paper, it was all there on a plate for him.

After the *Painkiller* tour, we were booked to do Operation Rock & Roll in the summer of '91 with Alice Cooper, Motörhead, and a couple of other bands.

✦

That was a tour I never wanted to do.

Furthermore, I didn't think it was right for the band. In the end, Glenn talked me into doing it, while everyone else was getting on my case about me letting the side down if I didn't. I was always going to lose.

But I still thought, *We've just done a whole world tour!*

Now, for various reasons, not least that the Gulf War was happening, here we were going out again, backed by a tough, camouflage-looking promo campaign. We were all pretty beat up after the *Painkiller* cycle as it was, which hadn't gone as well as was anticipated.

Even the record itself, as highly regarded as it seems to be nowadays, didn't have the kind of impact that we all hoped it would. I'm not totally sure why that was. As much as we can put a record through our rigorous series of tests, the only test that really counts is what your audience thinks. In the words of Metallica, who were everywhere at the time, nothing else matters.

Looking back on how things had gone with the previous albums, I think that we may have put some fans in a comfort zone with *Turbo* and *Ram It Down*. They were both very much of an era.

But the '90s felt different.

In making an album that was so far the other way in terms of heaviness, maybe a few fans thought it was too much. What they didn't realize until much later was that *Painkiller* was the last great traditional heavy metal album before all the subgenres took over: thrash, death, and speed metal. After they dominated the entire '90s and beyond, only then did fans start to appreciate what *Painkiller* was.

But back to the tour.

For some reason the tickets just didn't sell well. We played a few big shows where there was a fair amount of people, but then there were other nights where it was a bit patchy and you were thinking, *What's going on here?*

In retrospect, maybe you could lay a portion of the blame for poor ticket sales at the feet of promoters who were doing their best to operate in a very transient heavy music scene. Around that time, with metal dividing into its many subgenres, sometimes US tour bills would pair up bands that were really fantastic in their own right but who didn't necessarily belong on the same bill. Don't get me wrong, I loved all the bands we ever toured with in the U.S around that time, but even I couldn't ignore the fact that both their and our audiences were becoming noticeably different. It was what it was.

Similarly, in Europe, where we were on a bill with Pantera and Annihilator, I didn't feel we had the balance quite right there either. Both bands were good fun to tour with; we felt like Pantera's parents. Every night after the show, they'd be lined up outside our dressing room, hoping for any spare drink we had! It was so funny to see. We took them to visit the Colosseum in Rome with us; Dime busked in the street for money. It was hilarious, and definitely good times.

But, regardless, every one of these bands came from a different place in the metal world from us. Call me an old traditionalist if you like, but I always much preferred to be out there with someone more like Priest in an ideological sense—bands like Saxon, Accept, or maybe Dokken. I was never a fan of putting the younger, arguably harder-hitting bands on with us in the hope that the promoters would be successful in capturing *both* the younger fans and the classic rock fans. To me, it seldom worked.

As an example, a few years later I went to see Ozzy Osbourne at the Wolverhampton Civic Hall supported by Fear Factory. I couldn't believe how divisive that bill seemed. For the opening band there were maybe twenty kids down the front with Fear Factory shirts on, while the bars were absolutely rammed. Then, when Ozzy came on, you couldn't even see the stage! The combination just didn't mesh.

But that's what happened with the *Painkiller* tour.

✦

Despite the old issues and us being burned out, we did Operation Rock & Roll anyway and it really wasn't great, although there were some funny moments with Lemmy. I should say that Lemmy was always a pleasure to be with; we'd crossed paths many times over the years. Lots of people gave Lemmy a wide berth, but never me. He did collar me one day on this tour. It was in the daytime; he grabbed me round the neck.

"K.K.! Come and have a listen to our latest video . . . "

"Oh no, I can't. I've got to tune up."

"Come on, come on. Have a listen."

With that he manhandled me onto their bus and I should say that the last place you ever want to go is onto a Motörhead tour bus! Whenever we picked up a bus at the beginning of a tour, the first thing we'd say to the bus driver was: "Just checking, mate, were Motörhead on here last?" They were the one band you didn't want to follow; they were notorious for tour bus goings-on. It was an ongoing joke.

Anyway, he got me on their bus and I'm thinking, *How long can this possibly take? Five minutes at the most?*

The other guys in Motörhead were there too, crammed into this little space, when suddenly the penny dropped. *This isn't just one song, Ken*, I thought. *This is a whole fucking live concert video!*

So, there I was for two hours, cornered in there, with Lemmy singing in my ear. Can you imagine? He's smoking, he's drinking;

his breath in my ear. As great a lyricist as he was, fuck it was an ordeal! But me, being the sweet guy that I am, didn't have the heart to leave. I just tolerated it. Lemmy epitomized everything that was great about rock 'n' roll!

✦

The flip side was that we had all kinds of problems with Alice Cooper—that didn't help matters. Of the twenty or so shows, he was headlining two of them: his hometown and the last show, which was, I recall, in Toronto.

Throughout, he and his tour manager seemed to have a real problem accepting their lot, which, for the majority of the tour, involved being second on the bill to Judas Priest. I think they had other issues anyway; we'd hear arguing from their dressing room most nights. Then they'd come offstage late all the time and that generally made the whole tour something less than harmonious.

On the last night in Toronto there was all kinds of crazy upset going on during that day, mostly created by Alice's tour manager, from what I could gather. I wasn't happy at all, and eventually Scott and I had to go into the production room for a bit of a shouting match with them to let off some steam.

Because of all that, Scott and I ended up getting changed late; the rest of the band had gone ahead of us to the stage. Then our tour manager couldn't find the keys to the car in order to drive us to the stage, which was quite some distance away amid this big outdoor arena Everything snowballed.

The upshot of all of this was that, as our intro tape started, Scott and I were still in the damn car somewhere. Meanwhile Rob had already started to ride out onto the stage on the motorbike not knowing that, because the message had been relayed that the other band members weren't even onstage, the mechanical stairs had been lowered to their starting position.

Oblivious, amid all the smoke, noise, and dry ice, Rob drove forward on the Harley and crashed straight into the stairs.

Bang!

Rob was out for the count.

Scott and I were still in the car!

Somehow, we all made it to the stage and they started the intro tape again—oblivious to the fact that Rob was concussed. We even played the first song, "Hell Bent for Leather," with no vocals, none of us realizing that Rob was lying there somewhere under the dry ice. I think that's the only instrumental version of that track in existence. God it was a mess. It was real Spinal Tap stuff.

One thing had led to another that day, causing a domino effect that put Rob in the hospital after the show. And then that was it. Nothing more was said about it. We all got up the next day and went our own way, on planes to different places.

I went to Los Angeles for a few days to see my girlfriend Kyme before I went home and one thing that I don't think anyone knows is that I actually sat down and wrote a resignation letter on that airplane to LAX.

Like Dave Holland, I'd just had enough.

All the issues I had with management decisions and Glenn seemed to come to a head after that Toronto show; it was one thing after another. We shouldn't have done the tour. It wasn't a good tour. Everything was bad about it. The list went on and on.

I can't remember exactly how I structured the letter, but I probably just listed a growing number of things that most people probably wouldn't even notice but that really used to infuriate me.

Then, just to punctuate the fact that I was 100 percent on the money with my gripes, Rob *did* later leave the band.

He'd obviously had enough, too.

But he sent the letter (or was it a fax?) in and I didn't.

And that was it, really.

On reflection, I think I was always deadly serious about quitting by '91. It was just a question of when. And then, when Rob beat me to it, there didn't seem to be any point in sending my letter. I guess I thought the band was over anyway. I thought, *Forget it. There's nothing left to leave!*

For a few reasons, 1991 felt like it might be a logical end for Judas Priest anyway. During the tour, maybe sensing that the roof might cave in, Glenn had been putting the pieces into place for his own solo project. Whenever we were in Los Angeles I seem to remember him and Jayne disappearing off to see record companies in an attempt to strike up some kind of deal.

Eventually something was agreed, I think, and I'm pretty sure that if I had gotten wind of that, Rob would have, too. That might just have pushed him over the edge and made him think, "Well, if he's going to do that, maybe I should, too."

For me, the idea of people going off and doing solo projects while still in the band went against the grain of the Judas Priest ethos. I saw it as a lack of loyalty and, although I don't know for sure, Rob might have felt the same.

It certainly seemed to get the ball rolling on his departure but it's entirely possible, and I'll never know, that Rob himself had been planning to leave for a while, too. It's a case of which came first. Strangely, at no point at this time did I ever have a conversation with Rob about him leaving. There was just his resignation letter and no further discussion.

To complicate things, Rob's resignation came at a time when our manager, Bill Curbishley, was in negotiations with Sony that could have meant that quite sizeable sums of money would have come our way. Obviously, the cash would have been welcome. But because of Rob's departure that kickback didn't happen—which didn't seem in any way fair.

To backtrack slightly, when Rob initially resigned, he was asked if he could at least be discreet in the short-term so that in case he changed his mind for any reason, this windfall would still be in the pipeline for all of us and we'd be good to go.

He didn't change his mind; Rob was adamant about leaving. There was no going back for him. Worse still for us, he wanted Sony to support his new band project, which meant that whatever was in the offing for Judas Priest went down the drain.

Meanwhile, Rob could just pick up all the pieces in the form of sizeable advances for his new record and walk off into the sunset, while we'd be left standing there with no cash windfall and no singer.

Not surprisingly, we all felt incredibly bitter. And that's when the war of words with Rob started. It was time for home truths from us, and his manager, John Baxter, came back with some serious shit, too. I wasn't immune from any of it. He had a good go at us all, individually and collectively.

Looking back now, a lot of it was quite funny, really. It got down to being a complete shit-slinging exercise and most of it was a really good read! Sadly, none of it was going to improve the situation and, if anything—irrespective of the fact that the ink on my leaving letter was still wet—it brought Glenn, Ian, and me a bit closer together, all of which was rather ironic.

✦

In early '92, after all of the meltdown, I went out to the house I'd bought in Spain for a while to cool off. Normally I would be going back somewhere to start writing songs, but this time I went to Spain thinking something else: *What now?*

Rob had gone. Glenn was doing his own solo thing. There was talk of us putting out a compilation album (which did appear a couple of years later in the form of *Metal Works*). Really, the sole idea behind it was to appease the fans and keep them on board while we were on hiatus.

We discussed various other concepts around that time, too. I wanted to put out a "Priest on Fire" collection, a compilation of the fastest, most energetic tracks we'd ever done, back to back.

It seemed like a great idea at the time. I wanted to call it *Burning Sermons*, but it never happened. The idea got quashed for one reason or another. But despite that, I do like how the stopgap compilation turned out

So basically, apart from helping to curate *Metal Works*, there I was, sitting there in Spain with nothing to do. For the first time since joining the band, I felt isolated and confused. If Priest was over, I had no idea what I was going to do with the rest of my life. For a while I was just mulling things over.

From a financial perspective I was in a reasonably secure position. It had been a long haul, from 1970 to 1991. We'd worked hell of a hard for what we had. If that had been the end, I wouldn't have been destitute by any means. And I always had the pipe dream of what could potentially be done with Astbury Hall in the back of my mind.

As time passed in Spain, after weeks of soul-searching and over-thinking, two opposing thoughts solidified in my mind. The first was that Judas Priest really was over. Given how long it had been, that seemed plausible. The second was this desire to keep going and to really stuff it up Rob who'd said somewhere that Priest really weren't heavy enough for him, as well as all the other shit that went down at the breakup.

Now *that* seemed much more attractive. Suddenly, I was emerging from a bit of a fog with what seemed like clearer direction.

But, as one door opens, another one slams.

One night the phone rang at the kind of hour that can only mean something very bad. Groggy, I grabbed the phone from the bedside table and listened to the voice on the other end telling me that my on/off girlfriend Kyme had been killed in a car crash somewhere on the outskirts of L.A. that afternoon.

I put the phone down, numb, thinking, *I can't believe that she's gone . . .*

I really couldn't believe what I'd just heard, but I also sort of could. Although we were admittedly in limbo, in the process of breaking up (the visit to LA after the last tour had been the last time we'd seen each other), we were still very close. I was very fond of her; I was helping to fund her business; I cared about her future. Now she was gone. It was an extremely hard reality to level with at that time. I was absolutely distraught—not least when I heard later that it had taken the rescue team over twenty minutes to reach her because of the excessive LA traffic. That information conjured up a horrible image to me that she may have been in quite some pain and distress. I was devastated to think of what she may have been going through.

Eerily, though, I always knew Kyme was something of a loose cannon when it came to driving cars. She seemed to have no concept of the dangers around her. Once when I was on the *Turbo* tour and she was staying at the Astbury, she rolled the Ford XR2 of mine that she drove about in and somehow got it fixed before I got back.

Panicking, she persuaded a mate of mine who was a mechanic to repair all the bodywork and put all the other damage right. I didn't notice; I only found out much later—not that I'd have even really bothered about the damage or the cost. But I always saw a lack of awareness in her, about driving and a few other things. That was a huge bone of contention between us and it was one of the reasons why we were in the process of parting ways. Regardless, Kyme was a vivacious and very able woman with a lot to offer the world.

Sadly, driving was to be her downfall. I flew to LA to say my sad good-byes with all her family in attendance. I was one of those who carried her coffin. Later I had to go to both her apartment and her car to see if there were any personal effects that should be retrieved. It was very tough to do, and afterward I thought, *You really don't know what you've got until it's gone.*

◆

Throughout the mid-'90s, there were "How about we go out and find a new singer?" conversations among us, from time to time. I think we meant it; packing in Judas Priest seemed a less attractive option by then. But for one reason or another, nothing happened to force us into serious action.

Knowing our predicament, various people had been sending tapes for us to listen to for several months, but nothing concrete happened until Glenn finished his solo shit—which seemed to go on forever. Truth be told, his solo venture hadn't made much of an impact, and when he was released from his contract at Warner, per-hapse he thought, "Hmm, time to pick up the Judas Priest pieces, maybe?"

As usual, I just kind of went along with it when we eventually made the decision to actively seek someone to take Rob's place, and with that I started becoming a bit more enthusiastic about the idea of making music again. As a bit of momentum gathered, I spent more time back at England, going between Glenn's and my house, feeling my way on a few ideas for new songs. The Priest juices were beginning to flow again.

Uniquely, although the end of his solo project had triggered the re-forming, this cycle was being driven more by me than by Glenn. I'd been the player in Priest with the heavier taste and style, but that direction was always curtailed by what Glenn wanted. As was my way, I'd always given ground.

Now, for whatever reason, Glenn seemed happy to go along with whatever I wanted, and that in turn energized me to come up with conspicuously heavy material. This subtle shift in Glenn's and my working dynamic would be borne out by the nature of the album that we'd soon birth, with riffs and songs so heavy and uncompro-mising that they would settle the feud with Rob forever.

This'll show him.

Meanwhile, we were still getting sent tapes of singers. . . .

Eventually, after carefully listening to literally hundreds of them, we had to consider an extremely pertinent question: How many people can actually sing Judas Priest?

In the same way that only a few singers could pull off the AC/DC catalog, the same applied to us, maybe even more so because of those high wailing notes that Rob hit so well. The metal world is a small one when you're in it. We had a pretty good idea about who we thought could fit the bill. And there weren't many candidates. Ralf Scheepers, who at that time was singing in Gamma Ray, was definitely a possibility, but nothing came of that.

And then fate worked in our favor.

Scott met a girl somewhere who'd seen a guy called Tim Owens performing in a Judas Priest tribute band. He sent in a video and when we watched it we said: "That could actually be Rob."

He was that good.

So, we told him to get on a plane and come over to a studio we'd rented for a few days, where we got him to sing a couple of songs. In all truth, we didn't really need to even do that. But he turned up anyway, owned the songs, and that was it. Tim Owens was in the band!

While we were at this kind of reconvening-of-the-band reunion, I remember we all sat around a table one night and somebody said: "He's got to have a cool name. Lots of bands do it."

In my mind, I was adamant that we couldn't just call him Tim. It wouldn't have worked, just like a name like Norman might not have worked either. (No disrespect to any Normans reading this book!)

I thought of the name Ripper, simply because nobody else was coming up with anything better. If I'd had more time, I'm sure I could have come up with something even cleverer, but we needed something on the spot to go with. And believe me, it was a hard enough sell getting Tim to accept that he'd be called Ripper!

"But *why* Ripper?" he kept saying.

"Because you rip the shit out of the vocals, that's why!" I told him.

That was it. I kept pushing and pushing and it stuck. "Ripper" Owens just *sounds* cool.

On a personal level, Ripper was an absolute dream of a guy to work with. You couldn't have a better guy in a band. Better still, he brought with him absolutely no ego whatsoever, and everybody liked him straightaway. He took good care of himself, never abused himself or anybody else, and, better still, he played golf!

With Ripper on board, my view was that we were going to be Judas Priest, but a *different* Judas Priest. And the reason for that was that we *were* a different band. The positive thing was that we now had an opportunity to validate Ripper as a singer by approaching the music a little differently so that people couldn't draw a direct comparison with the Rob era. And I think we achieved that.

Ripper was younger, he was strong—it all made sense. As it turned out, Ripper's Priest baptism, *Jugulator*, was relentless. It was one amazing, punishing metal riff after another. A real riffmanac.

Whether it was a subconscious move to separate Rob's and Ripper's eras in a sonic sense or simply a product of the awkward, mid-'90s metal scene, *Jugulator* sounded, in most senses, quite unlike anything Judas Priest had ever done before. The guitars were tuned down a step, sometimes a step and a half; the riffs had groove to spare. Maybe the fact that Ripper was younger and came from a different place was significant, too. Either way we felt like we had a degree of latitude by virtue of his presence that made making a slightly different style of music a real pleasure.

And, amazingly, it all worked together, to the extent that if you heard it and saw the words "Judas Priest" on the cover, you'd still recognize aspects of our signature sound. In retrospect, *Jugulator* was a hell of a feat. I loved the album at the time and I still do today.

Now that we had a singer, *Jugulator* had the benefit of a fair wind at its back. However, one major problem still existed. The moment that Rob left the band, in effect leaving us without a label, we knew that some kind of dual-territory record deal with new partners was likely in the cards.

The industry wasn't getting easier at that time. There was so much uncertainty in heavy music with grunge around. The upshot of that was that from 1989 to 1990 onward, there were few superstars appearing in the metal world.

The big labels, the Warners and Sonys, were fine with that. They'd always have the Barbra Streisands, Michael Jacksons, and Shania Twains. Multigenre labels didn't have to worry about what was going on in heavy metal.

Because of all this, the Ripper-fronted version of Priest was never going to be an easy sell. Thankfully, SPV, the German label that took us on, focused on bands that had been dropped by major labels or new acts that weren't particularly lucrative. We were a bit of an anomaly in that we weren't technically either of those things, but they backed us anyway.

As it happened, SPV and CMC (the two labels we worked with in Europe and the US) both did us proud. As if to repay their faith and efforts, we went out on the road and made a really good go of things. Obviously, the gigs were smaller than we were used to, but the feedback we got from the audiences to the new material more than made up for it.

Ripper could do the Priest classics brilliantly but he also injected a new energy into the new tracks to the extent that people who saw that tour as teenagers, who saw me on stage with the Flying V, hammering out riffs like "Dead Meat" and "Burn in Hell," thought, "I want to be that guy!" And in some cases, they're actually doing it now. That's what being a musician is all about for me. Hendrix did exactly the same to me.

Despite all the positivity, we still had that age-old problem when, the moment we came offstage, the first thing some fans would say wouldn't always be, "Hey, guys, what a great show . . . "

Instead we'd get, "Hey, K.K., when's Rob coming back?"

There was a lot of that.

But, regardless, the album and tour ran its course.

Mostly the intraband dynamics were good, but there were definitely a few nights where I had issues with Glenn and his live performance. For me, there came to be a level of uncertainty where I wasn't really sure which Glenn was going to show up.

Would he be capable?

Or would the performance be what I considered to be a mess by my standards?

There were even some nights when Ripper would come over to me midsong, gesture over toward Glenn, and say, "What is *he* doing? Can't you do anything about this?"

Of course, midsong, there was absolutely nothing I could do other than make sure I was doing *my* job.

Consequently, going into the follow-up *Demolition* project, I had a lot more doubts than I'd had before. It was as if the enthusiasm and the newness of playing again as a band was already wearing off. It felt like by doing the first post-Rob project and it being pretty good, I'd exorcised something inside me.

But then, as the dust settled, I thought, *OK, but what next?*

I found it hard to generate any motivation to write songs for *Demolition*. There was something missing, and it wasn't just Rob Halford. I was definitely less engaged and it felt to me that Glenn picked up on that. He wanted to produce it himself because he'd decided that he wanted to upgrade the existing studio in his house. Then the idea was that we'd do some kind of money deal with Glenn to cover his costs. Even though we brought in Chris Tsangirides's help—and Chris, may he rest in peace, was a good guy and a good addition to any project—pretty soon I went off the boil with whole thing, thinking, *Hmm, I'm not sure about this . . .*

But anyway, I went through the motions despite almost walking away, in my own mind, from the album on a couple of occasions. We just about got there, I think, even though I hated the album cover and I told everybody at the time. I remember that we had a meeting to discuss ideas for it, and everyone was on board with the images that eventually adorned the cover. Jayne was there, Glenn was there, our production manager was there.

Sanity was not there.

"It's great. And it'll make a great T-shirt," they all said.

"For fuck sake!" I said.

I threw in a couple of my own ideas that, on reflection, weren't that great. I'd gotten a local guy, a friend of mine called Ben Davies, to knock up a few prototypes and all of them were better than that. They wanted the artwork to run all the way around the T-shirt and whatever. But none of that ever happened. The bottom line is that I lost the battle and that cover sucked!

Regardless of how I felt about the album, the artwork, or anything else, I did what I always did and gave 100 percent to the whole exercise. The *Demolition* tour was similar to the *Jugulator* run, only a little less fresh-feeling and satisfying.

Then, at some point after the tour in 2002, Sharon Osbourne called the office.

"Would you get Rob back in the band to do Ozzfest sometime? There's a lot of money on offer."

That was the gist of it.

"Umm, what?"

"Ozzfest 2003. Are you in?"

Sharon's reasoning was twofold. First, I'm sure that she saw that to have Priest on the bill with Black Sabbath would mean bums on seats. That much was obvious. Second, she probably thought that if Ozzy was ever unable to perform, Rob would be able to do stand-in for him at short notice, as he already had done on an Ozzy tour back in 1992 after he'd left Judas Priest.

"We'll think about it . . . "

Her question had come straight out of the blue, particularly given that during the "Ripper years" we'd had absolutely zero contact with

Rob. We discussed it, and from the start Glenn wasn't having any of it. I don't know why not.

I felt totally differently.

I realized that all the lethargy I'd been feeling at the start of the *Demolition* songwriting process was because, as much as I loved what we'd done with Ripper, deep down I knew that it probably wasn't going anywhere.

Above and beyond the immediate sense that it wasn't going to work with Ripper, I had this broader feeling that, from a career perspective, it was getting late in the day in the context of my whole life. I'd already "quit" the band once; I didn't want to feel like I was going through the motions for the time I had left. Furthermore, it was very obvious what the fans wanted. All in all, the timing was good on every level—not least because Rob's solo career was a sinking ship by that point anyway.

So, with all of these thoughts percolating, the idea of getting back together with Rob actually seemed most appealing to me. Furthermore, it seemed like it could actually happen because it made sense for both sides.

The way I see it, when Rob went out on his own he made several fundamental mistakes. He didn't put the right people around him, right across the board. But more importantly he didn't pick the right musicians and didn't go in the best direction musically.

Admittedly, it was an odd time for metal music, but even so, I'd heard on the grapevine the names of some of the musicians that Rob was maybe going to hook up with; it scared me at the time! I heard names like Steve Stevens for one, who was not only a good player but also an excellent songwriter and looked pretty good at the time, too. I remember thinking, *If he gets people like that around him, he'll do very well.*

But that's not what happened.

Rob never had the songs, and never got the direction dialed in. That first album with Fight, his new band, was just horrible. The songs had no character whatsoever. It's not to say that his some-what nameless and faceless musicians weren't accomplished. But the music was just not what Priest fans wanted.

On a business level, it was a mess, too.

John Baxter, who had come on board as one of Rob's love af-fairs while he was still on the road with Judas Priest, became his manager. This wasn't an uncommon scenario. I've known plenty of guys in bands who've hooked up with a groupie, possibly without knowing that he or she was a groupie. And then they end up getting married and the next thing you know he or she's managing him and it goes on from there. And that's what happened with John Baxter, except he had been a shoe salesman, I believe.

Anyway, from what I heard, Rob invested a lot of money into his management company headed by John, and in turn John managed Rob's financial affairs thereafter.

Managing Rob shouldn't have been a difficult task. Any manager worth his salt should have made some very good money for his cli-ent. But instead, it all turned into a horror story—which led to that war of words between Rob and us.

Despite these unresolved issues, with this lucrative Ozzfest of-fer implanted in my mind, I started conceding to the "one band, one voice" theory. Rob *was* the voice of Priest—end of story. Just as Jagger is to the Stones and Bruce is with Maiden. You say a band's name and you name the singer.

Queen? Freddie Mercury.

A couple of bands have achieved it with other singers, albeit with mitigating circumstances: AC/DC with Brian Johnson and, to a lesser degree, Black Sabbath with Ronnie James Dio. But as good as Sammy Hagar did, Dave Lee Roth will always be the voice of Van Halen for me.

So, there was a *heritage* aspect to consider with Rob and Priest that was inescapable to me. And I already knew, based on earlier comments, that that feeling was one shared by the majority of our fans. The evidence spoke for itself. Rob had sung on *British Steel, Stained Class, Painkiller*—all the great material that had propelled us to the success and notoriety we had. And in his own way, I'm sure Ripper must have known that.

It would be fair to say my mind was totally made up. And as if to confirm that my thinking was right, Rob Halford turned up at Astbury, completely out of the blue, sometime in late 2002 or early 2003.

It was so good to see him; Rob seemed more comfortable with himself than when I'd last seen him, possibly because he'd come out in 1998. That was the worst-kept secret ever anyway, and, as I've said before, Rob's sexuality was always of such little importance to us that his actual coming out only warrants one sentence here in this book.

Our working relationship and basic human friendship always towered far above anything as inconsequential as sexuality. I was always closer to Rob than Glenn ever was, so he probably saw me as the path of least resistance as far as building bridges was concerned. I was at Rob's mum's funeral whereas Glenn wasn't. It was that kind of bond: a certain closeness between Rob and me outside of the band. You can't break that kind of connection.

Because of our longstanding friendship, seeing Rob walk into my office at Astbury Hall felt normal. Neither of us batted an eyelid. Instead, we hugged like two guys who'd made some of the best metal music ever. It didn't feel in any way strange or awkward; it was as if we'd seen each other the previous week. He was the same Rob, albeit a little older and a few pounds heavier. And there were no apologies; it was all unsaid.

But as we talked, I felt the magic return as I shared the details of the offer that was on the table. (Sharon's offer now was for us to reunite for the 2004 Ozzfest.) As I did, the hairs on my neck stood up as the excitement gathered with the thoughts of what might happen: Priest back together again at Ozzfest, on the big stage, the fans appeased . . .

Rob wanted it, too. That much was obvious.

But for a while, in the days after our meeting, it seemed to me that Glenn still wasn't having any part of a Rob Halford reunion. In fact, I even seem to remember him almost scolding me for speaking to Rob at all, as if it was an act of disloyalty on my part. I've never understood where he was coming from with that attitude.

But the truth was that I was always the one who inherently knew what was best for Judas Priest. No, I didn't always get my way, but I like to think I knew what the right decisions were. And getting Rob back in the band was one of them. If there was a way forward at all, this was it. There was no way we could continue as we were after *Demolition*. We had a chance to jump off a canal boat onto the QE2.

Glenn eventually succumbed.

After seeing Rob in person, Glenn seemed to welcome him back. And then everything gathered pace at a rate of knots. Glenn and I did a few days' work in England, then we jumped on a plane to Rob's place in San Diego.

Out of nowhere, the Priest was back.

I should stress that parting with Ripper wasn't in any way an easy decision—although I don't think it came as a surprise to him. It's like a soccer team when its leading goal scorer leaves and is replaced by someone who doesn't score quite as many goals. Then, when an opportunity arises to get that top goal scorer back, what are they going to do?

It just is what it is. It's a career move, and not a personal one. It was all about bums on seats. And Ripper took it well. He was an absolute gentleman about it, as gutted as he must have been deep down.

From my own perspective—and maybe I'm just saying this to justify my actions—I thought that it might all be better for Ripper in the long run. Rather than always being known as a stand-in for Rob Halford, I thought he'd be better off looking to his own career and making a name for himself in his own right.

And nowadays I still believe that to a large extent, although I don't think Ripper has ever surrounded himself with quite the right people since he left Priest. Regardless, he and I remain on good terms and I'll always make a point of going to see him play whenever he's local. Ripper was, and always will be, top man in my eyes.

It never entered my mind to suggest that Rob sing any of the Ripper-era material once he rejoined the band. In the same way as I doubt Rob would ever ask me to play material that I hadn't worked on, I wasn't prepared to ask him to sing material that he hadn't been present for—although I suspect Rob wouldn't have had a problem.

When Ripper left, I just thought, *Let's leave that in the past.*

As great as some of these songs and riffs were—particularly on *Jugulator*—my feeling was that they should be preserved in time and not played again. Ripper, on the other hand, was free to play and tour with those songs and he did, with the bonus of being able to say "Tim 'Ripper' Owens, formerly of Judas Priest" in his promo material.

I say that, but while doing so I'm reminded of a call that Ripper put in to me, sometime in 2016, when he was taking his own band out for a series of small and relatively low-key UK club shows.

"Can you believe that they're stopping me from using the artwork?" he told me.

"You're joking?" I replied.

Seemingly Jayne Andrews had seen a picture of Ripper's tour poster, with the *Jugulator* cover art to support name recognition.

Now, to me, logic would suggest that anyone looking at this levelheadedly might have thought: "He sang on the albums, fair and square. So, if he uses the poster and a few people buy *Jugulator* or *Demolition* after the show as a result, then that's all to the good for Judas Priest. Everybody wins."

But that's not how Jayne saw it, from what I was told.

She shut him down and told him to remove the image. Any small semblance of recognition Ripper might have gotten of his legitimate Judas Priest affiliations went out the window. To me it was a very narrow-minded decision from a business perspective.

"What can I do?" Ripper asked me at the end of the call.

"You know the answer to that, mate," I told him. "There's nothing you can do other than what you've been asked."

CHAPTER THIRTEEN

WITH ROB BACK IN THE BAND, WE TOOK UP SHARON'S offer to appear at Ozzfest 2004, the first gig kicking things off in Hartford, Connecticut, on July 10.

The Ozzfest audiences really took to the re-formed Priest, and we reciprocated with what I felt were some of our best live performances. And as if Sharon had had a crystal ball when she first contacted us, her earlier prophecy came true.

The tour had reached Camden, New Jersey when Sharon called from the UK, where she was working on *The X Factor*.

"Ozzy is sick," she said. "Could Rob stand in for him at tonight's show? If he can't, we'll have to cancel."

Rob said, "OK, I'll do it."

And he did both shows, Black Sabbath's and ours. It was quite a feat, really. After all, it's always going to be a tentative situation when someone says, "Sorry, guys, Ozzy can't be here tonight, but here's a stand-in." In truth, Rob was probably the only metal front man who could get away with standing in for Ozzy without getting bottled off the stage.

As it turned out, it was a bit of a treat for the fans in that they were watching a bit of history. Rob put on an incredible performance.

The dynamics in the band with Rob back in place seemed fine; he was always fairly impartial anyway. One thing we did notice though was that Rob was now requesting the assistance of an teleprompter for the lyrics.

"You don't remember them?" I asked him.

"Well, not all of them," he replied. "It's been a while."

Christ. You've been singing "Breaking the Law" every night for the last twenty-odd years. Surely you can remember the words?

I even recall somebody from another well-known band having a dig at him in the press about it at the time. We just left it, though. Whatever got him through the shows was fine by us. Rob was cool about it all.

In 2004, Glenn's and my relationship, which was always a bit strained, seemed to be getting even more so.

At the heart of it, Glenn and I were always the human version of oil and water being mixed. That being said, we rubbed along pretty well for a long time and the reason there wasn't more friction than there could have been was that I just kept my mouth shut and tolerated behavior that I didn't like. As I've said, that's the kind of person I am: I avoid unnecessary confrontation wherever possible.

Should I have said more? Yes.

But for years everything rolled along pretty well so it wasn't worth rocking the boat.

Glenn and I are fundamentally different types of people. I like to think of myself as being a pretty open book. If you've read this far, you'll maybe agree. If I ever had strong feelings about songs, album titles, or artwork, I'd always speak up and keep my views out in the open.

Equally, if I thought Ian had been viewing someone through particularly strong beer goggles the night before, I'd have no issue saying, "Mate, what was *that* all about?" We'd both laugh, and it would all be good.

Glenn's and my relationship was never on that level. I could never, ever have even vaguely personal conversations with him. I never tried either. He was always much more introverted—I never really knew what he was thinking or doing in the background. The way Glenn was when he joined the band never really changed. Not just that, I thought that Glenn always seemed to find a way to influence decisions in the band in a way that I didn't like.

The origins of Glenn's influence began as far back as the *Stained Class* era. I always liked to contribute solos to our songs. I liked to think that my style of playing, totally different from Glenn's as it was, brought something valuably different to the table. I think some of the guitar solos on our early material bear that assertion out pretty well. In combination, our contrasting solo work gave Priest an interesting dimension.

But then, out of nowhere, this decision was made, perhaps unknown to everyone else, that Glenn would play the majority of the solos, and I, barring the occasional contribution here and there, would focus on laying down one half of the rhythm guitar sound that defined us for many years.

Rob accepted it, Ian accepted it, Les Binks, our drummer at the time, accepted it, and so did I, simply because it's sometimes best to give people leeway in the hope that it's all in the band's best interests.

I regret that now.

Looking back, I feel that there was greediness at work.

As years passed, Glenn applied an even tighter grip on band decisions when Bill Curbishley's management company put Jayne Andrews in charge of Judas Priest in 1985.

I should say without reservation that, from the very start, Jayne was fantastic at what she did. She was fastidious, trustworthy, and prompt in her communication with labels and promoters. If something needed done, you knew Jayne would do it. In some ways she was everything that a band could have wanted. She also seemed to have much more of an affinity with Glenn than any other member of the band. At the start, that was fine. I just thought, *Horses for courses . . .*

As time passed, decisions started being made, presented as faits accomplis, which I know for a fact didn't reflect my views or Rob's or Ian's. Summer touring was one such issue and, as I recall, it was Ian that raised it first.

"Why are we not touring in the summer? Surely that's where the money is."

"We've taken a view that the timing isn't right."

"Who has?"

We knew what the answer was.

Ian's gripe was legitimate, and I felt for him. He was never a songwriter in the band. That was his choice. Songwriters had a standing in the band, whereas nonsongwriters had to keep it shut, I'm afraid. Nobody discouraged him from presenting ideas—quite the reverse. If Ian had showed up with a great song idea at any time, all of us would have listened and welcomed his input with open arms. He knew that, and we knew that. Maybe he saw that there was already a battle on, like George Harrison must have had in the Beatles. But he never did come forward with anything.

This lesser role meant that Ian was more reliant on touring proceeds. He didn't have the luxury of publishing royalties that Glenn, Rob, and I had. So obviously, when Priest weren't touring in the summer, when the big arena shows and festivals guaranteed good money, Ian was quite understandably going to be in a tough position financially.

I was pretty sure that it was Glenn who was steering these decisions. Jayne was relaying information to us, the whys and wherefores of why we wouldn't be appearing at X and Y festival. But to my eyes, she was only acting as a conduit for Glenn. If Glenn said to Jayne, "The band won't be touring" for this or that reason, I'm sure she just thought, "OK then, if Glenn says that they're not touring, the band can't tour without Glenn, therefore they won't be touring at all."

And on it went from there.

The reason?

He had a family, and instead of wanting to be stuck on the road for months, he decided he'd rather be at home with his wife and kids. It wasn't every summer or every year by any means, but it happened too often for comfort.

None of us had any issue whatsoever with Glenn wanting to spend time with his family. But when that affected not only the financial landscape, but also the profile and platform of Judas Priest, it became a real bone of contention for the rest of us. I personally didn't like denying the fans all those potential festival appearances: Download, Graspop, etc. If you do one, you do them all, and in doing so you remain current.

But instead, people were saying to us, "Why aren't you out there?"

Not wanting to air dirty laundry in public, there wasn't a simple answer that we could share.

We all tried to lean on Glenn to compromise, but he wouldn't budge. And with the band's de facto manager always taking his side, it felt like we were in an impossible predicament—one that revolved around Glenn's schedule.

As long as Jayne was in place as the central hub, it seemed to me like Glenn would dictate how the major decisions played out. And he, in my eyes, confirmed that situation by always being the first to suggest gifts for Jayne at events like Christmas.

It should be said in Glenn's defense that it wasn't only his agenda that Jayne took control of. Gradually, she took her role as band manager to extreme levels. Sometimes it felt as if she'd rule offers and requests in or out without ever asking us. Beyond that she became far too defensive in my eyes.

If people wanted to interview us or record company executives wanted this or that—all of these things being part and parcel of being in a band—I really thought she took the idea of gatekeeping to an unacceptable level. It became embarrassing for me—and to this day I have no idea why she took that role on.

Regardless of all these simmering tensions, once we were all together in Rob's apartment in San Diego, pretty much all of the demos came together easily. It honestly felt like somebody had turned the clock back half a dozen years. It was business as usual. Glenn and I had assembled a few riff and song structures before we jumped on a plane to the US, and because I'd just learned how to use Cubase, I had it all stored on a laptop to take with me to Rob's home studio.

In that room we also had a small drum machine, a small multi-effect pod, a couple of guitars, and Rob sang vocals right there in the apartment. They were pretty decent-sounding demos, I'll say that.

The key to the recording of *Angel of Retribution,* most of which was done back at Old Smithy Studio in Worcestershire, was undoubtedly Roy Z. He was the vital new ingredient we threw into the Priest mixture.

Not only is Roy a very talented guy from an engineering perspective, but he's also a good guitar player. A producer who can also pick up a guitar is always a plus and in this instance that was definitely the case for me because it meant that I could do a lot of my solo stuff at home with just Roy and me in the room.

Up until that point I'd assumed that I did everything in a flawless fashion, simply because I'd been doing it for so long. But Roy showed me a different side to my playing—to the point that I often found myself thinking, *Hang on, he's making me do things that I wouldn't do if he wasn't here!*

"Oh, come on. Get that old '67 Flying V out and let it rip!"

"You think so?"

"Yes, mate. Let's get that classic Priest sound back."

Dutifully, I'd go up the stairs to the attic and return with a handful of those old stomp boxes and basic amps and that's pretty much how we went. In all the years I'd been in Judas Priest, it was a treat to be in a position where somebody was actually producing my guitar parts. That had never happened before.

And, by and large, that was a positive. Because he was always trying to listen to my playing through a fan's ears, Roy was successful in accessing aspects of my playing that I hadn't touched for a long time. If I went in a certain direction with a solo, while he was primarily there to record and engineer the sounds I created, he also felt comfortable to jump in as a guitarist to say, "Yes, mate—more of that!"

Then, after I'd done some takes, most of which I felt were pretty good, Roy would say something like, "Let's use that one, and that one. I hear some classic Priest in there."

Because I was always looking to move forward, I wouldn't have been open to these suggestions if Roy hadn't been there. He liked looking forward, but he also sought to look back. It was an interesting discipline all round—and just one part of the larger picture.

Like many albums, the bedrock of *Angel of Retribution* was the drum sound. We were adamant that we wanted a really solid drum track from which to build the album from the ground up. So, Roy took Scott to Sound City in Los Angeles to get the process underway; we pretty much left him to do that.

He pretty much locked Scott in a room and wouldn't let him out until he'd captured really raw, basic drum sounds with very few room sounds or reverb. And Scott delivered the goods. The track we got was incredibly tight, and it gave us something really good to work with.

This size also meant that, on some of the songs, we were able to back off the overdrive in a way that was completely atypical of

Judas Priest of that time. "Worth Fighting For" is probably the best example.

The trend at that time generally was to overdrive and compress guitar sounds to the point where they somehow became smaller, not bigger. Roy suggested that we wind it back somewhat; he thought that we'd be closer to that classic Priest sound from the '70s.

The irony is that those guitar sounds on albums like, say, *Sin After Sin* or *Stained Class* were completely unintentional. Back in those days we were desperately trying to find ways of getting more overdrive. Technology just wouldn't let us do it!

Getting the desired guitar tones was always a struggle for Glenn and me. He and I had always sought the right kind of distortion from as far back as *Sad Wings of Destiny* and, on reflection, not having it was probably of considerable benefit to both our techniques. The absence of gain or sustain meant that our clean playing would sound very scrappy if it wasn't perfectly accurate and phrased. Overdrive for a guitar player equals more sustain, and forgiveness, and for that reason Glenn and I spent pretty much our careers searching for ways to get the right kind of smooth distortion.

It was only once we started playing bigger gigs, where we could turn the dials on our amps up to the two o'clock position in conjunction with custom-made Rangemaster treble-booster pedals that we arrived at what would be the mainstay of our guitar sound for many years.

I tried several other things over the years, including a German wah pedal that, when I clicked it on along with the Rangemaster, would give me a tiny amount of additional boost. Even that small extra amount of overdrive was incredibly valuable.

Then later, when I was recording *British Steel*, I had an old Watkins Copicat that also had a volume control whereby whatever sound went into it could come out a bit louder. It still wasn't what I was looking for, but it helped in those difficult days in the late '70s and early '80s.

By the time *Defenders of the Faith* came around, I was installing a bass treble boost in my guitars. It had two boost settings that I was able to use for my live solos, at the flick of the switch. Then in the studio I was able to use them for the rhythm tracks as well.

When we later had pedal boards made by Peter Cornish in the early '80s everything was built in. In order to do it, whatever stomp boxes we wanted had to be dismantled whereupon Pete would use the carcasses and incorporate them into a square pedal board. Later he built us a rack-mounted pedal board that allowed my roadie to flick effects on and off whenever I was doing solos. That was one of the very first remote effects systems, I believe.

That's broadly how the progression of our guitar sounds went, so, on a track like "Worth Fighting For," the guitars are there but they're not overly distorted. And that was an intentional attempt to replicate some of our '70s sounds. Furthermore, from a stylistic perspective, it was totally new and welcome territory.

From a wider perspective, just being in the studio again with Rob gave us a lot of energy to make an album that I really, really like. Although most of the ideas came from me and Glenn in combination with Rob's lyric-writing sessions, there were others, like "Judas Rising," which had originated much earlier.

My recollection is that the song was first conceived by me, with Rob, back in the '80s, possibly around the time of *Screaming for Vengeance.* Why we didn't use it at the time, I have no idea. Maybe we had enough already; maybe we didn't have it quite right. But I knew when we were doing *Angel of Retribution* that here was a song that sounded a little retro and would therefore fit perfectly into the sound we were going for.

It didn't have the song title when we started reworking the demo; we just called it "Earth, Wind, and Fire" because Rob, as he often did, used scat lyrics simply to make the syllables fit.

Then, when Roy, Rob and I were trying to think of the hook for the song while we were sitting in my studio at Astbury Hall, suddenly the words "Judas is rising" came into one of our heads and we all thought, *Yes, that's it!*

Although we had no idea what might happen with the song "Lochness," we were specifically trying for something more dramatic and conceptual than we'd ever attempted. We all saw a certain degree of majesty in the idea. With retrospect, it was the gateway to what we would attempt next.

Unfortunately, as is often the case, not all of the fans got it. I suppose it's unrealistic to expect all of the fans to get everything you mean them to. And a lot of them really didn't warm to "Lochness", which was a shame because it was always Rob's dream to play that song live.

He had this image in his mind of the whole audience singing like a football crowd. You could definitely envision that working. But it never happened; we never did play it live. But I could play that song all day.

I actually pushed for "Judas Rising" to be the album title. Who wouldn't have? Rob was back in the band; we were making a new album—Judas Priest really *was* rising again. Everything about it made absolute sense to me. *It's going to happen!*

Then it wasn't the title.

That's another battle that I lost.

For the record I didn't like the word "retribution." To me, it was too new or too fashionable a word for Judas Priest. For some reason that I can't quite put my finger on, the word didn't fit with either metal or what we were about either.

Furthermore, I didn't like the angst in the word; it wasn't, in my mind, befitting of what the album stood for: a rejoicing period in Judas Priest's career, like when AC/DC came back with the great *Back in Black*.

Instead, retribution suggested bitterness, and I didn't like that. I'd have been quite happy calling it *Angel* of something . . . just not of retribution! But Glenn more than anybody else wanted it and that's what we went with.

When the album was finished, I remember thinking, *There's a lot of space in this production,* the only exception being "Demonizer," which was a reworked track from a previous writing session. To the trained ear, that should be really obvious. It's not quite up to the mark from a production perspective.

✦

It might surprise a few people to know that *Nostradamus* was one of my favorite albums to make. The idea was one of two that Bill came up with and he flew out to Estonia to present them to us while we were on tour there in December 2005.

The idea of lavishly curated concept pieces was hardly new for Bill. He'd had a production involvement in a number of impressive films that had stemmed from albums, not least *Tommy,* starring the Who's Roger Daltrey, and *Quadrophenia* and *McVicar.* Bill knew what he was doing, so when he came to us with an idea of this kind, we were always going to listen to him.

"I've got a couple of potential subject ideas for a concept album," he told us. "One is the mad Russian monk Rasputin. And the other is the French physician Nostradamus."

Immediately I thought, *Rasputin could be OK. But Nostradamus . . . now there's a great subject.*

Without reservation I'd say that *Nostradamus* was one of the best ideas Bill ever came up with. The whole concept appealed to me immediately. And then when you actually start to research somebody's life, you also start to become immersed in it and, by extension, you almost become part of them.

What also appealed to me (and fit with the kind of subjects Judas Priest was historically drawn to) was the era in which Nostradamus lived. For some reason the sixteenth century had such a dark mystique surrounding it. So many images were immediately conjured up in my head: plagues, jousting, the Spanish Inquisition—all kinds of dark things were going on that were in some way linked to the religious angles that Judas Priest liked to touch on.

After so many years of thinking about traditional songs within the framework of a standard album, to start thinking about a concept as broad and deep as *Nostradamus* would be like taking out my old brain and replacing it with a completely new one.

Because there was such a vast, empty musical landscape on which to start placing images, the primary issue at the outset was to establish what the parameters could and should be. To me they were endless. However, to make something that our audience—which, as was becoming common at the time, had increasingly short attention spans—would like, we had to decide what the album we'd call *Nostradamus* would be.

We settled on a double album, a risky enough proposition in 2008, and we approached the writing process in exactly the same way as we had every other Judas Priest album. The only difference was that sounds or ideas that in the past would be discarded because someone (like me) might say, "Sounds good. Just not for a Judas Priest album," were now not only accepted but actually encouraged.

During my own songwriting sessions, I revisited some parts that had been rejected for previous Judas Priest albums. The basis of "Alone" was an idea that I'd put forward for *Angel of Retribution*, but for some reason it didn't fly at that time. I never really knew why.

But when I reworked and reintroduced it under these entirely new circumstances, it fit in perfectly with what we were trying to do. The music spoke one word to me: "void." And that tied in perfectly with the song title, "Alone."

Similarly, many of the interlude parts between the songs—the connective tissue that held the narrative together—were created by me from bits of music that hadn't been accepted, for one reason or another, for previous albums.

Both Glenn and I had an abundance of ideas and as a result it all came together very easily. It seemed to be very quick at the time. I remember Glenn came over to the Astbury one day and said, "Let's dig out the guitar synths from the *Turbo* days." This was some of the earliest stuff that facilitated the conversion of analog signal to MIDI.

A little ominously, as I was pulling them out of a closet in the attic there were all sorts of accompanying pops and squeaks, bits falling off here and there. I looked at Glenn and said, "I think we need an upgrade!" And that's what we did. Technology had moved so far since 1986 and the new gear meant that if we wanted orchestral sounds or choir sounds, the guitars were set up to do it far more effectively and with none of the glitches that blighted the older gear.

It almost felt to me as if we were making a classically influenced album and not just a heavy metal album. Whenever I drove from my house to the studio at Old Smithy near Worcester, I did so with Classic FM on the car radio, there and back! I wanted to put myself in that place. It was all so fresh. It felt like we were merging two worlds.

The more I listened to classical music on the radio, the more I started to think, *What we're doing now has as much or more classical value than most of the stuff I'm hearing on Classic FM!*

✦

Nostradamus turned out incredibly well.

And then we dropped the ball completely.

As far as I was concerned, we were sitting on an enormous opportunity. Among us, we had lots of different ideas about how we could facilitate *Nostradamus*'s transition from a record to a legitimate stage production that could be franchised all over the world, maybe, and become our version of *Phantom of the Opera*.

"We need to go out and play the album in its entirety," I distinctly remember saying in one of our many meetings with Bill.

The way I saw it, at the very least we had to go out there and take the music to the audiences. That way, hopefully the music would be accepted as a legitimate classical work and people would become familiar with it to the point they would see a future show.

We should have gone out and done *Nostradamus*, from start to finish, at the Albert Hall, Carnegie Hall, and venues of that kind that had stages big enough to accommodate actors, illusionists, and whatever else we wanted to accompany the music, but that also were old and small enough to retain something of an intimate feel. Trans-Siberian Orchestra always seemed to manage it.

All of this, however, required a huge commitment from everyone to go out and do it properly. It just needed to be worked out in detail. It could have been amazing, with Rob as Nostradamus. I honestly thought it had the potential to be a Vegas show.

But we procrastinated. We had a tour looming, with us having to go out with all the familiar problems and me not enjoying it.

I thought we should have hung on to the *Nostradamus* idea and really geared up to doing it as a production in select theatres, where older fans would pay good ticket money to see Judas Priest doing something really extraordinary—a show not to be missed.

In the end we half-arsed the whole thing.

We went out on the road and just played a few songs from *Nostradamus* as part of a normal Judas Priest set list. Granted, most of them fit in perfectly but to me we completely wasted one of the best opportunities we ever had to take ourselves to a level above that of a heavy metal band.

The effect that decision had on the fans' reception of the album was profound. Looking back, I was probably stupid enough to think that there were enough people out there in the world who remembered what it felt like to actually sit down and listen to a double album, like back in the '60s and the '70s when people did just that with *Electric Ladyland* or whatever.

But by 2008, it felt like people's attention spans had shriveled up to basically nothing. Familiarity was the only way we were going to get *Nostradamus* across to the fans. Everybody knows that if you hear a song often enough, sooner or later your foot starts tapping and you think, "This is really good."

We needed to achieve that with *Nostradamus* via a spectacular live show, but the way we chose to present it meant that the level of familiarity we needed so much was nigh on impossible. The crying shame was that we could even have presented a *Nostradamus* production at a number of levels.

At the low end we could have performed the whole *Nostradamus* album with just Don Airey on keyboards to cover the orchestral effects. Then the next level could be a keyboard *and* a five-piece orchestra. And then we could have done it with a full orchestra—the deluxe edition!

In the end we did none of these things. We fell between stools. We hit no targets because we didn't see *Nostradamus* through. Fans couldn't relate to it and that was our fault because we hadn't delivered it to them in a palatable way. And that's it, really.

It would be good to think that in a few years' time people will go back and give *Nostradamus* a bit of appreciation. It might need one of us to snuff it, or someone like Justin Bieber to do a cover. Either way, I really hope it happens.

Despite my frustrations with how the presentation of the *Nostradamus* material had been handled, of course I went out on that last tour and gave it absolutely 100 percent.

To accommodate the changing capabilities of Rob's voice, this tour was the first time that we changed our guitar tuning from A440—also known as concert pitch—to a semitone lower. From a guitarist's perspective, I liked to do that because it reduced the tension on the strings enough to give my small fingers a little break. The overall pitch difference would sound barely noticeable to an audience anyway. But it helped Rob and me no end.

We started in Finland, on June 3, 2008 and a couple of weeks later we found ourselves in Bilbao for the Kobetasonik Festival, with a variety of great bands on the bill including KISS, Slayer, and Dio.

That night, after the show, I found myself standing at a bar sandwiched between Ronnie James Dio and Kerry King. I've known Ronnie for many years and always enjoyed his company whenever our paths crossed on the road, which really wasn't that often.

Similarly, Kerry was always great company, too. He was from one of the slightly younger generations of bands that followed in Priest's footsteps. That said, Kerry is a die-hard Priest fan. He knows more about Judas Priest than I do!

But these guys could drink.

By that time, I was probably just past my prime in terms of what I could put away.

"Come on, Ken, what'll you have?" Ronnie says.

"All right then, maybe just one more . . . "

"K.K.! What are you drinking?" Kerry says—an hour and three drinks later.

I'm thinking, *I'm toiling a bit here.*

"Go on then, mate. How about one for the road."

All this time, Kerry, Ronnie, and I are talking, laughing, telling stories from the past. It was wonderful to get that chance to spend some time with these guys for a night. But once Kerry starts buying, you can't stop him!

"I think I need to call a taxi," I say, slurring my words just a little.

Kerry goes, "Do that . . . I'll get you a drink while you're waiting." *Christ!!!*

Somehow, I got myself into the taxi; I barely remember leaving them. At some point on the half-hour drive to the hotel I passed out, only to be woken up later by that familiar warm sensation between my legs. I remembered it from childhood.

I can't believe this. I've gone and pissed myself!

I got out of the taxi, cursing myself. *Old man problems!*

There being no protocol for how to traverse a crowded hotel lobby as a fifty-seven-year-old musician with urine-soaked jeans, with a nod to the concierge on the way past, I slinked away to my room.

That night in Bilbao was the last time I saw the great man Ronnie Dio alive. What a huge loss he was to heavy metal music.

◆

Sometime in the weeks and months that followed my coming off-stage in Japan in October of 2009, following the *Nostradamus* tour, which then morphed into a *British Steel 30th Anniversary* run in the fall of 2009, I got the phone call from Jayne Andrews.

"How soon can you start writing again?"

For goodness sake, I've just gotten home. Can't you leave me alone!

To this day, I never knew the motivation for the EP. It was just one of a number of things that had been discussed in terms of what was next.

At that point I was of a view that we should just kick on and announce a farewell tour instead of recording anything new. Things weren't exactly great, attendances weren't startling, and the band's performances, to me, were somewhat lackluster. I suppose I just thought that a farewell tour was the best thing for the band as individuals. None of us was getting any younger. Rob's knees were playing up. Scott's wrists hurt. I had some ailments.

We need to be careful here.

Whether it was an instinct that came with being a bit older, I thought that if we were to get another year or two out of the band before something happened to one of us, we'd be lucky. At age sixty, touring was no longer as much fun as it used to be anyway. There were no groupies out there anymore and certainly no parties. The hotel rooms began to feel like prison cells. Everyone seemed to be moody and moaning. It felt like the furnace had been extinguished. My plan seemed to make sense—to keep playing live shows as long as we could. There were so many places we had yet to play. But, please, let's not lock ourselves away in the studio for months, or even years.

Nobody else agreed with my opinions about what should happen next.

Finally, we'd reached what seemed like a terminal impasse.

CHAPTER FOURTEEN

WHEN I MADE MY DECISION TO LEAVE JUDAS PRIEST, I thought, *This can be done in one of two ways.*

One, I could burn all the bridges by saying exactly what I thought.

Or two, I could bow out gracefully as best as I could.

At first, my thinking was to try to make the whole process as easy for everybody as I possibly could. So, in my initial resignation letter I said that I'd given it everything and couldn't imagine doing any more than I had already done in the band.

For the sake of simplicity, I think I may have used the word "retire" in my communications, simply because I thought it sounded better than "quit," and also because I thought that everybody of a certain age has a right to retire. I even offered alternatives as to how it could all be done to permit a smooth transition. All of this was done with the best intentions. Inside me, the real reasons why I was leaving were raging.

The truth of the matter was that all the reasons I'd planned to cite in my aborted resignation of 1991 were still applicable. In many cases those reasons had become even more valid with time and, inevitably, a few new ones had been added along the way.

Looking back now, it's a miracle that I stayed as long as I did in Judas Priest. Had it not been for my easygoing and non-confrontational personality, I'm certain that there would have been a punch-up, like UFO and Michael Schenker had, and that would have been it—I'd have been gone.

Really, that could have happened at any time after 1978.

That said, it was still one of those situations where I wanted to make a decision but didn't want it to cause a load of angst or to have people try to persuade me to change my mind. I'd made my mind up, didn't want to put anyone down or point any fingers, so the official line I gave at the time was that I didn't have anything more to offer.

I then added that I was happy for them to take on somebody to fill my role and that I'd also be willing to coach him or her in my parts, as and when required.

That offer was probably far above and beyond the normal call of duty. But that's how my nature works: I don't have it in me to be nasty and conniving. I always want to make things right and to make breakups as painless as possible, a bit like leaving your girl-friend who's dumping you with a car and a house. Or offering to help another girlfriend with her business after you've just split up.

People might say (and have said), "Ken, you're mad."

But the truth is that, even to this day, I don't really know how else to approach these kinds of situations.

Furthermore, I presented my departure in the way I did out of respect for all the fans who had bought albums, tickets, and mer-chandise, all over the world, for the forty years I'd been in Judas Priest. At the very least, I owed them that.

The problem was, when the band had their say with an announcement, they pitched it all slightly differently by regurgitating the word "retiring," and that the retirement had some connection to me not wanting to be away from the golf and leisure business at the Astbury for long periods of time.

As convenient an explanation as this might have sounded at the time, it just wasn't true. Everyone knew that the golf course development had been ongoing for several years. I'd successfully managed Astbury remotely, in one form or another, since 1985. No aspect of the business had impinged on my role in Judas Priest either. In fact, if anything, the very act of having another unrelated interest to focus on during Priest downtime had probably given me a level of balance that kept me going and excited. If I hadn't had the Astbury, I might have left long before I made the announcement in 2011!

So, it wasn't that I *couldn't* continue.

I didn't *want* to continue.

I'd just had enough on several long-standing levels, the most immediate that I just wasn't prepared to trek around the world again, getting older, treading boards with anyone whose onstage performance wasn't what it once was.

And this stuff wasn't even new.

We would play major shows in the early '80s where I had to grind to a halt because of something that Glenn did: got lost, missed choruses, sped things up too much. Casual observers wouldn't even notice these missteps, but it really did make me nervous onstage.

Furthermore, even before Glenn got onstage, he'd spend all his time in the dressing rooms just drinking and practicing his solos. Nothing else. He'd then walk onstage thinking, "As long as I can nail my solos, everything will be OK."

But in my opinion, far too often it wasn't OK.

For the record, I always thought from early on that Glenn was living the rock 'n' roll lifestyle on a few levels whereas I always

considered myself to be focused on trying to be a precision musician first and foremost—delivering as good a performance as possible, night after night. It felt as if our approaches were diametrically
opposite.

The final straw came for me on the *British Steel 30th Anniversary* tour when Glenn would often say things like, "I've never enjoyed playing live as much as I do now."

The irony!

Meanwhile, I'm thinking, *Yeah, great, buddy. You're, in my eyes
anyway, treating playing live like you're going to the pub for a night
out, while I'm the one going to work!*

I spoke to Glenn about it at several points but he just shrugged it
off. We even got Glenn's tech to water down the beer he had access
to onstage, which he was happy to do because, on some nights, it
looked like Glenn was too afraid to move off one spot. All of this
affected the whole band to the point that everyone seemed to be
going through the motions. To me, the Priest energy had slowed to
a walk—to the point that I genuinely started to feel awkward about
giving my natural energetic performance.

On these last tours, it felt as if some petty one-upmanship was
going on, too. Whenever we ended a song, Glenn always, always
had to make sure that the last sound that anyone heard came from
his guitar. To the outsider this might sound petty, but to me, having
been worn down over many years, it was big.

Glenn, for whatever reason, started getting sloppy when it came
to finishing tracks that are meant to come to a dead stop. I can only
assume it was the beer. But his long pull-offs became plain annoying to me. So, on a song like "Breaking the Law," where an abrupt
end creates impact, I was always of the mind that, if that's how it
was intended, that's how it needs to be onstage. But Glenn would
do some kind of elaborate pull-off instead.

Meanwhile, I'd be at the other side of the stage thinking, *Why?*

It wound me up to the point where I started retaliating. The band would stop dead, Glenn would do his long pull-off, and then I'd do a pull-off after his pull-off. It used to piss me off no end because it completely spoiled the ending of the song.

I don't intend any of this as a personal dig at Glenn—he and I go back a long time in a partnership that is deeply revered by heavy metal fans. I don't deny that. But I wouldn't be doing myself, the band, or metal fans any justice if I didn't state the opinion that on many occasions, particularly near the end, I felt that Judas Priest's live performances were suffering, to the point where I was going on every night thinking, *We're just not giving the fans an experience that I, personally, can be proud of.*

To this day, I stand by that view. Dave Holland had felt the same way in 1988.

◆

The second, and interrelated, irritant that pushed me inexorably over the edge was the subtle level of control that I felt Glenn applied through his relationship with management, specifically Jayne Andrews.

Ever since 1985, when Bill assigned Jayne to look after the band's affairs, this pattern had developed year after year. I put up with it for ages—simply because I knew enough about that personality type who, if they don't get their own way, they throw all the toys out of the pram. Meanwhile, nothing gets done.

So, barring a few boilovers over the years and the moment I almost quit in '91, I said nothing. I wasn't equipped with the required nastiness to counter the regime so I just tolerated it and I hated myself for doing so.

◆

I'm sure people will say, "So why *did* you put up with it, K.K.?"

Very simply, the reason I did was because I worked very hard to be in a band. It was my ambition to be a professional musician from an early age. I always acknowledged what we'd gone through to become successful. Not just that, I totally respected all the fans who'd spent money over the years and the record companies who'd invested in us to make the success possible. Therefore, I didn't want to throw that all away because of a relationship conflict that I was never, ever going to change, or win.

It seemed like I'd spent my life answering to people who were trying to control me one way or another: my dad, various bosses, record label people. I had hoped that being in a band would be different from all of that. I thought I'd be my own entity within a democracy, where there was respect for each individual at the top level.

But these things didn't happen. In my opinion, Glenn was and had been controlling me all along, albeit in a more subtle, hard-to-quantify way, with his various hidden agendas.

There I was, K.K. Downing, traveling in planes, boats, and trains to all corners of the globe to play for fans who seemed to worship me like I was a god, doing interviews, signing autographs. But, despite all of that, I still felt, *I'm in a bloody nine-to-five job here—and I'm still answerable to a boss!*

I was totally sick of it all.

Then, as if the realization that I was in this position wasn't bad enough, I had to stand there and watch my other band members being put in the same position! That's when it really dawned on me that, as hard as it was to walk away, I had nothing else to give. In a follow up letter to them I wrote words to the effect of "one of the main reasons I'm leaving is that I've hated you two, ever since 1985 when you started your regime."

And that was it. I'd essentially put the nails in my own coffin.

Another brutal blow to me came at Christmas 2010, when a documentary about the origin of heavy metal called *Heavy Metal Britannia*, made by the BBC, came on the television. I watched this very well-put-together program, seeing all of my friends and associates taking part. There was Sabbath, of course, Budgie, Gillan, Diamond Head, and even the Edgar Broughton Band, to name just a few. I was delighted to acknowledge that I had trod the boards with pretty much all of these artists, but as the program continued it became apparent that Ian and I were not included at all. Just Glenn and Rob were telling their version of the origins of heavy metal.

My heart sank.

After all of the hard work and dedication I'd invested in becoming the aspiring metalmonger from such an early age and all of the associated sacrifices, it just didn't seem fair that I didn't warrant so much as a mention.

How could this program possibly be made without me? I thought.

Even Edgar Broughton had three members featured. I began to wonder why our management had not insisted that I be included. It certainly wouldn't have been a hard sell to the producers of the documentary, as they would surely recognize that I, having been in Judas Priest since the beginning, would have invaluable input and knowledge to share about how it really all came about. Not just that, given that the heavy metal image and clothing was mentioned, wouldn't it have made sense to include the guy who was the first one in Priest to adopt full-on black leather and studs?

Apparently not.

Something about it all really stunk—so much so that it really was the last of the last straws. No one told me that this program would be the definitive story of the beginning of heavy metal.

To top it all, being asked by Jayne to start writing that Christmas for a five-track EP whereupon I knew I'd be expected to go back and forth songwriting and traveling to the studio through the dead of winter. At that point, I was absolutely done. I thought, *An EP? You're fucking kidding! After the epic* Nostradamus?

I'd reached that end point, and I knew I'd made the right decision when, the morning after I sent in my resignation, I woke up feeling completely unburdened. Thereafter, I had absolutely no regrets whatsoever. I knew I had given my absolute all in Judas Priest, and it was time to step away and let them continue in whatever way they saw fit.

And they just carried on, as I fully expected them to do. I paid very little attention to what Judas Priest was doing after my departure. Inevitably fans or friends would draw my attention to press or to the new album they released after I'd left.

Oddly, I found myself having no real opinion on their new music although it was unavoidable in my position to not hear snippets of tracks here and there. I felt a detachment that was both surprising and quite pleasant. For the first time there was no pressure on me whatsoever, and whenever I thought about the band along the way, I couldn't help thinking that the intraband dynamics probably hadn't changed in any way since I left. Glenn was still there, Jayne was still the manager; I had no doubt that the regime would still be alive and well.

✦

Obviously, leaving a band I'd founded and been in for all of my adult life was going to require a long period of adjustment. Whenever I used to come home from tour I always had a day or two when, although I was stationary, it felt like life was still moving at tour pace. Having walked away, I would never again experience that tour pace. Instead, all I could do was to focus on what post-Priest life held for me, and the hardest part for me always was maintaining what one might call normal relationships with women.

My relationship record has been, shall we say, checkered over the years.

On reflection, being in a band and being desired by women isn't the ideal grounding from which to enter into a normal romantic relationship. The rules of the road just don't apply, and that's a good thing on the whole.

However, when your relationships have been generally super-ficial and entirely founded on the fact that some girl wants the as-sociation of having had a dalliance, however brief, with a musician, then it's hard to then conduct relationships on normal terms. Then, when you add to the fact that the majority of the girls chasing you are twenty-five when you're now fifty-five, it only makes real-life dating even more of a minefield.

That said, I did try over the years, with very mixed results.

Back in 2003, while I was still in the band, I had just emerged, bruised and battered, from a long relationship. I'd met a nice girl in a pub six year earlier, and as well as being a couple in a romantic sense, she also became an important part of the day-to-day running of my business affairs.

After a certain period of time, this woman, whose body clock was understandably ticking, got broody and started needing a de-gree of commitment from me. In my cynical mind, what "commit-ment" meant was, you give me everything that I want, and we'll all live happily ever after. If you don't, it's not happening.

The problem was that commitment of any kind has always ter-rified me because of my family upbringing. The idea of marriage was scary enough, much less the thought of having children. I just lived with too many memories of growing up to ever want to bring children into the world. I knew that relationships didn't always run smoothly, so I never wanted a child of mine to have to cower under a table while his or her parents argued. I couldn't do that to a child. It was bad enough watching Carol's and my Alsatian hiding when we argued when we were young!

So, this relationship with the woman came to a head in 2001 when she realized that I wasn't up for long-term commitment. She then decided to get legal with me. I'd just flown back from Japan for Christmas and was in the midst of selling some land on the estate that was surplus to requirements. When I went into the lawyer's to sign the papers and draw the money, they said, "We can't do it."

"What do you mean you can't do it?" I said.

"Somebody has put a caution on your whole estate," I was told.

"Who the hell can that be?" I asked

And they said this woman's name.

The next day, I had to go and play a Judas Priest gig at Brixton Academy. I played what I thought was a good gig, but I'd be lying if I didn't admit that my head was in pieces. I was completely traumatized by the whole thing.

There had been no warning of this whatsoever. But when I went home to the office I found that she'd copied every single document I had while I'd been in Japan with the band. *Everything.*

I think that the situation was that, while she was thinking of moving on, her father, who was a legal exec of some kind, said to her, "You should get some lawyers behind you."

She went into the offices of a rather aggressive female-run law firm and told them her story. Then they must have thought, "Hmm, Ken Downing, international rock musician. What's he got? Oh, look . . . the Astbury estate and various properties here and in Spain. . . . "

I'm guessing they then said to her something to the effect of, "Go back to his office while he's away and gather all the papers you can find while we build a case for you. Let's see if we can nail this guy's balls to the wall."

I had to take an entire year out of my life to sort the mess out. I was on tour much of this time and had to spend all my free time assembling my case and going through literally tons of fax paper. The showdown came at the point when her lawyers contacted mine and said, "We want you to come to the negotiating table here."

I didn't go.

I knew very well that they were used to guys like me having a bit on the side, getting caught out, and saying, "I don't want publicity. I just want this to go away. How big is the check I need to write?"

At which point they say, "Let's start at half of everything he owns."

But this situation was different, and I knew it.

Without going into all the technicalities, I had to spend five days in court in Birmingham. It was all too familiar. Just like Reno, I was thinking, *I have no idea how this could go.*

Meanwhile, the press was there, various tabloid papers were there; that was all part of her lawyer's tactics to get me to cave in and settle out of court.

I didn't settle, and the case went my way.

There was still one problem: while all this was going on, the woman had been living in my house! It got to be an absolute nightmare, to the point that I had to go to Spain while a woman who was taking me to court was living in my home, like a bad movie. Until the case was over, the judge wasn't able to order her to leave, even though I offered to pay for fully furnished rented accommodation wherever she wanted. Predictably, her lawyers must have told her, "Do not accept the offer. Hold out. *Annoy* him."

I got a call when I was in Spain from one of my neighbors who told me that the woman was letting various people in my house. One of them I later found out was a new boyfriend she'd acquired—some sort of computer tech expert. The next day, my lawyer called and said, "You need to come home as soon as possible and get all your computers out of there."

Anyway, we won, and she declared herself bankrupt because she couldn't pay my legal fees. I took no pleasure from that whatsoever. It was all such a sad situation, because she was badly advised by her lawyers from the outset. Had she come to me and asked if I'd buy her a house to set herself up after our ways parted, I would have done it. But that's not what happened. The whole experience took so much out of me.

Thereafter I went into a number of other short-lived relationships with nice women who, on the surface, seemed to like being with me and were interested in the same things. But then for one reason or another, they just fizzled out, usually because of my ongoing commitments.

Then I found someone who I felt was as close to being that someone I might want to spend the rest of my life with than anyone I'd met for a long time. She was a little younger; she never lived with me—for a while it was great. She looked lovely, appreciated aspects of nature that I did, liked music . . .

I was thinking, *I could be very happy here.*

And then it abruptly ended.

I never knew what the precise reason was. Again, I was distraught, and this time I thought, *What am I doing wrong?*

Not long afterward I fell into a relationship by accident with a much younger girl and for a long while, barring the usual ups and downs, it worked really well.

Then I had a profound insight.

I suddenly realized that, regardless of their age, women would always be, and always had been, waiting around for me in some capacity.

Carol was waiting around for me when I was on tour in the early days of Judas Priest. All the others had been waiting for me while I dealt with either being in a band or whatever commitments I had with the Astbury or with helping to produce other bands like Hostile. I came to realize that the problem wasn't me specifically but more an issue of how much time I have to dedicate to a relationship. Just as I wasn't prepared to stop touring in 1985 to be with Carol, I'm probably equally unwilling nowadays to stop doing what I'm trying to achieve in business.

That presents problems with relationships, and that's what I found recently with the younger girl I was with. It suddenly occurred to me that she didn't need to be waiting around for me. She needed to have her own friends and to see the world while she's still young. I discussed it with her and she agreed. We parted on the most wonderful terms and we still email and see each other occasionally—just not on the same terms whereby her life hangs on my schedule. After all, I know more than most what it feels like to be in my position, although there's part of me that feels like, one day, we might end up back together.

The only exception to all of this was Kyme. She was the only girlfriend I'd ever had who very much had her own life. She was never in the habit of waiting around for me. Even when I was on tour and she was living at Astbury, she did her own thing. She had friends in England; she had many skills that could earn her money: hairdressing, manicures. She even went into business with a friend in Bridgnorth, opening a shop that sold handmade jewelry. I often wonder what might have happened if she hadn't died so tragically young.

What's the lesson to be learned from all of these relationship woes?

Well, it's not just the relationship issues that are a symptom of my upbringing and, by extension, the life I created for myself thereafter. My choice from a young age to avoid confrontation wherever humanly possible, despite witnessing more than my fair share of it, has caused me innumerable problems in later life.

In fact, to this day, I still find myself in a corner when it comes to business relationships with people who, for one reason or another, have to chest beat and get their own way. No matter what walk of life I'm operating in, I always seem to find myself in these situations where I'm being dictated to or controlled in some way by people of that kind.

Why don't you change, Ken? I have often said to myself.

The problem is, at sixty-six years old, that's easy to say, but much harder to do. The saying that "old habits die hard" has never been truer in my case. It's probably too late for me. I'm at the stage in life where I have to live with my past, one way or another. I'd be lying if I didn't admit that the shadow of my childhood still looms now and again.

The same applies to my sisters. Although we rarely discuss some of the unpleasant aspects of our upbringing, Margaret, Linda, and I share enough knowledge of what happened that we don't particularly need to say anything. Let's just say that our upbringing has affected all of us in our own peculiar ways, including my younger brother, Adrian, whose childhood was many years after the three of ours.

Since 2010 then, barring the odd guest appearance on music projects and the occasional production job for young local bands, like Hostile, the Astbury has been my sole focus.

✦

Even though I haven't been a member of Judas Priest since 2010, I'm still very much in contact, one way or another, with both the music industry and my past. Although it's highly unlikely that I'll ever play in Judas Priest again, I was nevertheless interested to hear about the Rock and Roll Hall of Fame nomination that the band received. When I first heard the news, my first thought was, *This could be interesting.*

Given that I remain to this day, from a technical perspective, at least a director of Judas Priest, I did receive some brief communication from Jayne Andrews about what the plan might be were the band to be inducted.

I thought it might be awkward to get together again. But given how much communication I've had, and still do have, with fans, the prospect of showing up at an induction seemed like just reward for all the hard work we all put in over the years.

Given how I'd presented my leaving the band, I was always curious what the fans felt about my decision to walk away. Part of me wondered whether a section of fans felt as if I'd somehow let them down by leaving Judas Priest. The other part of me wondered whether some of them might have seen and read enough over the years to be in a position to understand why I felt it was the right time for me to step away.

Either way, I couldn't control any of it. Once the announcement was out and the band took off into the distance with a new guitar player and a new tour, all I could do was get on with my daily life.

At no point did I feel the need to contact any of the band guys to explain further. As far as I was concerned, I had no reason whatsoever to ingratiate myself either. After all, I knew exactly how things had played out, and I suspected they did, too.

Scott Travis was the only member of the band to contact me after I left Judas Priest. He sent me a cool message saying that he respected my decision to leave.

As good as it was to hear from Scott, the fact that I didn't hear anything from Glenn, Ian, or Rob neither surprised me nor disappointed me much. I really think that they resented me for breaking up the band, which, on paper, was quite hypocritical because not only had Rob quit the band himself for twelve years, but also he, Ian, and Scott must have been totally aware of the ongoing issues I had with Glenn and Jayne over the years, as it was exactly the same for them.

The only thing that did surprise me was a comment Ian made in an interview where he said that nobody was missing or asking about me! And that Richie brought new energy to the band

OK, buddy. I know you're trying to toe the party line here, but there's no need for the put-downs! And wasn't it me who was complaining about how the band had slowed to a slow walk onstage anyway?

But really, I understood why it was happening and why it was coming from Ian. In order to maintain a band's image and identity to protect the dollar, it's important to always present the fans with a strong "things have never been better" façade. I get that.

Furthermore, because I thought it unlikely that Rob and Glenn would say anything about me directly, it appeared to me that Ian, who wasn't allowed to do press for all the years I was in the band, was now being pushed forward as the voice of Judas Priest!

It was all predictable stuff. I felt so relieved to be clear of all the subterfuge and head games that I felt had gone on from day to day.

✦

Nowadays, when I look back on my career in Judas Priest, I do so with curiously mixed feelings. It's still hard for me to believe that I even had the courage to walk out of the Yew Tree Estate as a frustrated young man all those years ago. Rather than venting my many frustrations via reliance on drugs, drink, or crime as many others have done, I focused on one thing only: my route to a better life. And that route, as we all know, involved picking up a guitar, plonking away, and never quitting until I had the tools to play in a heavy metal band.

Then once I was in a band, I like to think that—while I enjoyed some wild and hedonistic times along the way—my eye was always, always trained on the core values of what being in a band meant to me: being diligent about my craft while entertaining the fans to the absolute best of my ability. I know beyond doubt that I never for a moment wavered from those goals, despite being faced with some tough odds of various kinds over many years.

Did I contribute to a few bad decisions or missteps over the years?

Of course. I wouldn't be human if I didn't.

Did I make the odd mistake onstage and think, *What did I just do?*

Certainly. These things happen to the best of us. But the willingness to hone my craft and to respect my abilities was always unwavering.

On the other hand—and this may surprise a few people who hold Judas Priest in high regard as one of the biggest and best heavy metal bands of all time—I genuinely feel that we missed a lot of opportunities over the years. For one reason or another, wrong decisions at inopportune times, in combination with the wrong personalities in key roles, really held us back. Gull, as much as they gave us a deal when we didn't have one, made the mistake of not realizing our potential.

Arnakarta were a very helpful stepping-stone but they seemed to have a better understanding of the pop world at a time when we really needed a Rod Smallwood to gather up all the elements of what Judas Priest was, grip it tight, and take it forward with purpose. Instead, we lurched—sustained only by our own work ethic and determination to not let the graft we put in, up and down the country in a van, amount to naught.

In the grand analysis, I like and respect him as a person, but Bill must have known what was going on with Jayne and Glenn back in 1985. And in all fairness to him I am sure that he took steps back, time and time again, when he heard Jayne saying that the band didn't want to do this or that—all of which revolved around Glenn's preferences and schedule.

It felt like the only allies we really had were our primary record label, Sony, two other labels who were willing to come on board and support a Ripper-fronted Judas Priest through some tough times, and several radio personalities—Eddie Trunk and Joe Anthony particularly—who genuinely supported us through thick and thin. All these labels backed us; we couldn't have asked for more. Similarly, some radio show hosts couldn't have done more to further Judas Priest's cause in America.

So, the conclusion I arrive at is that we massively underachieved, in a financial and creative sense. And the fact that our best-selling album, *Screaming for Vengeance*, just sold 2.5 million copies tells you everything you need to know. We threatened to hit the really big time, but as much as it might have appeared to fans that we had, we never really did.

We never came anywhere close to Iron Maiden, Def Leppard, or Metallica numbers. These bands had records at that time that sold in excess of five or even ten million copies. Some of the bands with comparable sales numbers to ours would never be discussed in the same breath as Judas Priest about their significance to the genre. We had the reputation and the legacy, but for some reason we never backed it up with sales.

As much as things could have been so different, I still consider myself lucky to have had the chance to be in Judas Priest. I traveled the world, saw many countries and met the fans who love our music. The fans, for me, were always one the most important motivations for being in a band. Without them, I wouldn't have lived the life that I have.

To that end, all I've got to go on are the thousands of emails, letters, and photographs that I still receive daily, from all over the world. It's gratifying to know that people are interested in what I'm doing now, as well as wanting to know what I think about aspects of Priest's music, guitars, or really anything else they want to talk about.

Through my website and the occasional video updates, I have sought to keep the channel of communication open between me and the fans who have liked our music over the years. I created K.K. Downing's Steel Mill website for a few reasons. Firstly, I'd seen Rob and Glenn have solo careers, have their own websites, and sell merchandise. I thought, *Why shouldn't I do the same?*

After all, just because I'm no longer in the band and playing onstage when Priest are in their town, it doesn't mean that I didn't once shake fans' hands, enjoy a beer somewhere, or sign an autograph.

All of these things happened, and each and every one of these interactions I hold on to as tightly as I grip the musical legacy that I was part of with Judas Priest. As hard as it was to walk away, I comfort myself with the knowledge that I was so fortunate to be able to do what I wanted for a living for so long. I walked away on my terms, with no regrets, and with my integrity solidly intact. And I still have more life to live. These fans have been with me from the beginning, and many of them still want to read updates about not just what I'm doing, but also about anything interesting that's going on in the world of heavy metal. I've got a really loyal group of people in Finland who run my Website on my behalf. They're obviously huge Judas Priest fans, and massive fans of metal in general, as I am.

So, with all that being said, I would like to say thank you to my beloved bandmates for all the miles we have traveled together and for all the many shows we have played—and for everything else that we have shared, good and bad, along the way. It has been a privilege to have known and worked with you for so long.

Five years after I left the band, I became aware that Glenn had been diagnosed with Parkinson's disease. To his immense credit, he has done fantastically well in completing two successful albums and two successful world tours. I'm sure all of the fans would like to join me in wishing Glenn, and the band, continued success for many years to come.

My message to the fans is and will always be: "I'm here—the same fun-loving K.K. that I always was. Keep in touch."

♦ ♦ ♦ ♦ ACKNOWLEDGMENTS

WOULD LIKE TO TAKE THIS OPPORTUNITY TO THANK EVERY-
one who has played a part in making this book possible. First,
editors Ben Schafer and Andreas Campomar in the US and UK.
Second, US agent Matthew Elblonk and his UK counterpart,
Matthew Hamilton. I'd also like to thank my friends in Finland—
Jari, Pete, Kassu, Ville, and Kimmo—who run my website and who
have provided valuable input along the way. Finally, sincere thanks
to my co-writer, Mark Eglinton, for making the vision for this book
a reality.